POLE TO POLE

POLE TO POLE

ONE MAN, 20 MILLION STEPS

PAT FARMER

ALLEN&UNWIN

Allen & Unwin
Sydney, Melbourne, Auckland, London

83 Alexander Street
Crows Nest NSW 2065
Australia
Phone: (61 2) 8425 0100
Fax: (61 2) 9906 2218
Email: info@allenandunwin.com
Web: www.allenandunwin.com

Cataloguing-in-Publication details are available
from the National Library of Australia
www.trove.nla.gov.au

ISBN 978 1 74237 784 1

Internal design by Phil Campbell
Photographs by Anthony Bonello, Ming d'Arcy, Juan Femet, Gustavo
Garza, Nick King, Jose Naranjo, Eric Philips, Greg Quail, Jake Simmonds,
Javier Trujillo and Katie Walsh (unless otherwise credited)
Map and world dinkus courtesy of Quail Television Productions
Set in 10/14 pt Utopia by Post Pre-Press Group, Australia
Printed and bound in Australia by Griffin Press

10 9 8 7 6 5 4 3 2 1

CONTENTS

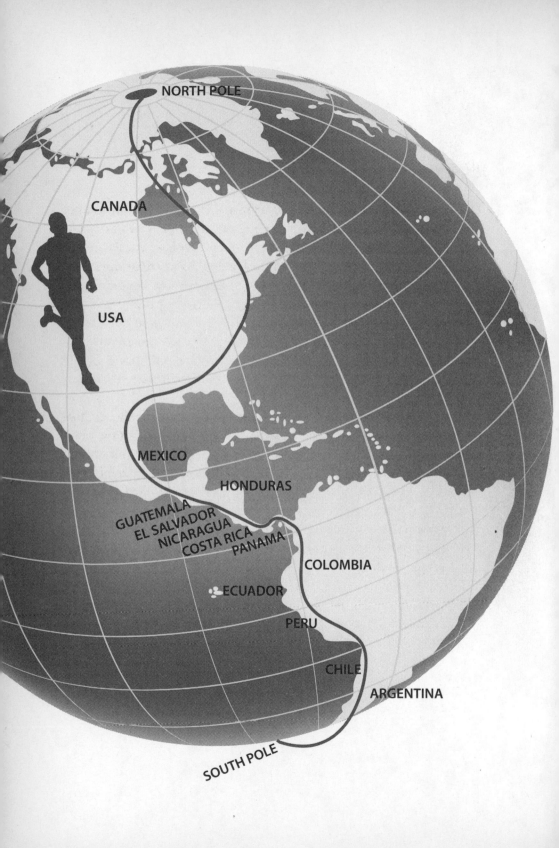

FOREWORD

One of the best things about being a journalist is that you sometimes get a front row seat to the world's biggest events and, if you are lucky enough, get to interview some of the players. I include Pat Farmer in that category. In 2011 we joined Pat at the beginning of his epic journey—to run from the North Pole through Canada, the United States, Central and South America to the South Pole—to raise money for Red Cross clean water and disaster relief projects. At first I, like most people I suppose, was sceptical. Surely no one could run 21,000 kilometres between April and February, averaging the equivalent of two marathons every single day through some of the most dangerous terrain on the planet?

Yet, as interview followed interview, and I saw how Pat, enduring everything from extreme weather conditions to braving polar bears, crocodiles, bandits, jungles and deserts, remained relentlessly optimistic, good humoured and determined to achieve his seemingly impossible quest, I began to think, 'You know, he might just do this.'

Now he has.

Pat Farmer's Pole to Pole Run is surely one of history's great endurance feats, and what makes Pat's efforts all the more commendable is that because of the funds he has raised, life is going to get better for thousands of people in impoverished and devastated communities all over the world.

Pat, you're an inspiration. Well done, mate. You did it. Now, rest up a little!

Karl Stefanovic

I dedicate this book to
the people of the Red Cross all over the world,
and to those who need their help

PREFACE

What a sight I was. In New York's Central Park in mid-January 2011, at one point with a blizzard raging around me, temperatures of –10 degrees Celsius, snow thick on the ground, day after day, usually dragging two 30-kilogram tyres attached to a leather harness on my back, plodding over the thick and slippery snow for hour after hour, kilometre after kilometre. I racked up 25 kilometres a day. I swear that the park's famous squirrels saw me pass and shook their heads in disbelief before sensibly retreating into their shelters.

Never let anyone tell you that Americans lack a sense of humour—New Yorkers, anyway. 'Hey, Bro . . . you trainin' for a chain gang?' yelled one passer-by from the cosy cocoon of his vehicle. 'Man . . . want me

Acclimatising in New York's Central Park before the trek.

to help you find the rest of your car?' offered another. Some just stood and stared at me as if I was mad. I was suffering, dragging those tyres through the snow, but I couldn't help breaking into a smile. Some people came up to me and shook my hand, recognising me from the TV interviews I'd done. Such moments lifted my spirits and helped me to keep going, both in my training and during the actual event: running from the North Pole to the South Pole, to raise money for International Red Cross clean water projects in the developing world. This book chronicles my run.

Who am I? I'm a 49-year-old single father of two children, Brooke and Dillon, with whom I live in Sydney. My beautiful and beloved wife, Lisa, died unexpectedly of an undiagnosed heart condition in 1998, aged just 34. I'm also an ultrarunner and have taken part in numerous national and international ultramarathons, usually for charity, including one in which I ran right around Australia—over 14,660 kilometres—in 191 days and ten minutes.

🌏 WHAT IS AN ULTRAMARATHON?

An ultramarathon is a run that is longer than the traditional marathon run of 42.196 kilometres, and an ultrarunner is an athlete who competes in such events. Ultraruns, in one form or another, have been staged all over the world since the late 1700s.

An ultramarathon can be contested over a specific distance—such as my run from the North Pole to the South Pole—or during a designated time, the winner being the athlete who runs furthest in that time—usually multi-day runs. The most common ultramarathon distances are 50 kilometres and 100 miles (160 kilometres), but I have competed in runs across the United States and around Australia, as well as, many times, from Sydney to Melbourne. Ultramarathons can take place on roads, in wilderness, over mountains, in open terrain, jungle, deserts, snow and ice, or on a running track; in blazing heat, freezing cold, gale-force winds, torrential rain or snow storms. They feature regularly on sporting calendars worldwide. Some 70,000 people complete ultramarathons every year.

Among the greatest ultrarunners are Yiannis Kouros, Serge Girard, Cliff Young, Ted Corbitt, Wally Hayward, Takahiro Sunada, Tomoe Abe and Suprabha Beckjord.

Why am I embarking on this epic adventure, running from the top of the world to the bottom? In 2001, I became a member of the Australian federal parliament and parliamentary secretary to the minister for Education, Science and Training. Unfortunately, though I stuck it out for nearly a decade, politics frustrated me. I wanted to actually make a difference, not simply sit in meetings *talking* about changing people's lives. In 2009, Brooke, Dillon and I spent our holidays at an orphanage in Chiang Mai, Thailand, helping children suffering from AIDS. Brooke read books to

I live to run.

the children and helped to feed and clothe the babies, while Dillon and I repaired the playground equipment and buildings, and built bikes. The year before that, I had travelled to India, Nepal, Egypt and Peru and seen for myself the real poverty that exists in this world: vast numbers of the world's population don't have clean sanitary conditions or fresh drinking water. These experiences influenced me profoundly and left me wanting to do something practical to help— specifically, to raise awareness of the poverty that exists in some of the world's poorest communities and to raise money to build wells and to provide clean sanitary conditions for them. And so, I planned a charity run of more than 21,000 kilometres, from North Pole to South Pole, with the aim of raising money to help the Red Cross. To get people's attention, in the hope that those who saw me would be encouraged to support my cause, my progress would be monitored and reported using the latest communications technology, accessible to classrooms, boardrooms and living rooms around the world. If we can get just 50 million people around the world following my run, a donation of just $2 from each person will raise my dream amount of $100 million, but I'll be grateful for whatever I raise.

Why do I run? I run because I need to contribute to mankind. Some people use their brain or creative talent to help others; my talent is in running long distances. I have always run for a cause. This pole-to-pole run is not about me being a martyr or a hero; I just have an innate need to make a difference on this earth. My parents and my late wife set me an example: they were always helping others. Maybe I am doing it out of guilt for living a privileged life in a privileged country, or for the sins I have committed. Whatever the real reason, this is what I do.

PAT'S ULTRARUNNING RECORDS

- World record for the longest tropics run (6307 kilometres in 83 days), 1999
- World record for 10,000 kilometres (129 days), 1999
- World record for crossing the Simpson Desert, 1996 and 1998
- Third in the world for 1000 miles (1600 kilometres) on a track
- Australian record for 13,383 kilometres (174 days), 1999
- Around Australia Long Run record (continuous running—191 days and 10 minutes—for 14,662.4 kilometres during my Centenary of Federation run), 2001
- 10 international ultrarunning records, including Western Australia border to border and Brisbane to Darwin runs, 1999
- Trans America Road Race: second place 1993; fourth place 1995
- First person to run 24 hours vertically, climbing up and down Sydney's AMP Tower (distance equivalent to running up Mount Everest in 24 hours), 1998 (repeated in 2006)

The cause

Every 15 seconds, a child passes away from a disease caused by lack of safe drinking water, inadequate sanitation or poor hygiene. I want to use my talent for ultrarunning to raise the money to make this dream a reality. By creating clean supplies of water and installing proper sanitation facilities—things we all take for granted in Australia—we can save lives.

In East Timor a child died before my eyes. In South-East Asia I

Safe water supplies are essential. *Courtesy of Australian Red Cross/Kim Batchelor*

saw children covered with needle-stick injuries in a dump; they were trying to break syringes down to sell the metal inside for bottles of water. It was a heartbreaking turning point in my life. I want to raise an enormous amount of money for such a cause. But to inspire people to donate I would need to do more than just stand on a soapbox and exhort the haves of the world to dig deep for the have-nots. No, I would have to make people sit up and take notice first, and then they might reach for their wallet or purse. I would have to do something that nobody had ever done before. And when I succeeded, people would say, 'Well, if Farmer is prepared to take on such an impossible and dangerous project, the least I can do is back him to the hilt.'

By running from pole to pole, I aim to highlight and help to prevent the needless deaths of millions of people each year through lack of clean water. Clean water and sanitation are vital to building healthy families and communities. They lead to fewer deaths from diarrhoea and improve maternal, infant and general community health, as well as the lives of villagers who often travel for hours every day to access clean water.

WATER AND SANITATION FACTS

- Unsafe water and poor sanitation have claimed more lives over the past century than any other cause.
- Wherever there is a lack of access to clean water and sanitation, disease and economic hardship are close by.
- 880 million people do not have access to clean water.
- 2.7 billion people do not have adequate sanitation facilities.
- Some 4 million people die each year from diseases associated with the lack of access to safe drinking water, inadequate sanitation and poor hygiene.
- 4000 children under five years old die every day from those same associated diseases.
- Dirty water and poor sanitation are the world's second-biggest killer of children; improved conditions could reduce this toll by two-thirds.
- Millions of people, mostly women and children, spend hours a day collecting water.

Source: The Australian Red Cross

The charity

My run would be filmed continually, and footage would be screened on my website and on television networks worldwide. People around the globe would be able to follow me as I ran: if I was eaten by a bear or fell through a crack in the ice, they'd see it! Hopefully, as well as savouring the thrills and spills, they'd be moved to donate money. Everything I raised would be managed by the Red Cross, which would channel the money to projects in collaboration with the International Federation of Red Cross and Red Crescent Societies and its individual national members. Red Cross water and sanitation programs form part of an integrated community health approach in which the organisation works with villagers to install communal taps and toilets and to provide hygiene education, such as encouraging people to kill germs by boiling water before drinking and by washing their hands and clothes regularly. The organisation also helps with the building of installed water systems, fencing them off from animals to avoid damage or contamination. Because of their record, the Red Cross was the first emergency coordinator called in after the tsunami in Japan in 2011 and Hurricane

Katrina, which devastated New Orleans in the United States in 2005. Its primary task was to set up sanitary conditions and clean drinking water for the survivors.

I admire the Red Cross because they don't give a hoot about politics, race or religion. They care only for helping those in need, and they keep their administration costs to a minimum: no more than 10 per cent of donations. It took me two years to seal the deal with the charity. They needed to be confident that I could do what I said I was going to, and that I wouldn't tarnish their reputation by failing. At first, they were sceptical that I could even start, let alone complete, the run. But once they got to know me, they agreed to be the conduit for the funds. The money I raised would be in safe hands.

Running for a cause—to save kids like this one. *Courtesy of Australian Red Cross/ Kelly Chandler*

The costs

Initially, I estimated that it would cost between $7 million and $8 million to complete the run. That would pay for polar guides, a logistics manager, a specialist support team and armed guards for the more dangerous areas of Central America and the Darién Gap. It would also allow for two fully fitted-out recreational vehicles to sleep in en route, stocked with media gear, food, water and medical supplies. Hotels are tempting when you're hurting, but if you leave the road and drive 15 kilometres or so to a hotel to spend the night there, it eats up precious time and also sends the wrong message. I prefer to rough it while I'm running and dream of a soft warm bed at the end. I hoped that the money we needed would be acquired from sponsors, but, to my surprise, nearly all of the corporations that I approached, in Australia, the United States, Asia and Europe, turned me down. I finally realised that this was not because they didn't believe in the cause; they simply didn't believe that what I was attempting was humanly possible.

So I had to cut my sail according to the available cloth. I *would* run from pole to pole, but I would do it on a shoestring budget, with a smaller support team, cutting corners by doing without anything—be it gear, food or communications equipment—that was not essential. I sold my house and car in order to raise the start-up costs. Some good friends also donated money.

The trek would be far tougher and more dangerous for the lack of financial support, but that would make it so much sweeter when I completed it. I would finish the run and make that money for the water projects or die trying: simple as that. I would never give up as long as my body allowed me to keep running. I'd succeed by doing what I always had done, taking it one step at a time, one day, one week, one month at a time. I would defy the cold, pain, polar bears, blistering heat and bandits. The way I saw it, unless a disaster befell me that I could not control, I couldn't fail.

I was blessed that at least some organisations understood what I was trying to do and, after looking into my history and track record, put their faith and dollars behind me. My hope, as I left for the North Pole, was that, once the corporations and individuals who initially turned me down realised that I'd actually started running, that I was doing what I told them I was going to do, they'd rethink and jump onboard. With so much at stake, with the chance to do so much good, I hoped they'd take the opportunity to show their support.

The quest

If I was going to make a difference, I wanted to make a *big* difference, and for that I needed to make a big impression. So I decided that I would attempt the greatest run in history: from the North Pole to the South Pole, via Canada, the United States and Central and South America. It was a run that had never before been achieved or, to the best of my knowledge, even attempted.

The poles are accessible only at certain times of the year, meaning that, beginning in April 2011, I needed to cover the 21,000 kilometres between them in around nine months, at an average of 18–21 kilometres a day on the ice and 85 kilometres a day—*two* marathons—everywhere else, be it jungle, mountain range or desert. I planned, apart from a couple of days off to equip the vans and brief the crew before we set off on the Canadian leg, to run *every single day*: rest and relaxation weren't on the schedule. At the poles, I would face winds of up to 140 kilometres per hour and temperatures as low as –40 degrees Celsius. If the horrific weather didn't get me, perhaps the polar bears, pressure ridges or treacherous ice chasms would. Then, there were the freeways of the United States, the searing heat of the Deep South, and the heat and energy-sapping altitudes of Central and South America, not forgetting their marauding bandits and drug runners. Not that my quest would be all doom and gloom. I would be meeting people from diverse backgrounds and testing my body to the limit. There would be the adventure that I crave. Also, I would be running through some of the most spectacular and compelling terrain on earth, from the vast and glistening ice floes of the Arctic to the broad plains of the United States and the tropical jungles of South America. How many people get to experience the best our planet has to offer at such close hand?

It was going to be a race against time. Actually, it would be *two* races against time: my daughter, Brooke, was sitting her Higher School Certificate in 2012 and I'd promised her that I would be home by then. I needed to reach Tierra del Fuego at the bottom tip of South America, then get to Punta Arenas, the take-off point for the Antarctic, by December, giving me a month to reach the pole and return. After then, the authorities do not allow entry, as the temperatures plummet from a summery –40 degrees Celsius to –80, and the days (offering 24 hours of light in summer) rapidly grow shorter until all is darkness.

Once I had completed my run, I would disperse the funds I had attracted and tell the world about my journey and about the plight of the people who had inspired me to make it. I was born with a gift— being able to run long distances faster and perhaps go further than any other person on earth. I'd be a fool not to use it.

WARMING UP

On January 7, 2011, I said goodbye to family and friends at Sydney Airport, bound for New York, where I was going to be doing some final training and trying to raise sponsorship and awareness of my run. The city was experiencing one of the worst winters in memory, and the temperature when I arrived was −8 degrees Celsius. Despite this, New York was filled with joggers, and they all seemed to congregate in Central Park.

While in New York I made television appearances, raised desperately needed funds for the run—and trained hard.

Every morning at five o'clock, I left my apartment in Harlem, strapped on two car tyres that I'd found in a wrecking yard, and ran the nearly 20 blocks to Central Park North. On the way, I passed convenience stores, hairdressers and cafes, parked cars with a metre of snow sitting on their roofs, and incredulous, rugged-up locals. Central Park itself was breathtakingly beautiful, a wonderful place to train. The lawns and paths were blanketed in deep snow, and the lakes were iced over. I was inspired by the resilience of the plants that survived the terrible cold, the dogs, squirrels and birds that turned the vast area into a snowy playground, and the people who told me they walked in the park every day, whether the weather was blazing hot or bloody freezing. As I did my two laps of the park each day—a distance of about 20 kilometres—I got to know its landmarks: the Sheep Meadow and the Lake, the rotundas, restaurants and ornate bridges.

The conditions replicated, in some ways, those that I'd be experiencing at the poles and in parts of Canada in the months to come. I would be pulling a kayak loaded with 100 kilograms of gear, so dragging the tyres through the ice and snow in Central Park prepared me, strengthening my back, core and legs. Before I'd left Sydney, I'd run thousands of kilometres, many of them pulling tyres on the sand at Coogee Beach. I'd also taken ice baths to acclimatise myself to the cold. I'd had olive oil with my cereal, because I needed the extra calories to cope with the cold conditions to come. This final period of serious training in New York, the culmination of months of physical preparation, was a beautiful few weeks. I could finally see my dream unfolding.

Of course, it was also hard work. But the people of Central Park made the physical slog easier to endure: the runners and strollers who stopped to jog or walk with me and chat. One fellow told me he never donated to causes, but he was going to make an exception for me.

PAT'S PLAN FOR SUCCESS

On the ice, I'll be hard-pressed to average more than 15 to 18 kilometres a day. The run from the North Pole to the southern end of the Arctic circle is around 700 kilometres, so this ideally will take me 40 or so days, although the constantly drifting ice and unknown hazards may play havoc with my plans.

After I get off the ice, I'll aim to run about 85 kilometres a day, at 10 kilometres per hour, maintaining that steady pace every single day that I'm on the mainland. I'll try to keep 10 to 15 per cent in reserve at all times: there's no point in busting a gut if I want to be able to start off again strongly, both physically and mentally, each day. Rob de Castella and Steve Moneghetti, both great marathon runners, ran only two marathons a year, because they gave those races all they had: they left nothing in the tank. But I'm going to be running two marathons a day every day for more than 11 months, and the only way I can accomplish that is to pace myself and not wear my body out. It's more about holding back when you're feeling good than pushing hard when you're feeling bad. I'm all about finishing this race, not being a show pony. I've been in races when blokes have shot out of the gate, and soon they've fallen by the wayside. No one cares who's in first place at the halfway mark. You hang in there, you keep going: it's like the tortoise and the hare. You have to make a huge effort but also make sure you finish. By running within my capacity, I feel I will be able to keep going until I reach the South Pole.

It's impossible to plan a run like this in every detail, because with such a totally new experience things can and will happen that we could not have planned for. All I can do is take care of the known challenges: make sure I have the best possible team that I can afford to support me, enough food and water, vehicles that don't break down. I'll need lots of luck, but I can't control that.

I have an economical running style. Economy of movement and having a good centre of gravity are very important. When I started out, my arms and legs flew everywhere, and it sapped my energy. I learned to run economically by observing ultrarunners Cliff Young and Yiannis Kouros and soccer players who move fast across the ground by running heel to toe and not lifting their legs too high. I keep my arms still and across my chest, as Kouros does: it dissipates lactic acid and pumps it around the body, stopping the muscles cramping up.

When I'm running from pole to pole, I'll conjure up images of things that are precious to me. In my mind, I'll visit my children in Sydney. I'll think of the good times I shared with Lisa. I'll imagine lying on the beach at Coogee, or enjoying a rich, creamy chocolate milkshake or an icy beer. And I'll be thinking, too, of the little face that epitomises the reason I'm running: the child who died before my eyes in East Timor because she had no clean water.

After six weeks of training and television appearances, an interview with the *New York Times* and several disappointing meetings with prospective sponsors, I flew across the country to Los Angeles, arriving on February 19. In contrast to icy Manhattan, on the west coast it was warm and sunny. It was so good to run in shorts and T-shirt again, instead of having to rug up each day.

My brother and logistics manager, Bernie, arrived from Australia, and Greg Quail, who would be responsible for filming, broadcasting and local promotions, also joined us, and we got down to business, planning what we needed to do before we drove north to Canada for more ice training.

I'll be thinking of my trip to East Timor to keep my motivation high. *Courtesy of Australian Red Cross/Kim Batchelor*

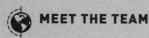

BERNIE FARMER

ROLE: Logistics manager

TASKS: Apart from mapping out my route each day and driving the main back-up van, my brother is charged with keeping me focused, monitoring my physical and mental condition and reacting accordingly. He is a great believer in careful planning, imagining all the possibilities beforehand and taking steps to ensure that all goes smoothly, being proactive rather than reactive.

EXPERIENCE: Bernie has been my logistics manager on many of my runs, including my run around Australia. A lifetime's experience of being my brother equips him to handle the mood swings that I am prone to when I'm doing it tough in the middle of a monster run.

GREG QUAIL

ROLE: Media expert

TASKS: To spread the word about my run so that those who saw me on TV, online and in newspapers or heard me on the radio knew that they could donate to my cause. Greg was responsible for getting the images of the trek broadcast. He and his cameramen and media technicians shot footage and broadcast from the poles and all the other regions. They also interviewed me at the end of each day's run about what had happened on the road.

EXPERIENCE: Greg is the CEO of Quail TV and a producer of television documentaries and drama.

We bought our two vans, a Winnebago and a Coachman, which would be our support vehicles between Canada and Argentina. They could sleep a total of nine people, and there was room in the Coachman for a mini TV studio. Each also had a shower, a loo and good sleeping space. Such comforts would make a big difference on the gruelling trek.

On February 22, we headed north. It was a great feeling to be on our way.

A few days later, we heard that the Nine Network had agreed to run regular video updates of my event on the *Today* show and to feature me on *Sixty Minutes*: fantastic news. However, I was beginning to feel a little worried that with all the lobbying for sponsorship and media commitments I'd been doing, I hadn't been doing enough training and that I was running out of time to reach peak fitness, despite the long distances I'd covered in New York and Los Angeles. I was spending too much time working on modifying the vans when I should have been training, because I couldn't afford to pay mechanics or refitters, and I was constantly on the phone begging everyone I knew for financial support. Then Greg called to say he had organised further sponsorship meetings in New York and Washington, and that I needed to meet him on the east coast as soon as we had set up our base in Canada. We were still very short of money to fund the trek. This trip took up extra training time, and I also became tired from driving hundreds of kilometres a day, because I couldn't pay a driver. Then, on March 1, I received some bad news. The doctor from the Australian Institute of Sport who was scheduled to be with me for the entire trek had fallen ill and so would not be able to come. We were unable to find—or fund—another medic at short notice. Who would have ever thought it would be so hard just to take the first step?

Letters and emails from home helped to keep my spirits up. One letter from my daughter said:

> People may call you crazy; let them. Really, they're the crazy ones. What do you think is more crazy: sitting at a desk and going home every day knowing that what you will do the next day will be exactly the same, or realising that you're greater than that and physically running from one end of the world to the other? You don't know what will happen tomorrow or the next day; you don't have to know, because today you've lived.

It was a hell of a drive up to Canada: more than 600 kilometres a day, through Oregon and Washington, then across the border to Vancouver. I couldn't help thinking that this was only a fraction of the distance that I'd be running, and it seemed so far, the country so vast, even without the ice and snow, and the endless mountains. It helped me to think about what two of my Australian heroes, around-the-world lone sailor Jessica Watson and long-distance swimmer Susie Maroney, had achieved against the odds. Jessica had had few sponsors when she sailed out of Sydney Harbour in 2009: people said she was committing suicide. Then, when she showed that she could accomplish her dream, sponsors flocked in and, along with the public, politicians and the media, were there to cheer her along the home straight.

On March 12, I picked up my new visa from the American consulate in Vancouver. Called an 'I visa', it's normally used by journalists, authors and filmmakers, and I qualified because I was writing this book about my run and would be appearing in Greg's documentary and the Nine Network reports. We had also secured CNN as a sponsor, who were going to pay for a weekly feed of the journey that would go around the world. It was a big coup.

While we were in Vancouver, Bernie and I were kept busy organising equipment, including the kayaks that we planned to use as sleds across the snow. When loaded with gear and food, they would weigh about 100 kilograms—around 30 kilograms more than me. We decided on kayaks instead of traditional sleds because they are better at bridging gaps between ice floes. There were lots of other things to do to make sure we had absolutely everything we'd need. At the North Pole, we wouldn't be able to take a stroll to the corner store to buy food, goggles or undies that we'd forgotten.

On March 18, I left Bernie and Greg in Yellowknife and flew to Longyearbyen in Norway's Svalbard Islands with the kayaks and other gear to meet up with my polar team: guide Eric Philips, satellite video uplink operator Clark Carter and cameraman Jose Naranjo.

The beautiful setting of Longyearbyen.

Longyearbyen is the world's most northerly town, indeed the world's most northerly settlement with a population of over 1000 people. Both Norwegian and German troops were stationed there during World War II. Although a bustling town with a busy airport, it remains picture-postcard beautiful because of its location amid the mountains and snow. The dwellings of the predominantly Norwegian, Russian, Swedish, Thai and Ukrainian inhabitants are painted in cheerful shades of yellow, red and blue. Yet, not too far away, at the North Pole, is a different world. There, the climate is completely unforgiving. We were going to be trekking across 670 kilometres of treacherous, continually moving ice, accompanied by winds of up to 140 kilometres per hour, temperatures of −40 degrees Celsius and, potentially, polar bears. No one ever knows what to expect in the Arctic Circle, because the conditions and terrain vary from year to year. It is impossible to tell beforehand whether the ice will be solid or breaking up, or too thin and deadly to cross.

 MEET THE TEAM

ERIC PHILIPS
ROLE: Polar guide
TASKS: To navigate through the treacherous polar regions, both north and south. He was responsible for 'reading' the ever-shifting ice, and he carried a Magnum revolver to protect us from polar bear attacks in the north. Being armed with such a heavy weapon sounds a bit over the top, but a revolver with its short barrel is more easily drawn and fired in freezing conditions than a rifle or shotgun. Eric's aim was to get me from the North Pole to Ward Hunt Island, Canada, safely and in good enough shape to run the rest of the way, and then to ease me across the ice on the final leg of the journey, to the South Pole.
EXPERIENCE: Eric is one of the world's few polar explorers and is well versed in leading expeditions to remote and dangerous environments. In 2001, he became the only person to cross the earth's largest icecaps—Antarctica to the South Pole, Greenland,

the South Patagonian Icecap and Canada's Ellesmere Island. On an 84-day ski trek to the South Pole, he pioneered a new route through the Trans-Antarctic Mountains. His adventuring philosophy, as expressed to *Life* magazine, appeals to me: 'We benefit from regularly confronting two key emotions—Fear and Passion. They are vital to achieving our potential, regardless of what we do, and shape the core of our biggest adventure—Life.'

JOSE NARANJO
ROLE: Cameraman
TASKS: As well as being my main cameraman on the ice, Jose is also my training master in skiing and mountain climbing.
EXPERIENCE: Jose is an experienced adventurer, skiier and mountain climber. He is a funny, brave guy who has the disconcerting habit of doing whatever it takes—including risking his life—to get a good shot.

CLARK CARTER
ROLE: Satellite video uplink operator
TASKS: To film and transmit one minute of film a day from the Arctic sector of the run.
EXPERIENCE: Clark is a 27-year-old adventurer and filmmaker. He works for the Australian Broadcasting Corporation as a news producer and also freelances as a cameraman and remote area communications consultant. In 2005 and 2008, with fellow adventurer Chris Bray, he traversed, unassisted, Victoria Island in the Canadian Arctic, a distance of 1000 kilometres, with homemade wheeled kayaks. They received the Australian Geographic Society's Spirit of Adventure Award. In 2010, Clark and Andrew Johnson travelled down the length of Papua New Guinea's longest river— the Sepik—from source to sea, hiking through 200 kilometres of thick jungle and facing down whitewater rapids, crocodiles, tropical diseases and bandits.

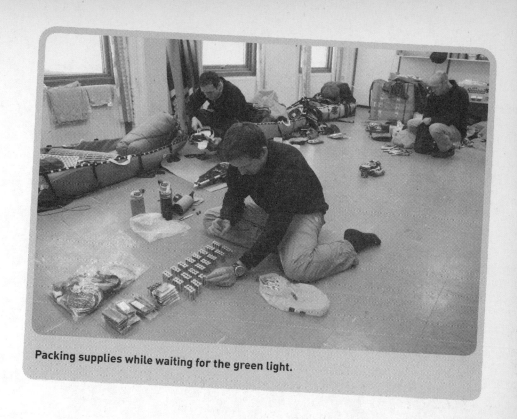

Packing supplies while waiting for the green light.

Altogether, we made quite a spectacle. We were camping in an aircraft hangar, and there were camp beds set up in every corner. The place was bustling with people madly readying gear and supplies for our trip and other expeditions. Those of us who would be doing the trekking laid out all of the food for the expedition and then packed it into bags for our sleds. Some of it looked a bit questionable, especially the more exotic freeze-dried curries that we were taking. But I figured that when we were out on the ice pretty much anything would taste good. (I was wrong!) One bonus was that I'd be expending so much energy that I could eat loads of delicious chocolate, nuts and Milo without worrying about stacking on weight. Keeping the kilojoules up would actually be a daily challenge.

In Longyearbyen, Jose also put me through interval training, trying to get me used to the repetition. I also learned to run on snow in snow boots and to cross-country ski. I had been planning to run in snowshoes, but Eric advised me that skis were more stable and better at traversing shifting cracks in the ice, which could be a metre wide. I had never skied before. In hindsight, I realise I should have learned, as

Getting into nick and learning to ski.

we would be spending up to 50 days on ice and snow, for heaven's sake. But, typically, I figured, 'How hard can skiing be? Everyone does it.' The truth was that it was damned hard to learn in such a short period. But I learned enough to get about on the snow. What was *really* difficult was dragging the kayak up hills while trying to balance on the skis and then being dragged downhill after the kayak, which would slide ahead out of control. Before long, I was covered in bruises.

On March 22, Eric, Clark, Jose and I headed out of Longyearbyen for a four-day training expedition in the icy wilds. While it wasn't nearly as extreme as the North Pole would be, the trial run was an important part of our preparation. As well as giving me a solid physical workout in cold conditions, it enabled us to finetune and test-drive the equipment we'd be taking to the poles. One bizarre piece of gear was a Hannibal Lecter–type mask that protected my face from the cold and warded off frostbite on the nose. I also tried out my new mittens, which had extra-deep finger compartments. Fingers and noses, being extremities, are very susceptible to frostbite. Our dry suits had a trial run as well: they are waterproof suits that let you walk or swim through water and clamber across sections of broken or thin ice without exposure to death-inducing cold and wet. We headed down to the water and watched Eric as he ran around on the ice and then jumped through a thin section and swam about.

We also did packing practice. Knowing how to pack and unpack our sleds quickly would make a huge difference to the team's overall efficiency. During the first weeks of an expedition, it can take as long as four hours to get ready to leave camp each morning. If we could reduce that to two hours, it would give us 40 extra running hours overall, which could prove decisive to the trek's success.

Finally, we tested our polar diet: freeze-dried curries, reindeer cabanossi, olive oil that we drank straight, and big blocks of butter that we chewed on like cheese and blended into stews and porridge, all to keep our kilojoules up so we could continue pressing on in the cold. On the ice, we would be carrying close to 30,000 kilojoules of food per person per day. Around 50 per cent of the food would be fat, to give us long-term energy, along with a balance of carbohydrates and protein to build up our muscles and help us to recover overnight. We would

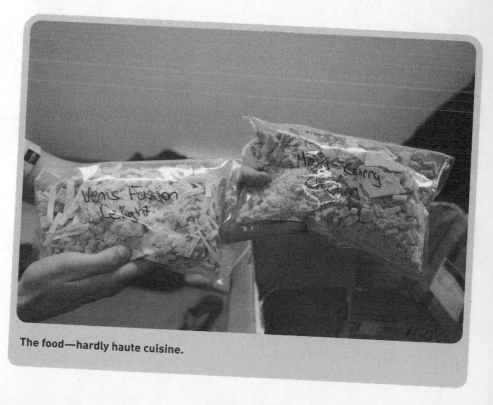

The food—hardly haute cuisine.

be stopping every 90 to 120 minutes to eat and drink (though I had qualms about those frequent rest stops, as we had so much territory to cover within a strict time frame).

To be frank, the training trip was hell. I had discovered in New York that I hate the cold, and here it was –22 degrees. My hands ached terribly. In the cold light of our imminent departure, I finally became aware of the huge task ahead of me and began to wonder if my run might not indeed be impossible. I kept my doubts to myself, however. The other team members were in high spirits, and we were in an impossibly beautiful part of the world. We even saw some wild reindeer!

The final few days at Longyearbyen were spent organising our communications systems. We were taking four satellite phones and two lightweight laptop computers with us on the trek, which we would use to upload footage to the internet every night. Temperatures as low as –40 degrees Celsius aren't great for electronics, and we had to put systems in place to keep the equipment running. Clark, our communications guy, had made an insulated, waterproof, shockproof briefcase to house the phones and computers: it looked like something out of

Eric takes a dip—something I was determined to avoid.

a James Bond movie. As a trial, we left the gear in its case out in the snow all night while it uploaded video, and in the morning we were delighted to find that it had worked like a charm.

While we were training in and around Longyearbyen, the Siberian team we'd hired to set up our base at Barneo Ice Station, about 130 kilometres south of the pole, had flown out to get started. First, skydivers landed on the ice to check that it was safe for a plane to land. Then, massive tractors were parachute-dropped out of jets, which were used to construct a runway, and building materials, communications gear, food and other vital supplies were airlifted in. While our team was there, Prince Harry and a team of British soldiers who had been wounded in Afghanistan flew in: they were 'The Walking Wounded', trekking to raise money for the families of those killed in the conflict. The people you meet at the North Pole!

Unfortunately, some atrocious weather also arrived and delayed the team's construction work at the station. Our departure date was pushed back indefinitely. This was a big blow: because of the limits to when we could get to the South Pole at the other end of the journey, a delay of even a couple of days here at the start—at 80 or more kilometres per day—meant having to make up the distance somewhere else on the road. And even if that meant running only 5 kilometres extra each day, that was an hour's more running—and an hour's less sleep—and it would all add up.

The news affected my morale, and I found myself dwelling on the first polar leg of the run: a leg over which I had very little control. It was impossible to predict exactly the conditions we would face, and I was concerned that the people trekking with me might not be able to go at the pace I needed to achieve: I was the only serious athlete in the group. In an attempt to banish the rising fear, I got up extra early, put 100 kilograms of snow in my sled and hit the hills. It's amazing what a couple hours of training can do to improve your outlook.

While we were waiting to leave, I painted Brooke's and Dillon's name on each of my skis, so when I'm feeling tired I can look down and draw inspiration from them. Brooke's name is on my right boot, the foot I lead with. She gives me direction and has done since she was born. My left foot is where my strength lies, and it keeps me stable, just like Dillon. If ever I feel I can't take one more step, I will look at these names and remember the old saying that when you think you've gone as far as you possibly can, you've only gone half as far as you're capable of.

I just wanted to get moving, because it was so cold standing still! While we were waiting, I filmed a segment with Jose, and I had to take a package of food out of my pack, but my hands wouldn't work so I dropped it. Then my lips were so frozen that I couldn't speak.

The last word from Greg Quail was that sponsorship was trickling in, but if an accountant looked at our books he'd be horrified. I also learned from him that my route had changed. Greg and David Mason from the Nine Network had come to believe that the potential to receive donations from the public would be greatly increased if I ran down the east coast of the United States rather than the west. They said that there would be more donors and more media coverage in the big population centres of Manhattan, Washington, Atlanta and New Orleans than in just San Francisco (which I had to skirt anyway) and

Comfort stops are in short supply.

Los Angeles. I acquiesced, hoping they were right. I transferred cash between bank accounts to make sure that Bernie, Greg and the crew left in Vancouver could drive across to the new pick-up point on the other side of Canada in the vans.

 THE PROPOSED ITINERARY

MARCH 2011
Polar expedition leader Eric Philips, satellite video uplink operator Clark Carter, cameraman Jose Naranjo and I gather at Longyearbyen, the Svalbard Islands, Norway.

APRIL–MAY
Fly to the Russian Arctic base Barneo, then to the North Pole. Ice trek around 700 kilometres to Ward Hunt Island, just off the northern tip of Canada, in 40 days.

MAY–SEPTEMBER
Resupply, then fly to the northernmost road at Radisson, Canada. Eric, Clark and Jose leave us here.

Road run approximately 9500 kilometres—through Canada, down the east coast of the United States, through Mexico and Central America to southern Panama.

Accompanying team include Bernie Farmer (logistics manager), my niece Katie Walsh (all-round duties and running mate), and Greg Quail (filming, broadcasting and local promotions), cameramen.

SEPTEMBER
Southern Panama to northern Colombia, 150 kilometres, incorporating the dreaded Darién Gap, hideout for bandits, drug and gun runners and insurgents, and notorious as one of the most dangerous places on earth.

A local guide and an armed security entourage join the group on this leg.

OCTOBER–DECEMBER
Road run nearly 10,000 kilometres from northern Colombia,
through Ecuador, Peru and Chile, to the world's southernmost city,
Ushuaia, in the Argentinean province of Tierra del Fuego.

DECEMBER–JANUARY 2012
Fly to the Ronne Ice Shelf, Antarctica. Ice trek around
1100 kilometres to the South Pole and journey's end.
   Eric Philips and a cameraman join us for this final leg.

The distances above are necessarily approximate—I knew that I
would have to detour around bridges that had been washed away,
run the wrong way on occasion and get lost in the desert so many
times it would be impossible to calculate the exact distance. But
how we got from the North Pole to the South Pole is the story of
this book.

In the end, we were delayed by four days, meaning that I was
behind schedule before I took my first step. One cause of our late start
was that we were bumped from our place in the queue by Prince Harry
and the soldiers. The schedule was looking almost impossible anyway;
I wondered how I'd make up the distance. Still, all I could do was take
one step at a time, one day at a time. I was still confident that I could
complete the task. My dream was to reach the South Pole on Australia
Day, January 26. For now, though, there was nothing left to do but
run . . . and run . . . and run.

STAGE 1
THE ARCTIC

April 5 to May 16

 DISTANCE TO COVER: Approximately 700 kilometres, depending on ice cap drift

 TERRAIN: Ice, ocean, pressure ridges and leads (splits in the ice)

 TYPICAL WEATHER CONDITIONS: Blizzards, bright sunshine, –30 to –40 degrees Celsius, winds of 130 kilometres per hour

 HAZARDS: Extreme cold and blizzards, falling through the ice into freezing ocean, polar bears, windburn, frostbite

 KEY EQUIPMENT: Kayaks for crossing leads and acting as makeshift sleds, skis and ski poles, snow boots, ice suits, tents, stoves and stove fuel, sleeping bags, navigation equipment, first aid kit, iridium phone, rope, fleece jacket and clothing, gloves, hats with ear covers and goggles to ward off the cold, sunglasses, frozen food

 PERSONNEL: Polar expedition leader Eric Philips, satellite video uplink operator Clark Carter, cameraman Jose Naranjo

APRIL 5

Today we got started, flying out to the Barneo Ice Station in a Russian Antonov 74 jet. Barneo Ice Station is the final gateway to the north for explorers and adventurers like me—just 100 kilometres away from the geographic North Pole. It opens in spring after Russian Hind helicopters locate a flat, smooth, stable surface on the ice for the base, and engineers build a runway that can accommodate supply and transport planes and a camp. The ice station closes down at the end of April, and each year it has to be rebuilt, thanks to the shifting ice flows at the top of the world.

Jose and me arriving at Barneo.

It's a sobering thought that I won't have another day off for another 10 or so months. During the delay beforehand, I was terrified that our expedition would be cancelled, like many other people's have been recently. But, at last, after what seemed an eternity, we were on our way to the North Pole.

> ### 🌍 PAT'S PREPARATION
>
> People ask me how long I've been training to run from pole to pole, and I tell them, 'All my life.' It's true: you can't just train hard for six months and hope to do this run; instead, it will be the culmination of everything I have ever done. Every run I have taken on in my life has prepared me for this ultimate test. I'm a better runner now at nearly 50 years old than when I was a young man. Of course, ultrarunning requires peak fitness and stamina, but, even more, it needs mental strength. It is this that keeps you going, putting one foot in front of the other, *never* giving up, even when every muscle in your body is screaming for you to stop. I will call on all my past experiences, the triumphs and the disappointments, every race, every training regime, the tricks I have learned, to succeed.

APRIL 6

Eric, Clark, Jose and I were collected from Barneo in a Russian Mil-8 twin turbine transport helicopter which took us to the North Pole, where the temperature was −30 degrees Celsius and a blizzard was raging with winds of up to 130 kilometres per hour: the dismount from the chopper was frantic.

The North Pole is located on sea ice around 3 metres thick. Under the ice there is nothing but ocean until you hit the seabed, about 4200 metres below. In the summer months, when we are here, it's daylight all day. In winter, it's perpetually dark. It is surreal being in this almost mythical place—the top of the world, a location that few people get to visit. I wish I had time to bask in the emotion, but there's work to do. Maybe when my journey is over I will allow myself the luxury of reflection.

Top of the world—dropped at the North Pole.

The Arctic is a humungous floating ice block, shifting this way and that. The landscape reminds me of the deserts of Egypt: both the tundra and the snow are fashioned by the wind. At the North Pole, the wind reigns above all elements. It pushes tonnes of ice across the ocean surface as if the ice sections are as light as pawns on a chessboard. The wind is the victor, and the ice bows before it and crumbles. We can hear constantly the groaning of ice rubbing on ice as the ice cap moves. There are pressure ridges everywhere—huge piles of ice formed when the wind and currents smash ice plates against each other, forcing them upwards, which are then snowed on and welded into place. There are also many leads—or splits—in the ice, and a lot of water.

Our first destination as we start the trek south is the edge of the northern ice cap. From there we fly to Ward Hunt Island, a snow-encased island 6.5 kilometres long and 3.3 kilometres wide off the north coast of Ellesmere Island, at the most northern tip of Canada. Ward Hunt is uninhabited and functions as another starting and departure point for expeditions to the North Pole. There is an airstrip and a hangar-like building. When we were ready to set out from the Pole, though, it was difficult to know which way to go! Obviously, we are heading south, but we also need to aim further to the west than where the island is situated, to allow for ice drift. This will become more difficult as we get closer to Canada, where the currents pick up. Thank goodness we have Eric with us as our guide.

Here's how things operate. We break up camp and set out between 8 and 9 am each day. Eric leads. I stay close to him. Clark and Jose are in the rear. We all drag our kayaks, which are laden with tents and other equipment and supplies. It's gruelling. We pull them over shifting ice, and up and over pressure ridges, and use them to ford breaks in the ice. We stumble, fall, bang our bodies against the ice. We keep going, taking breaks every two hours or so when Eric decrees. Around 4 or 5 pm we stop and pitch camp. Climbing into our warm tent, out of the freezing temperatures, the icy, driving wind and the glare of the sun is the best part of each day.

It has been an extremely hard first day. I've been moving gingerly on my skis, and we seem to have done nothing but climb over 2-metre-high pressure ridges, pulling our yellow kayaks—laden with a red pack of provisions and gear weighing 100 kilograms—behind us. After only two hours, I broke the bindings on my skis. Eric coughed a lot. I am worried that the equipment will not stand up to all the smashing around as we drag it over the piles of ice.

As we prepared to start out today, I felt like I was on the edge of a cliff, ready to jump off. I contemplate my past, and my future. There are a number of people whom I have helped in my life and a number of people I've let down. To those people I want to take this chance to say that I'm sorry, but I am who I am and hopefully the things that I do in the future will justify my single-mindedness and my determined attitude. In all of my runs, I have used positive visualisation to take me out of my pain, and never have thoughts of happy days at home with my kids in sunny Sydney, or arriving victorious at the South Pole early next year, been more beneficial to me than here. This event will call on every ounce of energy, every bit of will and determination I have just to finish, but my goal is not only to finish but to change the lives of many thousands of people worldwide. I will not give up.

The four of us—me, Clark, Eric, Jose.

APRIL 7

It has been our first full day on the ice, another incredibly difficult day. I knew this leg would be hard, but not this hard. Any sense of enjoyment has been ground out of me by the relentless slog. Every step is an effort. It hurts like hell. I know that later, when it's all over, I'll wish I could have revelled in trekking through the Arctic in the footsteps of great explorers, but as long as we're here, I now know, I'll just have to keep my head down, endure the discomfort, and make it through. This morning I didn't want to leave my sleeping bag, even though the temperature wasn't too bad: a comparatively warm –28 degrees! We commenced by boiling snow over the gas stoves for our thermoses, then adding a little extra to our porridge. The day was full of water-crossings and climbing over pressure ridges. Eric is doing a great job with the difficult task of navigation. I just wish we could move faster.

I wasn't prepared for the awesome spectacle of the pressure ridges, which are getting bigger. They are now ranging between 4 and 6 metres high, chunks of ice thrust up chaotically through the snow, some weighing as much as 50 tonnes. Our pace was 2 kilometres per hour—half what it should be—and that's damned frustrating. We must average 30 kilometres a day up here, but today we did about 15. Not good. Apart from not covering the necessary territory, we also found it difficult to warm up because of all the stopping and starting. Anyway, one day down, many more to go. It is so *cold*.

APRIL 8

The temperature on the ice today was –32 degrees. Being out in it was almost unbearable. Luckily, we didn't have too many stops: we are getting faster at negotiating the leads and the pressure ridges. But just when we thought everything was going well, Eric broke a binding on his ski. Just three days in and three bindings replaced: we have no more spares. I am gravely concerned.

We alternate sleeping partners in our two-man tents, so that we don't have a chance to get too much on each other's nerves. Inside, we have our sleeping bags, the satellite and iridium phones and

Our first pressure ridge—they would get much bigger.

computer, thermos flasks and a kettle, in which we boil snow for the thermos each day. And, of course, I have my trusty can of Milo, which I mix with powdered milk and boiling water. Each morning, we load everything from the tents, as well as the tents themselves, into the kayaks. Above the sleeping bags hang our boots, insulated clothing and dry suit, which all have to be de-iced when we take them off and hung up over the stove. The sleeping bags comprise three layers: an outside layer to stop the snow coming in, an inside layer to prevent vapour coming off your body and dampening the bag, and a sleeping layer rated to keep you warm down to –45 degrees Celsius.

APRIL 9

Since we set out, we have travelled almost 80 kilometres. This is just about okay. Clambering over the pressure ridges is slowing us down, as is Eric's insistence on frequent stops. Jose already has frostbite on the end of three toes. He says it will be okay; he just has to find a way to stop the ice from getting in his boots. A small mistake could prove very costly here. I hope and pray each day that we make it through this.

Our food is strictly rationed each day. No matter how hungry we are feeling, we can't eat more than our designated amount. If we do, it won't last the distance. We also have to make sure that there is sufficient spare in case we get held up, a possibility that is always on the cards.

Today we saw our first polar bear prints. A bear had passed this way a day before. The prints were enormous and I could make out the pads and claws. I gave a shudder, and I wasn't the only one.

This trek is the most painful thing I have ever done. The temperature is –36 degrees with strong winds. God help us.

APRIL 10

Today has been a reasonably good day, but we got off to a slow start. Apart from the fact that it hurts, the cold makes everything so much harder. Just doing up a zipper or a buckle takes ages, meaning that it's a major job getting dressed in the morning. My jacket is frozen solid and covered in ice: I was cold right from the start of the day, and nothing has improved.

Going to the loo is a major concern. Many of the children who have sent me emails have asked how I go to the toilet, and I reply, 'As fast as I can!' Terrible things can happen to your extremities in the Arctic. In fact, I do everything quickly out here: my meal breaks during the day are as quick as possible, because if you sit around too long you run the risk of turning into Frosty the Snowman. The only thing I don't do fast is getting out of my sleeping bag in the morning . . .

All I can do is eat plenty through the day to heat my body and give me energy to keep going. Tonight the cold is keeping me awake.

APRIL 11

We got off to a good start, but it was bitterly cold with a very strong northerly wind, which, thankfully, was at our backs. Our navigation is good, and it seems that we are headed just enough south-east (matching the drift) to put us on track for Ward Hunt Island.

Up here there are two kinds of water: water from melted ice, which is light blue, and the Arctic Ocean, which is pitch black. We are seeing a lot of black water. The ocean is black because the polar ice prevents

A wide lead opens before us.

any light from getting through. In places, it is 4000 metres deep. It looks very eerie. We had to don our dry suits to cross one lead that was about 30 metres wide. The water was black and deep, and it was a hellish crossing. The ice was very thin on both sides, making it extremely difficult to get out. You slip and slide and the ice crumbles, all the while trying to manoeuvre the kayak, and purchase is almost impossible to find.

As I write this, I am receiving texts from Brooke and Dillon; this gives me the strength to push on.

APRIL 12
. . . .

One of my ski bindings broke today, and the other one cracked. Eric blamed it on the way I ski, which is probably fair enough, though this doesn't explain his own binding breaking. Eric is treating us like school kids; he said that I need to be gentler on my equipment. He doesn't seem to realise that my sole objective is to get to Canada as fast as possible. He and I are clashing because we are both natural leaders.

Clark didn't film our barney because he is employed by Eric and wants more expeditions, but our disagreements are the dramatic stuff that should be documented, because they are the reality. We're not the Brady Bunch!

I have been forced to wear snowshoes and think I will just stay in them and hope they hold up. The problem with snowshoes is that wearing them takes a lot of energy and also makes crossing wide leads very dangerous. I have to pull my sled right to the edge of the lead and then jump across, before pulling the sled behind.

We have 625 kilometres to go before we reach the end of the polar region, and we're averaging 21 kilometres per day. If we can bump this up to 25 kilometres, we can make up a day's travel every four days. I know I'm a pain in the arse to my companions. I never let up on the need for us all to keep moving, going as far each day as humanly possible, so we can get back on schedule. 'Every kilometre counts!' I've said endlessly, like a cracked record.

APRIL 13
. . . .

Very cold start, –35 degrees. I didn't sleep much last night. At night—and I say that advisedly, because at this time of year it's daylight for

Above: The fairy-tale lights of Longyearbyen.

Left: So many options, but we're bound for the North Pole.

Above: Starting out with open hearts and high spirits—with Johan Ernst Nilson, another adventurer.

Below: My greatest fear—apart from not finishing.

Above: Unloading the plane in Barneo.
Below: Heading into the Arctic.

Above: My skis didn't stand up to the pressure.

Right: It's still freezing, even in the tent.

Below: Hauling the sleds.

Above: Tough going on a pressure ridge.

Below: Temperatures dropped to –40 degrees Celsius on occasion.

Above: A warmer day on the ice.
Below: Camping for the night.

Above: Relief

Left: Taking a break.

Below: Mountains in sight.

Left: Socks drying overnight.

Below: Getting closer to Ward Hunt Island.

Bottom: North Pole accomplished, waiting for the plane.

24 hours a day, which, although I was prepared for it, is bloody disconcerting—the prevailing sound, louder even than the screaming wind
outside the tent, is that of the shifting ice. It sounds just like two huge
pieces of metal rubbing together. I haven't washed in eight days. Being
so grimy is really uncomfortable, but it's part of everyday life for many
people who live on the street or don't have water.

I'm finding that messages from friends and strangers around the
world, telling me to keep going and never give up, are a wonderful support. It seems the word about the run is out there and getting louder
with every step I take.

APRIL 14
• •

A terrible day. From the first 100 metres, we struck walls of ice rubble
8 metres high. The whole place looks like a battle zone with ice chunks
of all shapes and sizes strewn everywhere as if the landscape has been
under heavy bombing. This is what happens when the elements of
wind and water play tug-of-war. All around us now, as we sit in our

Pressure ridge rubble—an icy junkyard.

tents, we can hear the groaning and the sheering of huge slabs of ice forcing their way through the snow-covered ground, buckling under the pressure from currents and wind more than 500 kilometres away.

I am bitterly disappointed at the distances we are covering each day. If we do more than 20 kilometres, Eric classes it as a good day, but I know we can go much faster and further each day. Eric insists on taking so many breaks. He is used to guiding tourists and adventurers on these trips, not ultra-athletes with a schedule to meet. I feel so terribly frustrated—and cold. Our clothing is covered in ice within minutes of leaving the tent each day, and I spend most of my energy just trying to stay warm at the slow pace.

It is an ongoing battle of wills between Eric and me. I have pleaded with him to make sure we cover the distance required before we take all these breaks. I keep suggesting to him that we should use the GPS at the end of the day to tell us how far we've travelled, and if we're short by 500 metres or a kilometre, then let's have a quick snack and push on and finish the day's distance. He structures our day around the time we have spent out, while I'm more concerned with the distance we've covered. I believe that if we finish a day's trek pleased that we have met our goal, then we will feel better disposed to get up and at it again the following day. Eric does not agree.

During one of our arguments, Eric said, 'Pat, you know nothing about the North Pole!'

I replied, 'No, Eric, I don't, and that's on purpose. All I need to know is what discomfort and pain I can put up with and travel the distance each day that I must to meet my goal. I don't need to dwell on what can go wrong.'

Eric is keen that I use him to guide me at the South Pole, and he's a wonderful guide. Many have tried to do what we are doing on the ice and failed. But if he joins me down south, I've decided that it will be on my terms: we'll move fast, and the camera crew will travel in skidoos. He'll do what I want him to do, rather than the other way around. I think by now he knows the strength of my will and my ability to tough out the worst conditions. Once, I told him that if the equipment and the ski bindings kept breaking I was prepared to complete the trek in bare feet if I had to, with or without him. He knew I was exaggerating, but I think I left him in no doubt about my determination.

APRIL 15

Trekking in the Arctic is the hardest thing I have ever done, and, when you consider some of the things I've done, that's saying something. I knew it would be tough, but not *this* tough. We're in the tent at the moment and have finished dinner; I hope this night, here in the warm tent, lasts and lasts. I don't want the morning to come, because that means I'll have to climb out of my sleeping bag and brave the −35 degree cold and bitter, freezing winds once more. I will put my jacket on in the morning and it will be covered in ice a moment later. At the end of every day, our gear and clothes are damp, and we try to dry them out at night but it only takes a minute for ice to form on them. Everything freezes instantly. You walk out onto the ice and straight-away your hands, toes, nose and ears ache as if someone is applying a Bunsen burner to them. It's excruciating.

We spent all day climbing and dragging our kayaks over wall after wall of broken ice. I wasn't prepared for the immensity of and diffi-culty presented by pressure ridges. Imagine you're in a scrap metal

Crossing a lead.

yard filled with car bodies and bits of bridge transoms and junk sticking in all directions out of the ground: that's what the terrain is like here. We scale each ridge, dragging our laden kayaks over the top, but they go on for as far as the eye can see. Today I was crossing a lead and banged my right knee. It's hurting badly. We slogged our guts out for 12 hours and covered 12 kilometres. That's depressing. Yesterday we did just 15 kilometres. These distances are nothing like what we should be achieving, and each day puts us further behind schedule. But there's not a thing I can do about it.

We've had to cross a lot of water. The leads can be a few centimetres wide, then the ice shifts and they're suddenly a metre across, and, before you know it, it's a lake. It is so dangerous. You might think, because the temperatures at the North Pole are in the –30s, even the –40s, that the ice there is hard, smooth and thick, and so easily traversable. But that isn't the case. The ocean in places is around 4000 metres deep, and the currents cause continual shifting of the surface ice. The movement literally drags sections of the ice cap apart, quickly and without warning, creating open channels of water. We passed a section of ice yesterday that was moving before our eyes. The ground shifted, then opened up, and a 50-tonne iceberg pushed up through the water. If you fall into a lead—easy to do—you can drown or freeze to death in seconds. It has been known for a lead to suddenly open up beneath a sleeping camp of explorers, with all lives being lost.

Each new obstacle has to be considered, analysed and dealt with safely. Swim across? Climb over? Look for a gap? Walk around? You have to make a call and follow it through. And when fatigue has set in, that's when mistakes are more likely. We haven't made any major mistakes yet. Apart from my bust-ups with Eric, we're pulling together as a unit and putting in the work. It's all we can do.

We must wear our dry suits at all times, because if you fall into that black, bottomless water without one, you're dead. Usually, we can bridge the leads with our kayaks, scamper across and then pull our kayaks after us, but increasingly we are having to swim across in our suits. I have never swum so bloody quickly.

My snowshoes are falling apart. There's no alternative, though, but to keep plodding on in them, because I'll have nothing else until we are resupplied via a drop of provisions and gear from a plane that is scheduled for April 25, which is ten days away.

Eric and Jose both broke ski bindings today, and a 30-centimetre hole was smashed in Clark's kayak when he fell on jagged ice. The resourceful Eric, who has been trying to repair our skis and boots, patched it with Kevlar rope. But no matter what, we'll keep going: we're going to get to Canada.

Physically, I'm fine. I've grown used to my nose and ears stinging terribly because of the extreme cold and wind, although the pain in my hands is like nothing I've ever felt. My knee is aching and I have a little bit of frostbite in one finger. Yet, agonising as that is, the mental pain is harder to bear. The short distances we're covering despite the high workload are a big worry.

It's hard to explain this place. It's beautiful and majestic, but terrifying too. I thought the North Pole would be flat and smooth, but mostly it's like bombs have gone off everywhere and turned the landscape to rubble. Yesterday, for 2 kilometres we had a good run, travelling relatively quickly over terrain that was for a change as smooth as an ice-skating rink, but instead of pushing on and making the most of it, Eric said, 'Let's rest up here and we'll get a good start on

The pressure ridges were getting bigger.

the smooth surface in the morning.' But then, when we woke up this morning, everything had changed. The smooth surface of the afternoon before had become pitted with pressure ridges thrust up in the night. The whole landscape had changed.

Brooke and Dillon have been sending me texts asking me what it's like, and I've been telling them everything is fine. I haven't mentioned the pain and the cold and the wind and the pressure ridges, or the ominous polar bear tracks I've seen. No point in worrying them.

This is so damned hard. There's only one solution to end the hardship: get to Canada.

APRIL 16

The day began sourly. Our gear took longer than expected to dry out, and we were ten minutes late starting off. Lately, Eric has been playing the sergeant major. I think the equipment failure, seven broken bindings and Clark's damaged kayak are on his mind. To top things off, our billy has a hole in the bottom, caused by continual crashing against ice platforms. Eric is spending two hours a night repairing equipment. He likes to do this work himself, and sees it as an integral part of his guiding duties. We stand around watching. The pain in my hands is almost unbearable.

I feel we are wasting too much time having breaks through the day. We had five today. They make us cold and cost us valuable kilometres, but Eric is not happy making changes to the routine he has always followed.

We sighted more polar bear tracks.

APRIL 17

Here's my quote for the day: 'Even bad luck has to run out sooner or later.' Each day feels like Groundhog Day, but I have to believe that we can make better progress. This trek is tough on our equipment and even tougher on our spirits, but I will not give up, I will push on, I will win. I must not lose my head, I must stay calm and focused. I can do this.

Tonight, we pitched our tent on a block of ice surrounded by water. Suddenly a treat: a seal popped its sleek head up out of the depths, looked intently at us and then dived under again. It was a sight to remember, but a worry too, because seals are the staple diet of polar bears. We sleep with the loaded Magnum and a flare gun, just in case we have an unwelcome visitor.

APRIL 18

I have all but given up on trying to push for faster times on the ice. Eric is intractable. White snow, grey sky and blue ice: this is my life day after never-ending day. This is a place where voices are frozen and silence is deafening.

APRIL 19

The end of this dreadful April is getting closer, thank God, but I am seriously worried about our schedule. Today, we travelled just 19 kilometres, and yet we worked so hard. The sleds are such millstones and yet a necessary evil, because they carry our food, fuel, camera equipment and tents. The camping costs us around four hours a day: two hours setting up and heating and two hours pulling down on top of breakfast and dressing. Temperatures of around −40 degrees make even the simplest tasks, like packing the sled or zipping up a jacket, epic toils. Eric is still insisting that we take five breaks a day. If I had my way, there would only be two.

I've been chanted the 'Serenity Prayer' to myself: 'Dear God, help me to change the things I can, accept the things I cannot, and have the wisdom to know the difference.'

We plod along. Eric, Jose and Clark are quite happy with our progress. They say polar expeditions are notoriously slow.

I am spending a lot of time replaying my life in my mind, from when I was a little kid through to the present. I try to keep things positive, but sometimes when I'm hurting, such as now, my pain is reflected in the negativity that I cannot prevent creeping into my thoughts. I wish I could apologise to Robert Cross for jabbing him with a pencil when he tried to take my book off my desk in third class. I wish I had been a nicer person through my teenage years, instead of the ego-driven, car-racing, girl-chasing loser that I was. I wish I had applied myself at school and made something of myself. Maybe then I

Our cramped but functional tents.

wouldn't be spending my life trying to prove to myself that I am some-body. It seems like the only good thing that I have done is to help bring Brooke and Dillon into the world, and for that I am thankful.

APRIL 20

I have a mild case of frostbite in my right index finger, which aches a little more than the other fingers; my nose and lips are blistered; my feet are finding it hard to adapt to the snowshoes, and consequently I have blisters on my right foot, and my left heel is severely cracked and painful. Yet I am more worried about my snowshoes breaking than my body.

Tonight, I burned the arm of my fleece on the gas stove while try-ing to get dressed in our cramped tent. Many of the children I met in Egypt had been burned by similar gas stoves, which they use to cook and boil water with. Sometimes, nine people were living in a tin shed only three times the size of our tent.

All I can say is that this is way harder than I thought it was going to be, and I *knew* it would be bloody hard. The distances we're covering each day, around 20 kilometres now, are colossal in expedition terms but still far below the 30 kilometres I need to be achieving.

The finish seems so far away—it *is* so far away—and I have to keep everything in perspective and not get emotionally overwhelmed by what I have to do. Little things—a text from the kids (who, it's comforting to know, are safe and warm at boarding school during the week and with my extended family on weekends), emails from supporters, news of donations, a corny joke with Eric, Clark or Jose, or word from Bernie and Greg about the resupply of food, fuel and batteries in a few days' time—lift my spirits to the heavens. (Dillon texted: 'Dad, u r my hero, I'm so proud of u, I know u can do this. Everything u do is an inspiration,' and Brooke said she stood up at school assembly and told everyone how I was going and that I made her so proud.) It's nice to know that we're not alone. Contact with the real world is important to me. Without it, I can lapse into feeling that the wheels have fallen off, that what I'm doing is a complete waste of time: Does anybody care? What was I thinking when I took this on?

Apart from being frozen, the aches and pains and wind- and snow-burn, physically I'm not bad, and, after feeling a little weak early on, with each passing day I'm getting stronger, which is reassuring because that's been the case on my previous treks across America and around Australia. Greg and Bernie, who are in relative civilisation at Yellowknife, preparing to drive across Canada to meet me at Radisson, Québec, at the end of the North Pole sector, managed to avert a crisis when Brooke and Dillon told them that their passports were about to expire. I ended up having a phone conversation with an official on my satellite phone, and he was incredulous. 'Do you really mean to say I'm talking to you at the North Pole?' I told him I'd say hello to Santa for him. But the passports were issued, and Brooke and Dillon will be able to meet me when I arrive in Canada.

Easter's here, although there'll be no chocolate eggs for us this year. We'll make do with the reindeer cabanossi, the consuming of which is a high point of each day, because it is full of flavour when a lot of our other provisions taste bland. My lunch pack is always full of broken biscuits, smashed to bits by the dragging of the sleds over the ice. I constantly snack on dried fruit and nuts and big chunks of butter, which I eat to keep my energy up.

I've said so many prayers since we set out. I say them when I'm on the ice, and I say them in my sleeping bag at day's end.

APRIL 21

I got a message telling me that the Canadian Air Force was coming our way as part of a search and rescue exercise. It was fantastic: our first connection with Canada. Although we are still 500 kilometres away from Ward Hunt Island, the Canadian territory somehow feels real and more attainable to me now. The plane buzzed us five times and on the last occasion swooped down so low I could see the pilot's face.

Clark reveres the wild. To him, this is a great adventure, something he will be proud to talk about for the rest of his life. I suppose that's the difference really: I have no time or emotions to enjoy the landscape. I just want to conquer it and get to Canada. The pressure of deadlines and my own and others' expectations make it so much harder, but that's my life.

Buzzed by the Canadian Air Force.

POLE TO POLE

APRIL 22

It's Good Friday, and this morning before we started I thought deeply about the sacrifice that I believe Jesus made for us.

It wasn't long before we ran smack into the pressure ridges again, but at least now the sleds are significantly lighter, because we have used most of our cooking fuel and food. Resupply is nearing. We are all looking forward to it, mainly because it will be proof that the outside world has not forgotten us. I read the letter that Brooke wrote to me every night and look at the photo she gave me back in January. They give me all the strength I need to keep going.

At lunch, after a cold, hard haul, I gave my portion of reindeer cabanossi to Eric, Clark and Jose. It's the only thing we eat with any flavour, but it's Good Friday and a small sacrifice that I felt was worth making for my mates.

APRIL 23

When we woke up, a snowstorm was blasting outside, and none of us wanted to leave the warmth of our tent. But of course we did. Outside, it was difficult to see, and packing up the tents was freezing and soul-destroying. It was a white-out, with the sky the same colour as the ground. When we started, we walked straight into a pressure ridge. It reminded me of the scene in *Willy Wonka and the Chocolate Factory* when Mike Teevee wanders into that huge white room.

Every step was a fumble, and many times today I fell over because I couldn't see the difference between a crest and a trough. Because there were no visible marker points to aim for, we relied heavily on the GPS and the compass, which made the going slow. We were regularly off-track and at one stage going in completely the wrong direction. If it's still like this in a couple of days, the pickup team won't be able to find us.

This has definitely been one of our toughest days so far. Right now, we're thinking that the only positive is that the wind might bring a significant southerly drift overnight. Here's hoping. The finish of this leg of the expedition can't come soon enough.

APRIL 24

This morning, it was still snowing and it looked as though everything had been sugar-dusted, like a Christmas cake. The ground and the sky were brilliant white. There were no shadows, because the sun was behind fog. The day went reasonably well, although a strong northerly headwind picked up at around 11 am—it felt like a razor cutting into my face. It found a way inside every zipper and flap. To take my mind off the pain, I thought about the juice bar back at Coogee in Sydney. In training, every morning I would run to the airport along the sea walk and back, then get a juice or a smoothie there as a reward.

We are all looking forward to the resupply tomorrow, even though it will mean that our sleds will be heavy again.

There is little light-heartedness in each day. There'll be the occasional joke, or a funny or inspiring text or email from home or from someone following the run, but mainly it's the grimmest of slogs. Moving forwards across this region demands total concentration: to slip on the ice or stumble while crossing a pressure ridge could mean a

Fully laden—dragging my 100-kilogram load.

snapped ankle or twisted knee, and that would be the end of the pole-to-pole run right then and there. And to top it all off, bear tracks are now plentiful.

Tonight, I'm in despair. I feel lower than at any other time since I set off nearly three weeks ago. One-third of the North Pole section of my run is behind me, and there are two-thirds still to go . . . And then there's the rest of the run stretching ahead. The South Pole seems a world away. It *is* a world away. I can't stop thinking about the extra distances I'll have to run each day on the mainland because of travelling down the east coast of the United States and the slow going up here. I'm finding myself irritated by the alteration to the plan. My unhappiness, of course, is exacerbated, maybe even created, by the hard going day in, day out, as I struggle with the terrible temperatures, relentless wind, rubble mountains of ice and treacherous leads. Have you heard that expression 'I'll see you when hell freezes over'? Well, this, I've decided, is hell.

APRIL 25

I'm blessed to be here in the Arctic. It is the adventure of a lifetime, and one that only a small number of human beings will ever experience. Well and good, but sometimes, like today, it is occurring to me that the vast majority who never experience the extreme conditions up here are the lucky ones. The wind this morning was horrendous, and it badly burned my ears and nose: my nose bled and my ears felt like they were being ground off. God, it hurt. And, to make things worse, my facemask was frozen solid because I left it out overnight, and I had to bash it around my knees just so it would take the shape of my face. When I fitted it on, it was like kissing an ice cube. My lips, nose and ears stuck to it. I shivered through to midday, when the wind finally died down. I don't complain to the others, as that could encourage them to slow down or spend more time in the tent, and we have to get to Canada on time.

We crossed a lead and then looked back to where we'd come from, and the whole area, the size of about ten football fields, was moving, visibly shifting. I could hear it happening as well as see it: the ice tearing apart and smashing together created a grinding noise that Jose likened to the shunting of goods trains. I held my breath in wonder.

Leads appeared and grew bigger before our eyes.

It was awesome and terrifying to realise the power of the currents and the wind that could so blithely trundle around these huge blocks of ice. It made me feel like we were perched precariously, bobbing on an unimaginably large ocean, and of course this is exactly the case.

Until I die, I'll be dreaming about the monstrous pressure ridges that, before our eyes, rise majestically out of the water to tower above us. It's like being in the middle of an earthquake, somehow. As we move south, there seem to be fewer ridges. We can travel for three hours without seeing one. But I've been told to expect masses of them just before we hit Canada, when the ice bulks up against the mainland.

A number of times in the past days, we've had to swim across wide leads. There is nothing else to do but hit the icy water and swim as fast as you can and get out again, and then dry everything off as quickly as possible, because the water freezes instantly. If the water gets on your skin and freezes, frostbite results, which, of course, can lead to the loss of the affected body part.

I received a text from Brooke this morning. 'If u can wait and not be tired by waiting, Dillon and I will be there soon, we miss u very much.' Of course, she was adapting Rudyard Kipling's great poem 'If'. This poem has been a constant inspiration to me in all of my adventures, and never more so than today. For years, I've been trying to get my kids to read 'If' and give its wonderful message a chance to sink in; it's nice to know that Brooke has.

IF

If you can keep your head when all about you
Are losing theirs and blaming it on you,
If you can trust yourself when all men doubt you,
But make allowance for their doubting too;
If you can wait and not be tired by waiting,
Or being lied about, don't deal in lies,
Or being hated, don't give way to hating,
And yet don't look too good, nor talk too wise:

If you can dream—and not make dreams your master;
If you can think—and not make thoughts your aim;
If you can meet with Triumph and Disaster
And treat those two impostors just the same;
If you can bear to hear the truth you've spoken
Twisted by knaves to make a trap for fools,
Or watch the things you gave your life to, broken,
And stoop and build them up with worn-out tools:

If you can make one heap of all your winnings
And risk it on one turn of pitch-and-toss,
And lose, and start again at your beginnings
And never breathe a word about your loss;
If you can force your heart and nerve and sinew
To serve your turn long after they are gone,
And so hold on when there is nothing in you
Except the Will which says to them: 'Hold on!'

If you can talk with crowds and keep your virtue,
Or walk with Kings—nor lose the common touch,
If neither foes nor loving friends can hurt you,

> *If all men count with you, but none too much;*
> *If you can fill the unforgiving minute*
> *With sixty seconds' worth of distance run,*
> *Yours is the Earth and everything that's in it,*
> *And—which is more—you'll be a Man, my son!*
>
> Rudyard Kipling

We're maintaining our rate of 20 kilometres a day, which is not enough. And because we're travelling on ice that is drifting north at a rate of 5 kilometres a day, we're really travelling only 15 kilometres. I pray that we find ourselves on south-drifting ice at some stage to even the ledger.

The resupply plane came and dumped our provisions onto the snow, and I have to say I was sad to see it leave. Opening the packages, we found that Greg Quail had included with the food and fuel a flask of vodka for Eric and Clark, six cans of Guinness, and an Easter egg each! So we did get an Easter egg after all. Unfortunately, the beers were frozen solid, but after some perseverance I got a taste of the golden nectar, which was great. What wasn't so great was the extra weight in our sleds when we loaded the new supplies in.

As we erected the tents tonight and I unpacked my gear, I looked forward to reaching Canada and then the warmer climates of the United States and South America, where it will not take four hours a day to set up and break camp, and where there'll be no de-icing of clothing and gear every night, or taking an hour to get dressed and undressed. I'll be running in shorts and a T-shirt, and at the end of the day I'll simply crash into my bunk in the campervan. The extra hours available to me will be spent running and resting. Bliss. I've had to go through what I am enduring now to realise how much easier that will be. I just have to be patient, and that's a virtue I do not normally possess.

APRIL 26

We slept in for an extra two hours to make up for the 11 pm finish last night, after the resupply. Just as we left our tents, a blizzard hit with blinding snow and incredible wind. We couldn't take any footage

Eric in his dry suit—without it, immersion means death.

of it, because the conditions were simply too bad for Jose to film in. We eventually struggled out and pressed on. Then came a calamity: after just five hours' trekking, Eric, not wearing a dry suit, fell through the ice and into the water up to his waist. The blizzard had prevented him, the most experienced of guides, from seeing where the ice was thin over the water. It was action stations as we pulled him out before he became waterlogged. We dried his boots and clothing as quickly as possible, before he was severely affected by hypothermia. All up, we covered just 5 kilometres.

We set up camp in the mid-afternoon. Our priority was to dry out Eric's boots and clothes so we could press on again tomorrow. As I write this, I'm still wearing my goggles and big fur hat, which will never be a fashion statement but keep me warm. Ice clings to my face and beard, which I've been letting grow. My nose is blue and scabby, and my lips are chapped and refuse to move when I try to speak because they are frozen stiff.

Disasters aside, I'm feeling strong and determined. I've fallen back into my mindset of past ultra events: not fighting nature, just accepting that it's there and that I have no control over it, and going with the flow of whatever Mother Nature with all her power hurls at me. Like I did in the heat in the Simpson Desert, the awesome sunrises I saw running around Australia and the endless raw and beautiful terrain of the American plains and deserts, I marvel at the Arctic Circle, curse it, cajole it, and try not to let it kill me.

Tonight, like all those people in the world who are *not* doing it tough in the ice at the top of the world, we're all enjoying our Easter eggs. As well as the eggs and alcohol, which amazingly landed intact, there were the essentials: food, fuel for our gas burners to heat the tents, cook meals and melt ice for our thermoses, new skis and boots to replace our busted ones, notes and goodwill messages. I wolfed down my chocolate egg, and it tasted indescribably wonderful. Unfortunately, it also triggered memories of one of my favourite Sydney haunts, a chocolate cafe where I often take Brooke and Dillon. We have steaming sweet hot chocolates, and waffles laden with rich chocolate sauce, strawberries and bananas. Oh, man. Heaven. It's a pity that those waffles will be off my menu for many, many months yet. I took the toy from my egg, a plastic robot, and for the rest of the polar section he'll be standing guard at the end of my sleeping bag to keep watch for marauding polar bears. Our Easter treat was a small pleasure, but it was the highlight of our journey so far. I shed a tear to think that people were thinking of us.

APRIL 27

Eric thanked us for looking after him when he fell through the ice and seemed determined to make up for the delay, setting a faster-than-normal pace, although he was understandably more cautious around the water crossings. The sun shone today, in contrast to yesterday's blizzard. We encountered a lot of powder snow and sometimes sank up to 2 metres down into it.

The new food is a pleasant change from the stuff we've been eating for the past three weeks. I spent the day singing to myself to take my mind off things.

By 4 pm the sky had turned dark, our shadows were no longer cast upon the snow, and it was difficult to see a contrast between hills and troughs. There came another dusting of snow followed by fierce winds.

We were close to finishing for the day, so we crossed one more tricky lead then quickly set up camp. Now, finally, I am in the refuge of the tent again for another night. The wind is howling. God, I miss Brooke and Dillon. I'm counting the days until we meet up in Canada.

APRIL 28

We started the day stumbling into the teeth of a raging westerly that blew us off course. In time, we got back on track. In fact, it seems likely that we may actually be on schedule and arrive at Ward Hunt Island on May 15 as planned. Of course, just when I was feeling positive, nature tripped me up. Crossing a lead, I stumbled and sank in up to the knee. I threw myself flat on the ground to make a bigger surface area on which to regather my balance and so was able to scamper forwards with just a soggy foot.

Mother Nature must have thought we were still too complacent, though, and chose to give us another wake-up call. The wind had died, the fog had cleared and the sun came out: we were all agreeing that

The deep black depths of the Arctic Ocean.

things were going well when a near disaster befell us. The leads of water we are crossing now are blacker than ever, as dark as engine oil that has not been changed for years. To bridge one wide lead, we had hooked our sleds together and were rafting across one by one, pretty much textbook stuff, when Jose thought he'd film himself floating across the water. He made it to the other side, where Eric, Clark and I were waiting, and told us that he wanted to shoot Eric telling the camera how we had just crossed the water. Jose lost concentration momentarily and stepped backwards onto a dodgy surface. The ice gave way, and in he went with a crack and a splash. I was close to him, and I grabbed him and held him up until Eric reached us; then together we hauled him out before the top half of his body went under. The ice was breaking up all around us, and it was a struggle to keep hold of him.

Jose was in the water longer than Eric had been when he fell in, and his clothing and boots were drenched. Although he was scared—as were we all—that he had hypothermia, he managed to joke that he had a swimming pool's worth of water in each boot. We hurriedly stripped off his wet outer garments and kept him running up and down on the ice to try to get him warm quickly, then we rolled him in the snow, covered him with it and rubbed it into his gear to absorb the salt from the water. Clothing that has been immersed in salt water takes an age to dry out over the stove in the tent, and the process eats up a lot of gas power.

A few moments more in that water and Jose would have perished, no question. It was fortunate for him that we were close at hand, because he would not have been able to haul himself out. Up here, we are close to death every day. You can't take your mind off the job for an instant.

APRIL 29

As usual, I am going crazy at the amount of rest time we are having. Today, we had to cross a lot of water, and, instead of pushing a little longer to make up the kilometres lost yesterday, Eric settled for 16 kilometres for the whole day. It's so frustrating. We could easily be ten days further on than this. I do understand that Eric needs to take Jose and Clark into account as well: his priority is to deliver everyone to Canada in good condition, and he is well on his way to doing that.

APRIL 30

The sun is noticeably higher in the sky, and the temperature is −21 degrees. Terribly cold, but, you'll agree, a whole lot better than −40. Consequently, the leads do not freeze over as quickly, and we seem to be constantly stringing the kayaks together and using them as rafts to ferry each other across the water. It's very time consuming, and just when I hoped our daily average distance travelled might increase to 25 or even 30 kilometres, we will only get 14 kilometres done today. It's devastating when you consider how hard we're working. We just can't speed up this leg. I feel guilty for sleeping and resting so much, even though we are hauling the sleds for ten hours per day. Fourteen kilometres is just not enough.

I have a song stuck in my head: Harry Chapin's 'Cat's in the Cradle', about a dysfunctional family and alienation between children and parents. I don't know how the song got in there, but I wonder if by taking on this vast challenge I am being true to Brooke and Dillon. I wish I had someone to talk to about this, but there has been no such person since Lisa died. I would not voice my inner thoughts to any of my companions on the ice.

MAY 1

What a bitch of a day. At dawn, I put my gear outside the tent while I was packing up, and it got blown away. I had to chase my foam mattress for 500 metres, as the wind did its best to blow it all the way back to the North Pole. On the ice, though we trekked from 6 am to 6 pm, we only covered 8 kilometres. The freezing southerly blew hard, straight into our faces. We moved forwards into it bent at a 45-degree angle, head-first into the gale. And there was so much open water that we were regularly hitching the sleds together to cross leads. It was −30 degrees again: my frozen lips refused to smile or speak.

Everything is difficult to do on the ice. Setting up a tent is normally a breeze, but not up here, with our aching tiredness and the wind that blows away everything that's not nailed down. It would actually be easier to lie down and die than continue, but I'll push on.

Rugged up and ready to go. My grin belies my trepidation.

MAY 2

Today, unlike yesterday, it was fine and still. Our bad luck may just have run out, as I had hoped. The temperature was back up to –21 degrees, and it was easier to navigate and identify the thin ice and crevasses. We pushed hard all day, and I felt sure that we had covered more than 20 kilometres. We hadn't: Eric informed us we'd only done 18 kilometres. Clark and Jose let out a 'Yeah!' I was disappointed that they were happy with such a short distance.

MAY 3

Such a beautiful day. There was no wind, the sun was out, and the temperature hovered around –18. I was able to duck outside the tent and go to the toilet with only my boots and thermal clothing on. This weather makes life infinitely easier. The kayaks are also around 1.8 kilograms lighter every day, as we consume our food and fuel. We have all noticed the difference in the weight, and if we don't have too many water crossings this should relate to faster trekking with more distance covered.

Today, we managed a creditable 21 kilometres. We had to cross some pressure ridges and lots of water, but we were very quick, on our game. It seems that everyone now knows just what to do when they come to a problem. I know these guys are doing their best. Even so, I felt lethargic today, as if I was running on empty. I just want to get out of these snowshoes and into some real running shoes.

Jose is sweating a lot more with the warmer weather. Tonight, we're sharing a tent, and he hung his socks over the top of the dinner pot. The sweat from his socks dripped into our dinner. He was genuinely surprised when I declined my share and opted for some dry noodles from the packet.

MAY 4

The weather has been perfect and the navigation easy. Hopefully, now we can make the most of it and start achieving some 25-kilometre days. My fear is that everyone is enjoying the better weather and they may forget I'm in a race against time. I worry that they will relax mentally.

Also, I worry that the weather will deteriorate again, which it can do in a moment. Instead of taking it easy and wasting the good conditions, we should be pushing hard.

MAY 5

The good weather didn't last. It was foggy and numbingly cold all day. I didn't sleep last night and felt like I had a fever: my sleeping bag was full of sweat. I didn't want to start the stove and wake Clark, so I got out of my bag and pulled it inside out and lay inside the outer layer. The show goes on.

MAY 6

We made 25 kilometres today, which means we have exactly 200 kilometres to go before we reach Canada. Visibility was good, and the temperature was –25 degrees, so it was smooth sailing. I hope we can do as well tomorrow.

We made just three lead crossings. One was the usual type, when we link two kayaks together to make a raft, one of us clambers across with a tow rope then sends the raft backwards and forwards until we are all across. Another involved laying two kayaks side by side in the water to form a bridge then walking over them. The third was more problematic: the entire ice mass we were standing on was moving away from the ice on the other side of the lead. I was in front, so I quickly unbuckled my sled, jumped across, then pulled the guys and sleds across, while the gap continued to grow.

It's amazing to think that we have travelled so far through the most forbidding terrain on the planet. We have had mishaps, but we have survived. It's getting warmer, though it's all relative, of course. As we've moved south, our pace has picked up and we're making more than 20 kilometres per day. We're more or less on track to reach Canada on time. What may hold us up are the large expanses of water we are now encountering. Some of the leads we traversed today were full of seals, and, as I've mentioned, seals are the staple diet of polar bears, so we are on full alert.

We're happy with what we've achieved up here, but every day is a grind. The North Pole section has become monotonous now, and I can't wait to see different country. I'm over ice and snow. It's too early to be thinking about the finish line, but I'm proud of my achievement thus far, because many people said I'd never survive the Arctic Circle.

In my mind, when I've completed the North Pole sector I will have completed one-fifth of the run. Seven hundred kilometres is nowhere near to 20 per cent of 21,000 kilometres, but the degree of difficulty of this first section is such that it accounts for more than simply the distance.

Because thoughts of being reunited with my children have kept me going, it broke my heart yesterday to receive a text message from Brooke in which she told me that she wouldn't be able to join me in Canada, with Dillon, because of school commitments. Instead, she'll fly over in the June school holidays, and we'll make up for lost time then. Happily, Dillon is still coming. It will be so wonderful to see my son. He says that I inspire him . . . Well, he inspires me.

I'm feeling happier and more confident today than at any time since I started this marathon. Having made it this far, I realise that there is a light at the end of the tunnel. I am going to get through this sector and tackle the rest in turn. Soon we'll be out of the freezer and into the frying pan.

MAY 7

Twenty three kilometres under our belt today, and we still have a chance to finish the North Pole leg by May 15. We have 180 kilometres to go to Ward Hunt Island, and we could really do with some luck in the form of drift going in our direction. You realise this earth is alive when you feel and see the ice endlessly moving beneath you. Sometimes it's like you're riding a moving walkway.

A Swedish guy, Johan Ernst Nilson, is also trying to make it from the North to the South Pole, although he is using a bike for North and South America and a dog sled team through Greenland. He is more than ten days behind us and in a lot of trouble trying to cross water. His sleds are too small and not buoyant enough to raft across, so he continually has to go around the leads. For me, Johan's problems highlight Eric's innovation and experience: I often think Eric is overcautious, but his job is to get polar expeditions safely from A to B; speed is not a priority for him. We are naturally at loggerheads, because I'm in a race against time. That said, I am glad he's my guide.

MAY 8

Just when I thought the really bad cold weather was over, along comes a day of –30 degrees (plus the wind-chill factor). My body froze, especially my ears, nose, hands and, for the first time since starting, feet. It makes the day drag when you start it in pain and that pain doesn't go away. Last night, I dreamed that my fingers were so cold that they shattered like glass and I was left looking at the bones in my hands. Then I bumped the bones, and they shattered as well and I had no hands, only a feeling that a blow torch was being applied to my arms.

One of the difficulties of this run has been the basic business of unzipping my fly to do a wee while wearing mittens. Each time nature calls, I pray, 'Please, please, please, God, don't let me wet myself.' The genesis of my little mantra was early on in the stage, when it was –38 degrees and I couldn't hold on long enough to get my fly open and ended up wetting myself. Some urine froze to my groin, and the skin blistered. I was in pain for days afterwards, as the raw skin rubbed against my gear.

Jose, all iced up.

MAY 9

After a good day's trek, it was decided by Eric and the others that instead of continuing further we should camp at a particularly picturesque pressure ridge, because Jose wanted somewhere nice to film. Quite frankly, that decision drove me crazy, and it still rankles as I write this some hours later.

MAY 10

Today was perfect weather-wise: great visibility and –21 degrees. Just after our afternoon break, I saw the mountains of Ward Hunt Island and Ellesmere Island 120 kilometres in the distance, and I was filled with joy. Finally, the end of this section is, literally, in sight.

We covered a worthy 22 kilometres today. I thought a lot about the last-minute change to my route through the United States, and I've come to the conclusion that it's a good idea after all. I have a great team around me, and, either in person or on satellite phone, we're constantly discussing the expedition and refining the details. We've all agreed from the start that this run is not really about me, and it's not even about running a route that has never been attempted before. The heart and soul of it is our mission to get funds to thousands of needy people worldwide through the Red Cross. I am serious about raising a lot of money for these charities. I run; people, hopefully inspired by what I am doing, donate money to the water projects. For people to open their wallets, however, they have to know that I'm running from the top to the bottom of the world, so publicity is key. I need to reach the maximum number of people possible as I run—through local and national media coverage, as well as at meetings and events along the route. I can appreciate that the east coast is definitely the way to go for maximum impact. Although it is out of my way, the new route also allows me to run through New Orleans—the city that was so devastated by Hurricane Katrina in 2005 and whose people have benefited from the American Red Cross's disaster relief program, to which I am donating as part of this run.

I'm desperately sorry that I won't be able to meet the people on the west coast of the United States who have supported me so staunchly, but I hope they will understand the reasons behind the decision.

While the route has changed, my resolve hasn't. It was always going to be tough completing this run, and now it's going to be even tougher because of the delays we've encountered. But this run has been my dream for so long: to touch the lives of so many needy people is all the motivation I need.

Manhandling the kayaks over a pressure ridge.

MAY 11

With the mountains in view, we worked hard to cover the final 120 kilometres. We started off well, but it wasn't long before we reached some of the worst ice rubble we've hit so far. However, with Canada finally in sight nothing can dampen my spirits. After two gruelling hours of lifting and hauling the sleds, our hard work was rewarded when we emerged into a good flat stretch to finish the day. I am sure that there's a guardian angel looking after me.

MAY 12

This morning was noticeably colder than yesterday. It's amazing how fast the conditions change here. My hands were freezing all day, and nothing I did made any difference. I tried clenching my fists 100 times each within my mitts, shaking them, and so on, but nothing worked. It was bloody uncomfortable.

Thank God the polar bears continue to leave us alone, although we have seen plenty of seals. The most awesome creature I have laid eyes on since we began the trek was a little bird I saw today. It was a surreal thing: it looked like a sparrow and flew very close to me. What was it doing up here, so far from food and a tree to nest in? It was heading north, so was obviously lost. The temperature was –30 degrees, and the air was thick with fog. The little creature was probably doomed, but it lifted my spirits just by flying by. It made me think that land must not be too far off. Perhaps Noah felt the same awe that I did when the dove returned to the ark with the olive branch in its beak.

Eric was picking his toes while cooking dinner tonight, and, along with the ice- and wind-burn scabs on his nose, it completely grossed me out. I am so ready to get on with the mainland part of this event, where I will have more say over the daily running of things, including the provision of meals. I am tired of rationing my food. How glad I'll be when I'm on the road and I can eat more! And I'll need to. I read at the zoo in New York that the male polar bear there consumes the equivalent of 95 hamburgers daily. I reckon I could give him a run for his money at the moment. There are around 20,000 calories in 95 hamburgers, and I'll be consuming around 8000 calories a day once I hit my optimum daily distance.

It's frustrating being able to see the mountains on Ward Hunt Island but not being able to ditch my sled and run over there. I snapped the frame on one of my snowshoes today, and I hope it will hold for the remaining three days on the ice. So far, I have broken six ski bindings, one snowshoe and two ski poles. It's lucky that my body is stronger than my equipment.

MAY 13

Navigation is now much easier, and as the early fog cleared our line of sight was perfect. The mountains of Canada and Greenland grow closer. But then the weather degenerated into another white-out. We've had a couple of them, now: days when you can't distinguish the sky from the ground because everything is white, with no gradations of colour or shadow. You put your foot down on what you think is ground and there's no ground there at all. On such days, the potential for disaster is always present. The pressure ridges, as predicted, are much bigger here. Earlier they were around 50 tonnes; now they're

Ward Hunt in sight—the end of the beginning.

100 or 200 tonnes. Yet the winds and currents still bowl them around like kids playing marbles in the school playground.

We've been making 22 kilometres a day for the past few days. Our sleds are lighter again, because we're getting through our fuel and food. Food has become our main topic of conversation. After nearly 40 days on the ice, there is a sameness to our activities each day: we try to stay alive while moving forwards over the ice and snow. It's a little monotonous. If we focus not on our hardship but on food, it becomes easier to keep going. We try to one-up each other with our descriptions of the things we love to eat. Baked dinners, cheesecakes, even Big Macs get plenty of mentions. I boasted to Clark how I could polish off ten Cadbury's Flakes in a flash.

This afternoon, as I set up the tent, I felt elated. I've damn near beaten the North Pole leg. Surviving this most terrifying section has set me up, in a way, for the rest of the run. I feel that I will have credibility keeping pace alongside me. Before, I was saying 'I'm going to run from the North Pole.' Now, I can say 'I *ran* from the North Pole.' Bernie has warned me not to be complacent, however. He reckons that traversing the Antarctic may prove much more difficult than the Arctic, despite the absence of polar bears; he says it's even colder and windier down there. And still to be faced are the murderous bandits of the Darién Gap, the heat, the enormous distances . . . Have no fear, I'm not resting on my laurels.

Still, this has been a great day. We're just 50 kilometres from Canada. The terrain that we saw before the white-out was breathtaking, so majestic. On Ward Hunt there's a mountain that resembles an Egyptian pyramid: a perfect triangle. The mountains of nearby Ellesmere Island are rugged and green. To think I'm seeing these sights from the North Pole side: a view not many humans have enjoyed.

I continue to worry about someone falling through the ice into the water, and at every water crossing my heart races, especially when it's Jose's turn to go across. He insists on standing right on the edge and filming, and the ice at those points is often only 10 centimetres thick. When he puts his eye to the camera, he doesn't think about his footing or surroundings, and this makes me extremely nervous. Until we are safely on Canadian soil, I shall worry about this section of the run. I've

White-out—when you can't tell the ice from the sky.

had no control over this leg, and I've found it difficult to deal with. I am being prickly at times and in the main not concealing my frustrations from the others: I am past pretending. Still, as Eric has rightly said, we are four alpha males, and not everyone can lead. On the ice, he is the boss.

We should complete the North Pole run in two days' time. Today, Eric arranged with the airline to pick us up off the ice and fly us to Ward Hunt Island.

MAY 14

Our focus has shifted to our departure from the ice. The others are starting to plan what they will do next. Today, I took a special paperclip from my pack. On the plane to the pole, just beside the altimeter, was a Russian paperclip that was bigger and more robust than normal ones. I used it to scratch the word 'If'—the title of the Rudyard Kipling poem—on the back of my landing badge, which we were given instead of a boarding pass. I gave the landing badge to another expeditionist on the flight who was later going to climb Mount Everest with his father, and I told him to present it to his dad. The thought of them together on an adventure touched me and reminded me of the relationship I had with my own father and that I have now with my son. The expeditionist had told me that his father had encouraged him to read 'If', just as I have encouraged Dillon and Brooke to read it and live by its message. I kept the paperclip and will carry it with me every step of the way, to bring me luck. When I'm finished, I'll give it to my children.

We picked up the pace and found ourselves in huge fields of clear ice; there was some ice rubble but nothing we couldn't negotiate. We were all excited at the prospect of getting off the ice. It seemed the fates were smiling on us.

Then came a huge downer. Despite Eric having been continually assured by the airline that they would be picking us up tomorrow, they broke the news that because tomorrow is a Sunday the pilot and co-pilot will be having a day of rest and not flying. Eric's jaw dropped when he heard this. He reminded them that the flight had been booked for days, but they refused to budge.

Eric accepted the news easily, and told us there was nothing he could do. This drove me mad. I was cranky about his defeatist attitude, as well as about the airline not picking us up. We were so close, and now we were being held up because a pilot and his mate wanted a day off! I couldn't believe it. We should have had all this cleared beforehand, so false hopes could not be raised.

At that point, I started off fast on my own, in the direction of Ward Hunt Island. I didn't want to wait around if we could get to a suitable spot before Sunday. The others followed me, Eric calling, 'Pat, slow down . . . slow down.' We arrived at a pressure ridge zone, and, our sleds banging against our legs, we punched our way over it. We called the airline again, told them where we were and asked if the plane could come straightaway. They refused and said that the plane would be with us first thing on the morning of May 16, but that we had to trek another 14 kilometres to the proper landing zone. Eric told them that it was perfect terrain for landing where we were, but the airline was adamant.

We set up our tents. My mind is consumed with the question of whether we will get safely off the ice. At the North Pole, nothing is certain; there's always an 'if'. There have been too many things in this leg that I've had no control over: I've had to stick with the group, drag the sled, eat what I've been rationed, do exactly what Eric has said. I've had no independence. I am a man who needs to be master of his own fate. I don't like not being able to fix situations and get on with the job. I so needed to get off the ice to start the Canadian sector. I was in pain with frostbite. The others were also affected. Eric's face was a mess. Jose, particularly, was doing it tough.

I keep saying the 'Serenity Prayer': keep calm and accept, accept, accept—that is my lot.

MAY 15

• •

We scrambled our way over, through and around the mountainous pressure ridges until at last we found ourselves at the landing strip. We have set up camp for our last night in the Arctic Circle and wait for tomorrow.

MAY 16

We've done it. After 43 days and nearly 700 kilometres, I stood on the southern edge of the polar ice shelf. I have survived the North Pole—the section of my run that I feared the most—and am in one piece, as are my companions, although two of them, who fell through the ice into the water, are lucky to be alive. Trusting that the plane would arrive on schedule, while we waited for it we finished the last of our rations. Between us, there were high-fives, hugs and cries of 'Canada, we're coming to get you!'

I feel joy and relief at having so far succeeded. I am also desperately tired and sore, and my cheeks, nose and lips are red and raw with ice-burn. My fingers are numb; I've been told that I'll have no feeling in them for another fortnight. There's no doubt, though, that my overwhelming feeling, as I stood with the North Pole at my back and the rest of my run stretching out ahead, was immense excitement. We would soon be flying to Ward Hunt Island, where Dillon would join me the next day.

I don't think I'll be back at the North Pole in a hurry.

About to leave the ice after our gruelling trek.

The expedition was long, difficult, dangerous and things broke, stuff went wrong but the team held it together and it was a very successful trip. Eric Philips was amazing. He has a wealth of information and knows how to manage a team. Pat Farmer, who may I add, had never done anything remotely like this or set foot in the Arctic before—took the daily toils and troubles in his stride and proved he is one tough cookie. Jose Naranjo was, as we expected, a fun guy who not only managed to ski the distance, but film the whole adventure—the good times, bad times and ridiculously cold times! It was a great experience for me and no doubt will hold off my need to visit cold and unforgiving environments for some time.

Clark Carter

STAGE 2
CANADA

May 17 to June 6

 DISTANCE TO COVER: Approximately 1350 kilometres

 TERRAIN: Roads leading through wilderness, plains and mountains, rural villages, bridges and cities

 TYPICAL WEATHER CONDITIONS: Cool to warm days, up to 30 degrees Celsius, changeable conditions turning rapidly from fine to showers

 HAZARDS: Black bears, flies, mosquitoes, tripping over while entranced by stunning scenery, the security guards at Parliament House, Ottawa

 KEY EQUIPMENT: Cap, T-shirt, shorts, running shoes, rubdown table, cameras and media gear, needle for puncturing blisters

 PERSONNEL: Logistics man and chief back-up driver Bernie Farmer, assistant and running mate Katie Walsh, camera operator Nick King, film editor Jake Simmonds, cook, nurse and masseuse Emma Cohen

MAY 17

If we thought we were going to have a comfy and relaxing flight to Ward Hunt Island, we were mistaken. After existing in temperatures of –30 degrees, I didn't think I'd ever grizzle about the heat again, but the conditions in that plane were stifling. It had no air conditioning, and we four were jammed in tightly, along with all our gear and the kayaks. We had to stand up for much of the flight. But the lunch made up for the discomfort. After a month and a half of dehydrated food, we were treated to delicious sandwiches with real bread and fresh fillings. I could feel them doing good.

Happy to have made it to Ward Hunt Island.

When we arrived, we waited at the airstrip for Dillon's plane to arrive. At last, the plane descended from the clearest, crispest, bluest sky and rumbled to a halt. My heart pounded as I stood waiting for the door to open and the passengers to disembark. Suddenly, there was my son.

Dillon saw me and his face split into the biggest grin. I was crying behind my dark snow glasses. We ran to each other and embraced. 'Son,' I said, 'it's so good to see you! I've dreamed about this moment for so long.' I held him tight and was overwhelmed by love for my boy. I said, 'How have you been?' and he said, 'Good,' and I said, 'How's Brooke'?' and he said 'Good,' and when I asked him how he was getting on at school his reply was the same. Teenagers! Then he reached into his bag and produced a packet of Tim Tams. I scoffed four in one gulp and gave the rest to Eric, Clark and Jose. They'd earned them.

The pilots had told Dillon that he must be one of the youngest people ever to have stood there, on the edge of the ice shelf. It was special for me to be able to show him the view. I pointed out the direction of the North Pole, Ellesmere Island, Greenland and Russia. I doubt he's likely to forget the experience.

My son Dillon arrives.

We all flew south from Ward Hunt Island to Radisson, Québec, in north-eastern Canada. Radisson is a small town of just 300 people, but it has the amenities we needed, such as an airport, petrol stations and mechanic garages, motels for me and the crew, cafes, and a good road, the James Bay Road, to take us directly south the 600 kilometres to the next major town, Matagami.

Waiting in Radisson for us, a sight for sore eyes, was my new team, who will accompany me south. Bernie was there, of course, and with him were my niece, Katie Walsh, who will be my fitness and movement specialist and general crew member, camera operator Nick King, film editor Jake Simmonds and cook, nurse and masseuse Emma Cohen. All will be combining their specialised roles with every-day duties that must be carried out to keep the run rolling smoothly. They had already driven across Canada from Yellowknife in the vans. I discovered that a third van had had to be bought to house everything. One will be driven by Bernie, which he, Katie and I will sleep in; one will house Nick, Jake and all their gear; and the third, which has a kitchen, stores a tonne of equipment and tows a hyperbaric chamber to aid my recovery after each day's run, will be driven by and slept in by Emma. Nick and Jake's media van is amazing. Inside, as well as bunks, toilet, sink, table, chairs and shower, are a satellite termi-nal, computer, printer, tangles of wires, double adaptors and video camera positioned so it can be pointed out of the back of the van, to capture me running and talking.

If I thought I'd died and gone to heaven when I was munching those sandwiches on the plane to Ward Hunt Island, I *knew* I was in paradise when I climbed out of my Arctic gear, took a hot shower and sat on a real toilet. After a debriefing session, we prepared to set off into the wilds of Canada.

MAY 20

· ·

I said goodbye to my North Pole comrades. Clark and Jose were profes-sional in their work and friendly, good-natured colleagues and mates. Quite simply, I could not have negotiated the pole without Eric. He was worth every cent of the money that we'd paid him. My farewell to Eric was simple and brief; there was no time for fanfare. 'See you at the South Pole,' were my parting words.

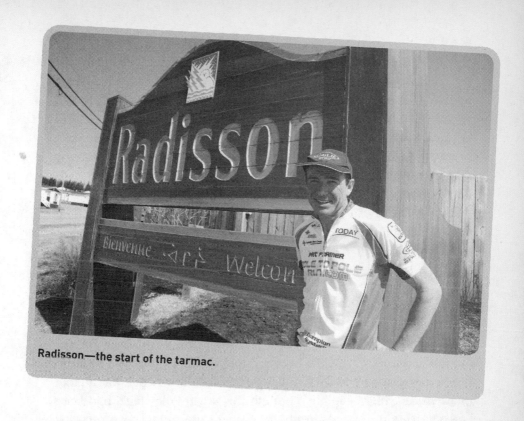
Radisson—the start of the tarmac.

I spent five days at Radisson recovering from the exertions on the ice and catching up with my son. Dillon and I were joined at the hip, walking everywhere with arms around each other. Greg, Nick and Jake filmed me at Radisson standing in front of a big green novelty signpost with arrows pointing to major cities of the world. I posed beneath it and addressed the camera: 'Well, we're in Radisson, northern Québec, the northern-most point of my run down the east coast of the US and on to the South Pole. Now there are lot of cities on this signpost, but I have to say that the one I'm looking forward to arriving in most of all is Sydney, my hometown, 1550 kilometres away.'

At one point, we recorded some footage of me in which I appeared cheery and positive, and my cheeks had a rosy glow. (I didn't explain that this 'healthy' complexion was due to snow-burn and was stinging like mad.) Weighing me down, though I kept on smiling, was the awareness of the distances before me. From Radisson, Montreal was 1265 kilometres, New York 2000 kilometres and Washington DC 2350 kilometres. There was still a long way to go.

MAY 22

I set off on my first road run, a 30-kilometre stretch due south from Radisson, and Dillon joined me for the last 2 kilometres. Bernie had set the distance for today at just 30 kilometres because he did not know what condition I would be in. In fact, I was a bit shaky. At least, at the end of a day's run, I can now climb into my portable hyperbaric chamber, which pumps oxygen into my system and helps my cells and muscles recover. It's like a big blue cocoon that we tow in a trailer behind a van; after I've spent time encased inside it, I feel I can float like a butterfly.

MAY 25

Today Dillon was driven back to Radisson to connect with the plane for the return flight to Sydney and school. It was really sad saying goodbye; I felt hollow after he left, and my world went quiet. He was helpful and nurturing while he was here. He and Brooke will be coming over together in the June holidays, and that knowledge was all that made our parting bearable. Through the North Pole stage, had I not had thoughts of my kids in my head, inspiring me to keep pressing forwards over the ice, I could easily have curled up and died, saying 'I just can't do this.' Thoughts of Brooke and Dillon made my success possible.

With Dillon gone, Bernie, ever mindful of the distance still to be travelled, decided that it was time to get stuck in and refocus. I had to run 80 kilometres today, down the picturesque route towards the town of Matagami, on Lake Matagami. As I set off down a long, straight highway with less and less snow on the ground the further south I ran, I revelled in being able to stride out in my T-shirt, shorts and running shoes on firm ground in fine weather. I felt like someone had unlocked my prison shackles. Until the South Pole, I will have no further need for skis, sleds or polar gear! I was as free as the sparrow that flew close by me at the North Pole, and I hoped that my fate will be a happier one than that beautiful lost bird's.

And I'm running really well. The roads have been almost devoid of cars. Flanked by wooden telephone poles, they wend through thick pine forests that stretch out on either side as far as we can see.

Even the foxes think I'm mad.

Making the transition from the ice to the road will take a while. I've been told that strange things could happen to me in this period. Today was hot, and the sky a brilliant blue. The temperature rapidly climbed to 30 degrees Celsius. Just nine days ago, I was plodding over the ice in temperatures of –30. That's a difference of 60 degrees in just over a week! My body has been rebelling, with my blood pressure soaring and my veins like thick red ropes. My skin still stings from frostbite, and there is no sign of a return to feeling in my fingers. Making things worse is that I am being attacked continually by the biggest, nastiest mosquitoes I've ever seen.

The daily distance we covered on the ice towards the end of the North Pole sector was 20 kilometres, whereas now I'm doing 80 kilometres a day, and I'll be increasing that to 85. The other major difference is my footwear: on the ice, I was wearing boots and snowshoes, which shortened the length of my calf muscles, so I have to take it easy these first few days before they lengthen again, or I'll risk tearing a tendon, which could end my quest.

The food, of course, is way better.

MAY 26

We've settled into a daily routine. Bernie wakes me at 5 am, and we determine the day's route. I get dressed, warm up, stretch, take my vitamins with a cup of tea and start by walking briskly for a kilometre or so. Bernie and Katie follow me in their van. Katie gives me cereal and a fruit drink, which I have while walking. Throughout the day, I have a drink every 5 or 10 kilometres, depending on how I'm feeling and the weather conditions. I eat according to need. At lunchtime, by which point I should have covered 45 to 50 kilometres, I don't stop but eat sandwiches, pasta, fruit or nuts and have a drink on the go. I then buckle down for another 30 to 40 kilometres.

The media boys film and photograph me along the way. I have to fit in with them but don't like stopping and starting: it jars my rhythm and costs me precious time. But I do it, because we have to get the message out via film, photos and interviews so people will donate.

By the time I have run the required 80 or 85 kilometres, it may be dark. I have a massage, rubdown and snack, then a long, hot shower to banish the aches and pains. Then dinner: pasta, steak, vegies, pie or whatever is going. Often I fall asleep before I finish my meal. Bernie or Katie shakes me awake, and I shuffle off to bed. Sometimes, if it's not too late, I do some email correspondence, conduct interviews and catch up with the crew on what has happened while I've been fixated on my running. Katie may read out Facebook messages and emails.

I feel confident. I *know* at this moment I'm going to finish this crazy run. Bernie has warned me not to be so relieved at surviving the North Pole that I let my mind relax and become complacent. I mustn't forget that my task is enormous and that I'm just starting. There are many, many hurdles to overcome. For now, though, I'm pleased to be here. It's all good.

MAY 27

The weather has been changeable today. One minute it was 30 degrees; the next it had plummeted to 0 degrees and it started snowing. The pain from my frostbitten hands returned with a vengeance. Now that I'm running 85 kilometres daily, my body is shouting, 'Stop doing this to me!' But I'm paying it no heed: I will achieve this epic goal if I listen to my mind, not my body. Of course I'm hurting. Apart from the remaining Arctic ailments, I have blisters and bruising and am experiencing stomach cramps.

Earlier today, I put my North Pole sled up for auction on the website of my sponsor the SOC Exchange. Frostbitten fingers crossed that it draws a good sum for the cause.

MAY 28
••

We've seen some awesome wilderness scenery: vast mountains and pine forests dotted with the occasional cabin and teepee. The sky is a light, clear, brilliant blue in the day, and the air is so very clean. Often, in the late afternoons, a wind blows up and clouds move in, and the temperature cools. Awesome, too, has been the power of the water and lake systems up here: there are spectacular rapids in the rivers that I've crossed and run alongside.

At the end of the day, Katie wrapped me in a warm jacket, because the temperature was falling fast, and she gave me a good, deep stretch. My calves were tight and sore. Apart from having run 85 kilometres, one of the reasons for my soreness is the slope of the road. Because in Canada it rains and snows a lot, the roads are built with a steep camber, so when I'm running, the foot closest to the centre of the road is hitting ground 8 centimetres higher than the other foot. I can't swap sides, because for safety I have to run on the same side of the road as cars drive on—in Canada the right side—so as I run, my right calf muscle is being stretched longer than my left. Being out of whack like this causes all sorts of complications, leading to strain and pain in my ankle, knee and hip joints and in the base of my back.

I take a combination of vitamins in the morning and afternoon to try to counteract the effects of the stress on my body and mind, the varying weather conditions and occasionally insufficient nutrients in my diet. Antioxidants help muscles to recover and repair, and magnesium stops cramping. Another important vitamin I take is glucosamine, which helps to reduce swelling and inflammation in the joints, because in this run I'll be taking approximately 20 million steps, which will cause a hell of a lot of wear and tear.

Tonight, I met a friendly Inuit bear hunter, and he told me about

About to savour moose stew.

his work and gave me a container of moose stew and dumplings that his mother had made. (Moose is tender and not as gamey as you'd expect!)

MAY 29

We are currently 60 kilometres south of Matagami. When we were in the town, I did a live cross to a Canadian TV news show. The telecast sparked donations to the website: fantastic! The Canadian people we've met have been friendly and generous: nothing seems to be a problem. They've been curious about what I'm doing, and when I've explained to them my quest, they've been very supportive. I need big turnouts if I'm going to raise the necessary donations; that's why media coverage is vital. So far, because I've been off the radar in the North Pole and out of contact with other, more sensible humans, the donations have been disappointing. But I keep telling myself that as I cross Canada and the United States, passing through big towns, appearing on TV and being interviewed for newspaper articles, the donations will begin to roll in.

While we were in Matagami, I also found time to tuck into a lasagne and a chocolate milkshake in a cosy restaurant. What a treat! I haven't yet forgotten the freeze-dried curries.

This morning, I was just getting started and was up the road from the vans, loosening up, when a big black bear crossed the road in front of me. It was the first time I'd ever seen a bear without bars in front of it. The bear gazed at me and then lumbered on into the bush. I ran back to the vans, yelling, 'Hey, come quick, there's a bear up here!' I grabbed a camera and was about to charge into the foliage to try to take a picture but then thought that chasing a bear into his lair might not be so wise. So far, we've also seen two wolves and plenty of squirrels, porcupines and geese.

We passed Stark's Knob today, where, during the American War of Independence, the American General Stark held the Brits at bay until reinforcements arrived and forced a surrender. I've never been a great reader, preferring to experience life first-hand rather than vicariously, and being in these places brings history to life for me.

MAY 30

• •

Now I'm on the road and running alone, and not having to worry about falling through the ice or banging into pressure ridges in white-outs, my mind can roam free. Today, I pondered building a home back in Australia when I return, and what work I will do when this journey is over. I have a dream of starting an organisation that helps adventurers achieve their dreams as I'm achieving mine. I'm a devotee of positive visualisation, and as I run I conjure up images of me finishing this event on time, fit and healthy, and having raised millions of dollars for the needy.

I'm not feeling strong at the moment, as I'm still recovering from the ice. I suspect it will take me another two weeks to get over the damage I did to my body in that sector. My facial sores are healing in the warm sunshine, but my fingertips are still feeling very corky. When the weather cools or a snow flutter descends, they ache so much I can't concentrate on running.

Blistered feet come with the territory of ultrarunning. Tonight, I found a blister the size of a 20-cent piece on the base of a toe. What with all my other aches and pains, and concentrating on the run, I didn't know it was there until I cooled down and was on the massage table. By tomorrow, though, the toe will be like brand new and ready to carry me for another 80 kilometres.

> ### 🌐 PAT'S BLISTER FIXER
>
> I've had thousands of blisters in my time and have worked out an effective way of treating them. The worst thing you can do is leave a blister unattended, hoping it will go away: it will split open of its own accord, leaving a gaping wound that is easily infected. Instead, grab a sterilised needle and thread and carefully pierce the blister. Ever so carefully, push the needle through and out the other side, then cut each end of the thread so it is left in the blister. This allows the fluid to weep out through the cotton, and in a short time the blister will dry out. All that's left are two tiny dots. Then, cover the area in second skin: jelly encased in plastic with micro-holes that allow the sore to breathe and repair itself. Finally, stick a small tape bandage over the area to prevent dirt getting in.

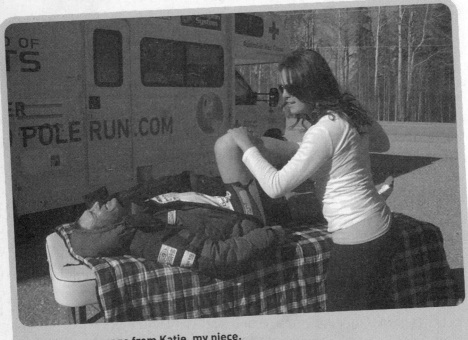

A welcome massage from Katie, my niece.

Above: Arriving from the Arctic in high spirits.

Below: Sights few boys have ever seen—with my son Dillon.

Above: A heart to heart with Dillon.

Below: Running through pines—typical Canadian terrain.

Top: Getting used to the road.

Above: When one pair isn't enough.

Left: Feted in Canada.

Above: The streets of New York.

Left: Rendezvous with Sam Kille in Central Park.

Below: Why I'm running.

Above: Celebrating my birthday with Bernie.

Below: Athletes together in Central Park.

Above: The Lincoln Memorial—he ran a hard road too.

Below: The whole Pole to Pole team with our great supporter, Kim Beazley.

Above: Brooke, Dillon and me—family ties.

Right: What a way to spend the 4th of July—Turner Field, Atlanta.

Below: Running through Washington.

Left: Gladiator—at Turner Field.

Above: The Pat Farmer Day proclamation —I didn't know whether to laugh or cry.

Below: Brooke and I—blazing heat and a gathering storm.

MAY 31

I saw a tree snake on the road today. The little fella was in grave danger of being squished by the trucks and cars whizzing by. I stopped, picked him up and placed him safely in undergrowth at the side of the road. Forrest Gump meets Steve Irwin.

I did an interview via satellite phone with Chris Smith on Sydney's Radio 2GB, bringing listeners up to date on the past few weeks. It was good to hear his broad Aussie accent. Chris introduced me on air as a masochist, and I didn't disagree.

We are at a town called Val-d'Or, and have covered nearly 1000 kilometres since Radisson. The biggest problem today has been the flies that hatch in huge numbers at this time of year dive-bombing me as I run. Otherwise, I'm feeling good. My legs are loosening up, and I'm back in my stride. It goes without saying that running on bitumen is a whole lot easier than on ice, and my diet now is steak, pasta and salmon fishcakes, which beat plastic-tasting dehydrated food hands down. Not a night passes when I don't thank God that I'm no longer

On the road, with the vans bringing up the rear.

sleeping on a block of ice. I'm grateful that I have such a wonderful support team, and the film footage the guys have been shooting is spectacular.

The Narellan Rotary Club has bid $2500 for my sled, which is great news. Hopefully, other organisations will try to outdo them. Whoever wins will have a sled that has been dragged through some of the most dangerous and beautiful terrain on earth; best of all, the money will go to those without clean water.

We will be in Canada for another week and then enter the United States. I think of milestones such as borders, or the end of months, or 500, 1000 or 2000 kilometres covered, as mental goals and feel a sense of achievement as I achieve each one.

JUNE 1
• •

There was an article about my run in the *Sydney Morning Herald*, which is great for publicity. Every day, I'm inspired and sustained by messages of support. It's a treat to put my tired feet up at the end of a day's run and read the emails, texts and Twitter and Facebook posts. Here are some that I've received over the past day or two:

> Kwe kwe ['hello' in the Algonquin language] we met briefly on Hwy 117 May 29th, you are an awesome inspiration, spoke to one of your staff n just wanted to offer some words of encouragement, and hope you enjoy the rest of Algonquin territory as you run thru Verendrye parc, safe travels, may good spirits guide you, we pray for not only health n success, but for this great man we know as Pat Farmer . . . madjibiton [run]!!!!
> *Marc Hunter*

> Keep going Pat we are thinking of you down here in Tassie and I am spreading the word of your great run at every speech I give so hopefully people will give to your cause and support you.
> *Deborah De Williams, Running Pink*

> Hi Pat! Great going! I saw your campers stop by my horse farm just before Amos. I was up on a scaffold welding and was wondering what you were running for? Now I know. I waved at you in

recognition of your efforts and in respect for your courage. Here is something nice a friend of mine found that represents you: 'A hero is someone who has given his or her life to something bigger than oneself.' (Joseph Campbell)
Cony Pard

Good day Pat! I've been tracking your progress (with increasing admiration might I add!) since Radisson! Do you have an ETA for Ottawa by any chance? Some friends and I would like to see if we could drop by in person to cheer and welcome you and your team to town! (and who knows, buy you a Gatorade or two!). Keep on running mate!
Patrick Henrichon

Hello Pat Farmer. Saw you running in Gracefield, Quebec this morning just before noon and again near Kazubazua, Quebec, around 4 pm. You are very courageous in your quest, keep up your spirits. Will try to see you again in Ottawa, Ontario, this

Overwhelmed by well-wishers in Canada.

weekend. A donation will be made to the Canadian Red Cross shortly in your name. Good luck and enjoy the beauty of our country as you pass through it.

Paul Paiement

JUNE 3

We're 200 kilometres north of Ottawa, at the end of another good but bloody long day, 85 kilometres covered. I'm sitting on my bunk in the van, my feet in iced water, taking some time out to reflect. A lot of people who have been following my run have taken to calling me the fittest guy on earth, some kind of Superman. But I'm just the same as anybody else. I ache, and I'm tired at the end of a day's run. Mentally and physically, there is nothing left in my tank. The only difference is that I keep backing up, so tomorrow morning I'll get up before sunrise, put on my gear and hit the road again. It's more about will and determination than about physical ability. I've got a strong will, and that's what's driving me on at the moment. It's one very ordinary body that I'm pushing from one end of the earth to the other.

JUNE 4

We're right on schedule. Further along the route, Greg Quail is organising local dignitaries to roll up to fundraising functions, so I've been pacing myself to coincide with the events. There would be little point in a mayor and townsfolk turning up at the appointed time and place to meet me and donate, only to discover that I was still 300 kilometres away or had passed through the day before. The public has been incredibly friendly, cheering me on and wanting to know what I'm trying to achieve. One Native Canadian offered to put us up in teepees on his reservation.

The section of Canada we've seen, with its wide open spaces and vast national parks, is a beautiful place. The terrain I'm running through now reminds me of the road from the Blue Mountains down to Sydney, with rural land, cattle pastures and horse studs interspersed with quaint towns, all linked by a wide highway. The further south we go, the more frequent the towns and the heavier the traffic. We're seeing many mighty logging trucks, huge behemoths that roar by at 130 kilometres per hour. The percussive shock as they pass shakes the trees—and me. We've left the wilderness behind and must be alert to traffic.

JUNE 5

Today, our timing was perfect. It was a thrill to run through Ottawa—capital of Canada and the first major city on my run—on the very day that saw the official opening of the country's 41st parliament. I ran into the city in the morning, a crisp, brilliant, blue sky day, and made straight for the magnificent Parliament House, perched high on a hill on the Ottawa River. A grand and stately mansion with towers and spires, it reminded me of the British Houses of Parliament in London.

The first person I bumped into as I entered the forecourt of Parliament House was the Sports Minister, Bal Gosal, who congratulated me on my run and what I was trying to achieve. I presented him with one of my running T-shirts and thanked him for the hospitality of his countrymen.

There was frantic activity and great pageantry outside parliament:

Outside Parliament House, greeted by Sports Minister Bal Gosal.

hundreds of police and army personnel, marching bands, dignitaries, and a real-life Mountie dressed in his bright red uniform, wide-brimmed hat and shining brown leather boots with gleaming stirrups. He explained to me what was going on and presented me with a maple leaf lapel badge. He told me how the Governor-General, David Lloyd Johnston, would be admitted to the House of Commons by the Usher of the Black Rod, who would pound on the door until the Prime Minister, Stephen Harper, bade him enter. The Governor-General would then deliver the opening address, known as the 'Speech from the Throne'.

Then Herb Davis appeared and took me and the camera crew into the building. Herb, a big, gangling, larger-than-life bloke, has managed newspapers, community-run dental clinics and fisheries, and has directed documentaries, hosted Canada's longest running radio program, *The Fisheries Broadcast*, and been a fish exporter. As international manager for a telecommunications company, he negotiates with government agencies in Argentina, Thailand, Malaysia, Spain, Brazil, Peru, China, Vietnam and Pacific Island nations. He obviously took a shine to me and believed in my cause, because nothing was too much trouble. Travelling at a brisk jog, he zoomed us down the corridors and into an area where the ministers and other bigwigs were gathering. He introduced me to many of them then led us through magnificent stone rooms, chapels, wood-panelled corridors and a huge, imposing circular library. Then security, which had been growing more intense as the hour of the opening neared, pounced, and we were chucked out. It had been a marvellous experience.

Before we left Ottawa, I

In Parliament House with the remarkable Herb Davis.

paid homage at the statue of the great Terry Fox, a Canadian distance runner and basketball champion who lost a leg to osteosarcoma but in 1980 ran across Canada with an artificial leg to raise money for cancer research. In his Marathon of Hope, he ran 5373 kilometres over 143 days before the cancer, which by then had reached his lungs, forced him to pull out. He died nine months later. Today, the annual Terry Fox Run is the largest one-day fundraiser for cancer research in the world and has raised over C$500 million for the cause. Terry, you're no longer with us, but you're an inspiration.

JUNE 6

Next stop was Montreal, which, hard to believe, is almost at the end of the Canadian leg of my run. It has taken me exactly 16 days to run the 1350-odd kilometres: an average of 84 kilometres a day, which is good, considering the time we spent getting things together in Radisson.

Montreal, which is located where the Ottawa and Saint Lawrence Rivers meet, is an impressive city with its striking mix of modern and older buildings. I'm hoping I can remember some of my schoolboy French because it is the largest French-speaking city in the world apart from Paris.

I was interviewed by a reporter from a local TV news program as soon as I ran into town. He asked if he could call me a freak of nature, and I jokingly said that would be fine! I used the opportunity to broadcast my message to people to dig deep. From there, I was ushered to Montreal City Hall, where I was invited to an official reception and signed the city's Book of Honour. On a page headed 'Monsieur Pat Farmer, Ancien Membre du Parlement Australien, le Six Juin, 2011', I signed my name. I thanked the people of Canada for all their support and donated one of my running shirts as a memento. The mayor called me 'a marathon runner with a heart of gold' and on behalf of Montreal made a generous donation to the Canadian Red Cross.

As I ran out of town earlier this evening, across a bridge spanning a wide, rolling waterway, I realised that when I think of Canada, I'll always think of the rivers I crossed. That's fitting, because water is what my run is all about.

North Pole . . . tick. Canada . . . tick. Two stages down, many more to go. Tomorrow I'll be in the United States.

STAGE 3
UNITED STATES

June 7 to July 29

DISTANCE TO COVER: Approximately 4000 kilometres, through Vermont, New York, New Jersey, Pennsylvania, Maryland, Washington DC, Virginia, North Carolina, South Carolina, Georgia, Alabama, Mississippi, Louisiana and Texas

TERRAIN: City streets, busy highways, rural roads and many bridges

TYPICAL WEATHER CONDITIONS: Searing summer heat with tropical thunderstorms heading into the southern states

HAZARDS: Extreme heat, heavy rain and lightning strikes, speeding vehicles that whizz by missing me by centimetres, smog, the notorious Fat Boy burger, officious cops, my aching body!

KEY EQUIPMENT: Cap, T-shirt, shorts, running shoes, hyperbaric chamber, rubdown table, cameras and media gear, litres of cold water, Nurofen, needle for puncturing blisters

PERSONNEL: Bernie Farmer, Katie Walsh, Nick King, Jake Simmonds, Emma Cohen

JUNE 7

Today we left Canada at the town of Rock Island, Vermont, and entered the United States at Derby Line, Vermont, which, as far as I could see, was the same town. Vermont produces more maple syrup than any other state in the United States, and its attractions don't end with that delicacy. It also boasts excellent skiing, snowboarding, fishing and hiking. In autumn, the leaves of the trees blaze bright red and deep brown. Lake Champlain, along whose banks I ran as we headed south, forms a large part of Vermont's western border. I ran through green fields, up and down rolling hills and on relatively quiet highways. As dusk fell tonight, I sat on a whitewashed wooden bench on the bank of Lake Champlain and had a quiet reflection on how far I've come and the things I've seen and experienced. And I allowed myself a quiet moment of pride at the distance I've covered, while not being able to deny a private shudder at the immensity of the run ahead.

JUNE 8

The temperature reached 30 degrees Celsius in Canada, but today, my first full day of running in the United States, was *really* hot. The temperature hit the high 30s. Knowing it would be a scorcher, I got off to an early start before the sun rose, gulped down some cereal and tea on the road as I walked briskly to warm up, then I was running again.

I make it a rule during the day not to stop running except for a toilet break, a quick meal or an emergency. Never will I go backwards. Today, however, with 15 kilometres to go before the end of the run, we came upon a young man whose motorbike had broken down and wouldn't start. He was stranded kilometres from any town. I made an exception for him, because so many of his countrymen, while I was training in New York and in the short time I've been running on my official journey, have shown me such goodwill. Being a motor mechanic by trade, I tried to help him start his bike. Bernie, who also knows his way around a motor, lent a hand. Unfortunately, the problem defeated us. Not even giving the bike's tyres a kick or a couple of push starts helped. We had no choice but to leave the bloke to seek assistance from a bike specialist. I hope it all worked out well for him. We said goodbye, and he thanked us for doing our best.

My friend Greg Quail, media manager of the expedition, ran with me for a few kilometres today. He levelled with me, breaking the news that while we were getting good media coverage for the run, donations to the Red Cross were not as high as we'd hoped they would be by now. He said the challenge was converting the media attention into actual donations. I didn't mince words: I told Greg that the sole reason for this run is to raise money. Ways and means *have* to be found to increase the donations. That's his job. In the meantime, mine is to keep running.

JUNE 9

Greg woke up this morning and could hardly move. He gave it his all running beside me yesterday. He asked me how I did it, 85 kilometres a day, every day. I explained how I break down the distance mentally. Towards the end of each day, when I'm hurting, I divide the remaining kilometres into lots of 10 kilometres, then lots of 5 kilometres, until there are only a couple to go. On very tough days, I ask Bernie to stop the van just 2 kilometres up the road ahead, so I can see it in the distance, and I make reaching the vehicle my goal. I know that if I catch up to the van five times, I will have run 10 kilometres. It's easier to chase something you can see than something that is out of sight.

This is why, in long-distance running and bike races, a competitor will try to stay in view of the lead pack; if they are in sight, you can hang in there, but once you lose sight of the pack it's mentally harder, and often a competitor will drop out of contention. At the end of each 5- or 10-kilometre stage, I have my team give me a drink or a snack, and this little treat also gives me something to look forward to.

I have a similar philosophy pertaining to the whole run. If I thought of the total distance I have to run, 21,000 kilometres, I'd crawl under the covers on my bunk and maybe never emerge. So what I do is break the distance down into one-day lots. I know I have to do 85 kilometres a day, day in, day out. I can handle that.

Ultrarunning is 90 per cent mental. It's about focusing on the goal, seeing success clearly in your mind and never letting that image go. One step at a time, and you can do anything.

JUNE 10

Today was a difficult day. After the hot sunshine of the last two days, I found myself running most of the day in torrential rain. I asked the crew to go ahead and try to find a hot cup of coffee and something sustaining to eat. In Shoreham, they found the Halfway House restaurant, a cosy diner, the kind you see in rural American movies, which was fine, because we were in rural America. As I came to a halt outside, I took off my wet weather gear, my wet shoes and socks, and went in . . . to the cheers of the diners. One bloke came up, shook my hand and told me I was his new hero. They gave me hot coffee and a huge slice of blueberry pie, baked fresh that morning, with a big scoop of

Running through the downpour.

fresh cream. Delicious. It was almost my daily intake of 8000 calories right there in that pie. Certainly, it was fuel for the next 30 kilometres. It hardly touched the sides as I scoffed it down.

I talked to the locals about what I'm doing, and one fellow with white hair, wearing a black T-shirt, nailed it. He said, 'I bet you've been told a million times that what you're attempting is impossible. Well, my philosophy is, if your dream is big enough, the hurdles, the facts that say you are biting off more than you can chew, don't matter a damn. You can do anything you set your mind to.'

As I left, Laura, who runs the Halfway House, gave me a laminated menu, so any time I feel down-hearted on the road I can pick something from it and the crew can whip up grilled ham and pineapple, steak, rhubarb pie, maybe even blueberry pie. I reckon they'll have trouble topping hers!

One of the great things about this expedition is meeting new people. And, America being America, everyone has a story to tell you. This afternoon, I bumped into a champion arm wrestler. His sport, like mine, is often seen as a pastime for oddballs, so we got on fine during our brief chat. I asked him the secret to arm wrestling, and he told me it's all in a special grip that allows you to control your opponent's hand. Do that before he does it to you, and you're on the way to victory. He had bulging biceps that looked like they were carved from steel. I was tempted to ask him if he was up for a job as my bodyguard when I run through the notorious Darién Gap between Panama and Colombia.

A woman who donated to the Red Cross website, inspired by my run, told me she was eternally grateful to the organisation for the help they had given her and her family when her home burned down when she was five years old. She invited me to have a dip in her swimming pool. It was tempting, but I had to thank her and keep running.

JUNE 12

· ·

We're in upstate New York, about 120 kilometres north of New York City. Maybe it's because a full-on media day in the Big Apple on June 15 is looming, maybe it's because I've had a fragmented, frustrating day on the road being filmed, meeting wellwishers and doing a long radio interview on the phone with a broadcaster in Boston, but I'm feeling jaded tonight. I ran 80 kilometres today. The terrain was awesome,

The map tells me what I already know: there's a hell of a way to go.

with fields and mountains and deep green forests and rivers where beavers had built dams. I saw a deer and a fawn dash from the foliage. But my body feels like I ran 180 kilometres.

We have a young man on board now, Anthony, an Aussie who lives in Canada, who's normally an ice documentary cameraman. His job is to film me running and talking about the expedition. We get on well. All the crew and I get on, but I'd be lying if I said there's never any tension. I suppose it's inevitable when you get a crew of dedicated professionals, each wanting to do a hard job the best they can, living together in a confined space. It's just the way it has to be, I guess.

Something that irritates me is when the film guys tell me to comb my hair or to swap my sweaty shirt for a clean one, so I'll look good on camera. I know where they're coming from, but to me that's fakery. Ultrarunning is a sweaty and dirty business.

Bernie sees me suffering, and because he has been with me before, he says, 'I know this is tough, brother, but keep going!' We argue, he says a few foul words, as do I, and we keep moving.

I get short and shitty with the crew from time to time, but what they have to understand is that it's my job to get from A to B, on foot every day. I have to do that no matter what the weather conditions are, or whether I'm feeling happy and fit or unwell and down in the dumps. I *must* meet my target every day, and I feel terrible if, for whatever reason, I fall short. We have so far to go. I have to get to the South Pole. There is no plan B.

I told the crew yesterday, 'I might make running long distances look easy, so you think everything is rosy, but, let me tell you, inside I'm hurting, my mind is twisted, I'm trying to visualise positive things to block out the pain and the boredom. To you guys it's just another day. If a film shoot doesn't work out you can film again, or have a break and play pool in a diner en route. I can't.'

I haven't been sleeping well, and that makes me feel ragged and fractious during the day. Pretty much all that's keeping me going are the thoughts that I've covered a lot of territory—nearly 3000 kilometres so far—I'm on schedule, and in 11 days, on June 23, when their school holidays commence in Sydney, Brooke and Dillon will be joining me on the road for three beautiful weeks.

I've been surprised by how welcoming the Americans have been, just like the Canadians. The drivers are all being kind to me. My experience running on Australian roads is that drivers resent me sharing the roadway and scowl, shout and hurl abuse or heavy objects. Here, motorists wave and pip their horns, pull over and thank me for running through their town and for trying to raise money for the Red Cross. The other day, an incredulous driver saw the decals on our van and the big sign 'Pat Farmer . . . Pole to Pole', and he yelled out to us, 'North Pole to South Pole . . . *Sheeeiiit*!' Yesterday, a band of hundreds of bikers complete with tattoos and headbands going to New York gave me a wave. They were older guys, part of a club, enjoying the freedom their Harley-Davidsons give them. They respected what we are doing.

Occasionally, we annoy people. Bernie parked the van across a driveway, and a little old man with the world's worst hair dye job stormed out and told us to get the hell away. Bernie was courteous and friendly, and the man soon realised he was overreacting and that we were no threat to his little world. By the time we parted ways, he was smiling and wishing us well. We've found that most bad situations can be defused by humour, diplomacy and courtesy.

I'm very thin: thinner than I've been in years and certainly thinner than when I started this run. I need 8000 calories a day to fuel 85 kilometres of running, but I'm not consuming enough. Katie has just acquired an application for her iPhone that will monitor the number of calories I ingest and my metabolic rate. I have to give some serious thought to my diet—what I'm eating and in what quantities—otherwise my body will fail me as the run wears on. I need large amounts of protein in the form of meat and fish, and of carbohydrates provided by rice, pasta, potatoes and bread. Along with that, for balance, I need fruit and vegetables, sweet treats for my mind as well as for my body. And I need to keep hydrated by drinking lots of water.

Today, as I often do while running, I was playing mind games with myself, and my thoughts took me in a weird direction. I was thinking back to when my hands were hurting during and after the ice, and I transferred that thought into a scenario in which I was running on the road and a truck zoomed past me, and its side mirror smashed into my hand and broke it off. When I fell onto the road, another truck ran right over the hand. I could see my hand completely flattened on the road. It wasn't so much a daydream as a day nightmare.

I think of my kids every day. I know they are proud of me. When this run is over, it will be wonderful to be close to them, enjoying their school activities, revelling in their growing into adults. I'll be there for them every minute. My heart bursts when I realise that, despite what I must do for the next eight months, this run will end one magic day, and then I'll be back where I belong. Meanwhile, I will contact them via text, phone call, email or letter every day. I am so excited that they will be with me in little more than a week.

Dillon has settled down a lot. He was unhappy when he returned home after joining me in Canada. It was hard for him to go back to the rules and regulations of school after the freedom he experienced on the road with me.

I've been buoyed by a letter from a group of Australian ultrarunners who were preparing for a 100-kilometre race and felt the need to contact me and say that they were thinking of me. They said I must be the greatest ultrarunner our country has produced. Am I? There have been some beauties. I don't think I'm in their league. Still, kind words from peers mean a lot.

Today, as I ran through neat and pristine farmland, past red

Going offroad in upstate New York.

barns, streams, cattle and palatial homes festooned in US flags and yellow ribbons to honour the soldiers in Afghanistan, I kept thinking about the bloke in the Halfway House restaurant in Shoreham who remarked that if the dream is big enough the facts don't matter. My family, my team and my close supporters have been the only people who have believed from the start that I can do this. To all those who are so logical about it, my dream to run from pole to pole is impossible to realise. I believe that if I can dream something, I *can* make it happen. We live in a technological age in which if something doesn't compute many think it can't happen. They said the early explorers wouldn't realise their dreams—Magellan and Columbus and Cook. The naysayers don't live free, don't think free; they don't challenge the accepted norm. If I can inspire others to push their boundaries, that will be one more benefit of this run. Dream it; do it.

Every single thing I ever wanted I've had. I fell in love with Lisa and wanted to marry her and I did, and our life was wonderful right up to the moment when she passed away. I wanted kids, and I have Brooke and Dillon. I wanted to be an ultrarunner, and I became one.

I wanted to be a politician, and my nine years in Canberra are in the history books. I wanted to run from the North Pole to the South Pole, and here I am, on a highway in upstate New York doing just that.

Bernie made me laugh today. He has a broad Australian accent, and though the Americans understand most of what he says, they simply cannot work out what he wants when he goes to a diner or store and asks for 'oatmeal'. One shopkeeper made him write down the word and then said, 'Ohhh . . . you want *oatmeal*!'

JUNE 13

As I ran towards New York City, yesterday's bad mood returned. It's part of my psyche that if I say I'm going to do something, I do it. I have always been this way. When I was planning this run and seeking sponsorship, I said to company heads, 'Look at my track record. I have run around Australia, across the Simpson Desert, twice across America, along the Great Wall of China. I will die before I fail to complete this run from pole to pole. Please sponsor me. I won't let you down.' That the executives doubted me made me angry.

We went to Telstra and the big banks, and to the major petroleum companies—Shell, BP and Caltex. The guy at Shell wouldn't even give us cards to buy fuel. BP was mired in the Texas Gulf oil leak scandal, and helping me would have given them much-needed positive publicity, but they turned me down. Again and again, after we made our pitch, the executives would tell us how much they admired our plan, and then a few days later we would receive from them the standard letter: 'After much consideration, we really appreciate the goal you have set for yourself and we wish you well in your endeavours, but unfortunately at present we are unable to help.'

Tonight, we're in Chappaqua, a picture-postcard town about 50 kilometres north of New York. It's a neat and wealthy place—not a McDonald's or Burger King in sight. It's home to former US president Bill Clinton. Greg was keen to hook us up, not because we're both ex-politicians, but because Clinton is a runner. Unfortunately, he's out of town.

Greg had better luck connecting me with a superb masseur, Rob Silverman, who lives in Chappaqua. My body was as tight as a drum, but Rob is immensely strong and worked at my muscles relentlessly and without mercy. I yelled as he dug his steel fingers deep into my sinews. For all the pain, though, he did me the world of good, and afterwards I could move much more freely. He has agreed to give me another going over before I get too far south.

Ultrarunning is an extreme sport. A run-ending fall, from stumbling on a gutter or pothole or just an uneven surface, is always on the cards. There are also real dangers to avoid: in the Arctic, I was wary of polar bears; here in the United States, it's semitrailers hurtling by me, or side mirrors on cars and vans that can clip me and knock me down. Still to be encountered on this run are bears, wildcats and snakes, kidnappers and bandits in the Darién Gap and deep crevasses in the Antarctic snow. I could contract food poisoning or a serious disease. There'll be blisters, sprains and bruises, maybe stress fractures. I've yet to have anyone throw objects at me from passing vehicles. I'm serious: it has happened to me many times in Australia. When I was running around the country, some galoot threw a beer bottle at me, and it hit me on the buttock and caused such deep bruising that I was laid up for some time.

Trying not to get distracted by the scenery—a slip could end my run.

Falls, wild animals and diseases apart, I know that simply taking the millions of steps I need to in this run is damaging my body. The physical stress is enormous. It has been known for ultrarunners to suffer injuries to feet, ankles, legs, knees and hips. Neck, shoulder and arm injuries are common. Ultrarunners lose muscle tissue as well as fat; their immune system can take a pounding. Some runners have damaged their heart. I've been told that I could be dooming myself to an old age of stiff joints and pain. I don't listen; I don't look that far ahead in my life. I may not be alive in ten years' time. When I was competing in the Trans-America race, I suffered a bad stress fracture in my leg, and the doctor said I would never be able to run again unless I pulled out of the race. I refused to quit. I figured that I was on the other side of the world running my best in this race, and I didn't know if I'd ever have the chance to do so again. I happily accepted the risk and ran on.

If I can inspire people to make donations to the Red Cross, it will be worth it. I've been luckier than most ultrarunners, who give the sport away in their 30s or early 40s. I've survived as long as I have because of my economical running style, my small frame and my resilience. Mental toughness and determination play a part too. I guess I was born to run.

I'm trying not to dwell on what lies ahead. When I've done New York, I'll worry about Washington, then Texas, Central America, South America and the South Pole. If I obsess about the challenges I'll be facing tomorrow and in the months ahead I could go out of my mind, so I've made a decision: There's no point in fretting today about what I'll come up against tomorrow.

A word about the location of my massage. We set up a table in a little memorial square near to where we had parked the vans, in the car park of Chappaqua Railway Station. Memorial squares are common features in many US towns. They are kept in pristine condition, and the gardens are tended daily. The centrepiece in Chappaqua is a monument depicting an American eagle along with the inscription 'For God and Country we dedicate this symbol to keep forever living the freedom for which they gave their lives.' The names of local men killed in five wars are listed underneath. The Americans are a proud race.

Afterwards we all gathered at a local tavern for a delicious meal of ribs, steak, pie and other standard American fare. As when I entered the Halfway House in Shoreham, the patrons stood and cheered me and wished me well. The local media flocked and fired questions at me. Thank goodness I turned down all the kind offers of a second and third drink; otherwise, I would be in no shape to run tomorrow. I enjoyed myself and relaxed more than I have for a time, but the bottom line is that with the dining and the media interviews I didn't get back to the van until after midnight, and that means I won't have enough sleep.

Here's another thing I'm trying not to dwell on: if we don't receive an injection of funds from sponsors, we'll be hard-pressed to finish, or even to travel much further than South America, let alone to the South Pole, where we will have to pay for guides and skidoos. All I can do is keep running and hope the money comes.

JUNE 14

As I run, I try to notice the sights and sounds, the scenery, what people are doing on the route. Running through the United States, I've been aware of the smell of dead animals on the side of the road. Roadkill is everywhere—deer, cats, dogs, possums, birds, rats—poor creatures that tangled with a passing vehicle and lost and now lie decaying on the roadside or in the bushes nearby. When I think of this run in years to come, the acrid smell of death will be in my nostrils.

Sometimes things I experience spark memories, and I go with the flow. I see a tennis court and I remember playing tennis with my brothers and mates when I was a kid growing up in Sydney's western suburbs. The aroma emanating from a diner will take me back to the time when I was running in my neighbourhood and would pass my home and smell Mum's cooking, meaning I had a pressing decision to make: be strong and run on, or weaken, go inside and help myself to her beautiful rich pancakes or roast lamb. I bask in the memories and my legs keep working.

Bernie was giving me a briefing the other day and I grinned at my recollection of the time when I was running across the Simpson Desert and Bernie was my logistics man and ran a kilometre or two with me. Unbeknown to Bernie, I was miked up so I could talk to a television van that was covering the run. One of the reporters was the beautiful Rachel Friend. Bernie was telling me how he was sure that Rachel fancied him. His every word was heard by Rachel and the crew in the van. Every time she encountered my brother afterwards, she reminded him of it.

I've been having problems with the crew, including Bernie. For various reasons, usually a communication breakdown, a couple of times lately I've become separated from my support team and have ended up running extra kilometres while I try to find them and they search for me. These are teething problems that will be ironed out. I told them, 'My job is hard. Yours is comparatively easy. We *have* to communicate. If I'm in a vehicle and I hit the top of a hill I can coast to the bottom, but when I'm running I don't go anywhere unless I keep on running. Nothing happens unless I pick up one foot and put it down in front of the other. A kilometre is no big deal if you're travelling it in a van, but to a runner a kilometre equals 1000 metre-long steps.' When I was running through the North Pole I was hard on my team when I thought they were wasting time. It's the same now that we're on the roads of the United States. I am ever aware that in the scheme

Skyscrapers loom ahead as I enter the Big Apple.

of things I haven't come far at all. I have just six months to get to Tierra del Fuego at the bottom of South America.

Bernie and Katie lost me today, but for a change there was a lighter side to the debacle. I like to invite supporters, my crew and visitors to the expedition to run a few kilometres with me, just to get an idea of how it is for me. We chat; they work up a sweat. With us for the past few days has been a writer covering the pole-to-pole run. The writer, who is in his early 60s and reasonably fit, and I set out from Chappaqua at dawn to run 5 kilometres. The plan was for Bernie to catch us up and drop the writer back at the car park by the railway station where we'd spent the night camping, while I ran on. Well, the writer and I jogged up some pretty steep hills leading out of Chappaqua. He was doing all right, running easily, until after a while he started gasping for air. He told me that in his view we had run much further than 5 kilometres. On consideration, I had to agree. Where were Bernie and Katie and the bloody van? After another half-hour's running, the writer, whose face was by now scarlet, declared that he was sure we'd run 15 kilometres. I looked at my watch, and he was right.

We stopped, and the writer declared that he was going to walk back to Chappaqua and get the team there to contact Bernie by phone and tell him what road I was on. Just then, Bernie and Katie pulled up in the van. They had taken a wrong turn. It was an honest mistake, and we all know that stuff-ups are inevitable. My anger didn't last long and soon all was forgotten.

Compounding my angst is that I'm making the run on such a ridiculously tight budget, and without a doctor or a proper masseur. I can't afford the specialised high-energy food that I need. If the vans break down, it'll be Bernie and me trying to fix them. If the crew gets lost, as happens, because I run on ahead before they are ready to follow or they, or I, take a wrong turn and we become separated, as well as running further or backtracking (which, as I said, I refuse on principle to do), I run the risk of tripping or stumbling and getting hurt while I'm distracted and worrying. A later end to the day when we are trying to find each other means I have less sleep. I tell them that their job is to get inside my head and *know* where I am. If they can't do that, they are of no use to me. Thankfully, I'm confident the problems will be resolved, and, anyway, our flare-ups are soon over and done with.

The streets of New York—Bronx locals cheer me on.

JUNE 15

Finally, I'm in New York. The last time I was here was in January, when it was −10 degrees and I was dragging tyres through the thick snow in Central Park. People laughed at me and wondered who the crackpot was. It feels good to be back, with the North Pole and Canada under my belt.

It's been a full day. I've done the rounds of the talk shows, whipping up donations for the cause and proving that I am a man of my word: when last I was interviewed here, I said I would do this run, and here I am doing it.

First thing on today's agenda was to run from the tip of Manhattan to Central Park, where the media, including a crew from the Nine Network's *Today* show, were waiting. I had a special running companion, a member of the New York fire brigade, Denis Sweeney. He has completed nine consecutive New York marathons and is one of the brigade's finest runners. We joked about the number of cats he's rescued from trees as we ran to the fabled park. On the way through upper

Manhattan, we stopped off for a coffee at Tom's Restaurant, which has been featured in the TV show *Seinfeld*. At Central Park, I was greeted by Sam Kille of the New York chapter of the Red Cross. He whisked me off to stand before the cameras of the popular Fox morning TV show *Good Day New York*. Afterwards, I caught up with another New York fireman, Kevin White, and a fire brigade paramedic, Dave Kruysman, who has lost a leg but doesn't let that stop him helping others. He runs with an artificial leg in triathlons. I never cease to be knocked out by the human spirit.

Then appeared a group of cyclists from one of my sponsors, Champion Systems, who make all my running gear, and their leader Scott Kaylin, who challenged me to a race around the park. I was tempted but had a lot of media engagements still to meet, including the live cross with *Today*.

One of the highlights of this wonderful and most satisfying day was the reception in my honour at the Australian consulate on East 42nd Street hosted by Consul-General Phil Scanlan. They turned on a fine party, and Phil introduced me to some Manhattan movers

Two of New York's finest: fireman Kevin White and paramedic Dave Kruysman.

and shakers. Everyone backed my run 100 per cent. In my speech of thanks, I told the gathering about a poem that inspires me every day of my life: Linda Ellis's 'The Dash'. 'It doesn't matter if you are the Queen of England or Pat Farmer,' I told the gathering. 'When you die, on your gravestone will be engraved the date when you were born and the date when you died, and separating those dates will be a dash. The dates aren't so important. What *is* important is what the dash between the dates represents, the life we've lived between birth and death. The dash stands for the sum total of our lives.'

I finished my talk to the dignitaries and guests at the consulate with a vow: 'I promise to everyone here tonight that I will complete this run from the North Pole to the South Pole, just like I have completed every single thing I have ever taken on in my life.'

Phil Scanlan offered a toast to the expedition and called on all those present to wish me 'a safe and healthy and robust onward journey'.

The support I've been shown in New York has been satisfying, and I feel my message is really getting out there now.

JULY 17

This morning, I ran out of New York City and into the state of Maryland and fell foul of the law. Just as I was setting out behind Bernie's van across a 3-kilometre bridge, I was stopped by a policeman who sternly warned me that there was no pedestrian access to the bridge. I told the officer that I was running from one end of the earth to the other for the Red Cross and asked if he would contact the bridge authority to see if an exception could be made for me. He ordered us not to move from where we were and drove off to do so.

If permission was denied, what in the world could I do? I'd be stuck. As usual, on principle, I refused to retrace my steps, so if I couldn't run over the bridge I would have to either swim across the river and risk drowning in the rips and currents that we could clearly see from the banks, or buy an oar for the kayak we kept in one of the vans and paddle across. This was not good. Whatever option we took would soak up precious time.

After 20 minutes, the police car returned and the cop got out. I was expecting the worst, but what he told me was good news. Because

Striding out on a no-pedestrian bridge after my run-in with the law.

of the humanitarian aspect of my trek, he had been instructed by the authority to tell me to run on right across the bridge. I could have hugged him. I sprinted the 3 kilometres across, with the police officer, the lights on his car flashing all the while, bringing up the rear. Another hurdle cleared.

JUNE 18

Not long now and Brooke and Dillon will be here with me. I'll be somewhere in Virginia when they arrive. The plan is for Katie to collect them at Washington Airport and drive down to meet us. From their emails and texts, I know they can't wait to see me. It's good that we're mates as well as father, daughter and son. They're promising to bring me some new music on their iPods, and Brooke, who can really sing, will be entertaining us. I've made a mental note to buy her a guitar along the way.

I've been so lucky with my kids. The loss of a parent can mess up young lives—lead to social and drug problems—but they have always coped, even while missing their mother desperately. It has helped our relationship that every chance I've had I've taken them overseas on my humanitarian trips as a politician and on behalf of the Red Cross. Because they've seen the plight of people in the developing world with no clean water, or suffering from AIDS, they understand why I do what I do, and my absences from home are easier for them to bear.

I took them to Thailand's Agape Children's Home, which cares for children with HIV/AIDS and was established by a Canadian woman, Avis Rideout, in 1996. We had a short holiday, but the trip, I made clear to Brooke and Dillon, was about working with the kids at the orphanage. I told them to get their crying over before they left home.

I was so proud of them, as they rose to the occasion. Brooke was brilliant. They say babies turn adults into children and children into adults, and this was the case with Brooke. She read to the little ones, fed them, gave them love. There was one baby whose mother had died of AIDS, and the child had contracted the HIV virus from her. Many at the home believed that you could catch AIDS from simply touching a person who has AIDS, but we knew that was not true. Brooke simply picked up the baby and cuddled it. The others gasped. That child is now thriving.

Dillon and I rolled up our sleeves and built a playground for the home. We made play equipment and bought life-size wooden elephants, horses, lions, tigers and zebras and concreted them into the yard. We erected soccer posts and cubby houses and painted them in bright colours. We constructed five bicycles from old discarded parts.

After we returned to Australia, I raised the funds to buy a bike for each of the 58 children at the Agape home. They all rushed out of church on Christmas Day to find the bikes waiting for them. The trip to Thailand awakened in Brooke and Dillon a need to help the less fortunate.

Every parent wants to leave their kids with something, and it is my dearest wish that Brooke and Dillon become decent, independent, compassionate adults, treating everyone the same, with courtesy and respect. I want them to be leaders, not followers. When I was on the ice, the other guys were procrastinating one day when the weather was truly frightening, but I simply kept on going through the blizzard and over the pressure ridges. They saw me pressing on, and they followed. That night, I texted to Brooke, 'Never be afraid to take control because this world needs leaders.'

I would love Brooke to be a doctor one day. Not so she can afford to drive a Mercedes-Benz and live in a nice home, but so she can heal people. Her mother died of heart disease, and if she became a cardiologist that would be a nice symmetry. She has other plans, however, and has set her heart on being a singer, songwriter and dancer after studying at the Sydney Conservatorium or perhaps the Juilliard School in the United States. Dillon has no idea what he wants to do when he grows up. He's a typical 13-year-old boy. At school his favourite subjects are basketball and lunch. He's not bad at maths but has no interest in reading.

JUNE 23

After five days of running on busy, dirty and, it has to be said, otherwise nondescript urban roads from New York City, I arrived in Washington DC, seat of the United States government, where Barack Obama, his wife, Michelle, and their kids occupy the White House. The Obamas weren't there to welcome me, of course, but Allen Lew, the

In Washington, just like Forrest Gump.

city administrator for the District of Columbia, was. I've given away so many shirts on the route that I was left only with some miniatures to give to Allen as mementoes.

I went to say g'day to the great monuments of the city. I have no time for sight-seeing on this run, but there was no way, having come so far, that I'd miss out on paying homage at the mighty Washington Monument, which is ringed by US flags, and at the Lincoln Memorial. I doffed my cap at the foot of the great statue. Its plaque reads, 'In this temple as in the hearts of the people for whom he saved the union the memory of Abraham Lincoln is enshrined forever.' On the way to the memorial, I visited the Reflecting Pool, which was created to reflect the images of the monuments along the Mall. It featured in the movie *Forrest Gump*, whose lead character, who runs and runs and runs, I have so often been likened to by both foes and friends. Unfortunately, the pool was a construction site—no water at all, just tractors and churned-up earth.

I couldn't leave the national capital without dropping in at the American Red Cross headquarters on E Street NW. There, I was given

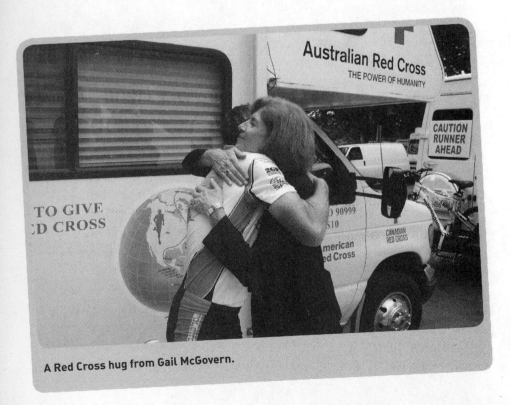

A Red Cross hug from Gail McGovern.

a warm welcome by Gail McGovern, president and chief executive of the organisation. 'You're amazing. It is such a privilege to meet you,' she said. When I had stopped blushing, I told her that the honour was all mine, and so it was. The American Red Cross, just like its branches around the world, including Australia, is a magnificent outfit. The visit was a timely reminder of why I am doing this pole-to-pole run and gave me a surge of strength and determination to run on to Antarctica.

As I prepared to leave, Gail said to me, 'Can I give you a Red Cross hug?' I readily agreed that that would be a good idea. She was later interviewed by reporters and camera crews and said, 'Pat Farmer is a remarkable inspiration. I'm so privileged that I had the opportunity to meet him and his generosity and his work shining a light on the Red Cross societies around the world is overwhelming. He lifted my spirits, raised my heart, and I just can't wait to tell friends and family and potential donors what he's doing on behalf of the Red Cross.'

My final stop in Washington DC was at the Australian embassy, where I was met by an old political foe and all-round good bloke Kim Beazley, the former leader of the Labor Party, who is now Australian ambassador to the United States.

'G'day, mate, how are ya?' Kim bellowed and gave me a huge grin. 'You look just like you did when I first saw you running around Australia.'

When interviewed by TV reporters later, Kim said, 'Pat's a great achiever and a great fighter, and this run would be just about the toughest battle in his life. And he's been involved in politics, which is a bloody hard life. So to do something even harder than that is special. He's done so well so far, and all of Australia is right behind him, looking forward to that day when he's racked up another enormous athletic achievement and he's standing proudly at the South Pole.' Kim's kind words and genuine hospitality made me feel a giant.

Despite our differing political philosophies, Kim and I have always been mates. We first met when I was running around Australia in 1998, before I entered politics. The Australian parliament acknowledged my run by letting me sit on the floor of the parliament, an honour usually reserved for presidents and royalty. Kim that day came over, shook my hand and offered his congratulations. When I took my seat as the Liberal member for Macarthur on the benches opposite Kim in his role of Labor leader, nothing changed. We were always friendly.

Leaving Washington—on the road again.

We often met up in the Parliament House gym. As well as his enormous workload, Kim's advisers were always at him to change his image by losing weight. Kim was a fine minister for Defence when Labor was in power, and a good opposition leader when it wasn't. I respected him, and so did our leader, Prime Minister John Howard.

In Washington DC, Kim was genuinely glad to see me, and he promised to discuss with the Australian ambassador to Mexico, Katrina Cooper, ways to iron out any problems I may encounter there. Mexico is a place where, I've been warned, there may be red tape and confusion.

I've been heartened by some excellent coverage of my run in local newspapers. Typical was an article, headlined, 'Australian man aims to run from North Pole to South Pole', which portrayed me as a lonely figure running alongside the traffic on US Highway 1 just north of Richmond, Virginia. The reporter, who interviewed me while running alongside me, was astonished by my quest, and after writing of my adventures in the Arctic, Canada, and my qualms over the Darién Gap and the South Pole, he heartily called on readers to donate to my website to help the Red Cross.

JUNE 27

They're here! Today, on a lonely rural road in south Virginia, after three months, came the moment I've dreamed of, my reunion with Brooke and Dillon. They'll be with me for the next three weeks, until it's time for them to return to school in Australia. Katie drove back to Washington DC and picked them up at the airport. They'd been held up for a day due to missed connections and lost luggage, and were dead tired. They saw me from the car, a tiny speck on the road in the distance. They approached slowly and quietly to take me by surprise. Then, at last, I sensed someone close behind me and turned, and there they were.

My children piled out and swamped me in one of our big Farmer family group hugs. There were tears, and everyone tried to talk at once. Brooke told me she couldn't believe how skinny and tanned I am. I put my hands on her cheeks and looked at her to see how much she had changed in the six months since I've seen her. She's had her braces taken off her teeth, and now her ears are pierced. She looks pretty good to me. Brooke was still emotional an hour after the rendezvous.

Teary reunion—Dillon and Brooke are here.

While we're together, Brooke and Dillon will run alongside me for a few kilometres a day in Virginia, North and South Carolina and Texas, and we'll say goodbye in New Orleans. Brooke, who is worried by my wasted frame, says she'll make sure I eat nutritious food while she's here. We'll take quiet time together to share memories of Lisa.

When I ran around Australia on the Centenary of Federation Run, Brooke was four and Dillon was one, so they've hardly any memory of that event. Then I stopped running to be in politics from 2001 to 2010, so for most of their growing-up years I've been a bloke in a suit in Canberra. That wasn't the real me. As well as raising money for the Red Cross, this quest is giving me a second shot at being the man I know I am. The kids are seeing their father for real now, running again. I told Brooke I am once again the man her mother fell in love with.

The kids know the sacrifices that they are making—not having me with them for an entire year, perhaps losing me forever if something bad happens—are not about me realising a personal dream, but about attempting to end the suffering of communities across the world who have no clean water and whose lives would be saved if water pipes and wells could be installed in their villages. The kids accept that I sold the family home and went into debt to fund the run. They believe that if we raise the money it will all have been worth it.

As well as Vegemite, Tim Tams and lots of hugs, my kids have brought me the gift of music, in the form of an iPod loaded with Katy Perry, Justin Bieber and Delta Goodrem songs. Brooke will sing and play for us each night. Bernie managed to buy that guitar for her, at a music store we passed back on the road. As usual with Bernie, his happy-go-lucky personality appealed to the bloke who owned the shop. He recognised Bernie's Aussie accent and asked him if he knew Tommy Emmanuel. Of course, Bernie, who plays guitar, is a fan of the great Australian guitarist. The proprietor then asked Bernie what he was doing in the United States, and when Bern told him about my pole-to-pole run, the fellow gave him a second guitar free of charge as a thankyou memento.

JUNE 28

Today we crossed into North Carolina. I am getting through this trek. Having the kids here has totally changed the atmosphere of the run:

their happiness, enthusiasm and charm have defused the tension of past weeks and brought everyone together. They have many interests, and conversation is now about more than just running and routes and who stuffed up. Today, we're all best mates again.

When we were in the Arctic, I banged my knee on the edge of a lead. For a while it was fine, but it has recently started giving me grief, and I need to have a competent masseur work on it and maybe even strap it. I don't want the injury to become chronic. That said, I'm running well. As I've mentioned, ultrarunning is about mental toughness, and if I'm feeling positive, as I have been since Brooke and Dillon joined me, it shows up on the road. I have now covered almost 4000 kilometres and have worn out five pairs of running shoes.

More and more now, as word spreads, I'm being stopped by members of the public—and a number of police—who want to chat and wish me well, take a photo and, most importantly, donate. Many people long for adventure in their own life, and some, after meeting me, have said that they're going off to make their own dreams come true by doing something they might not otherwise have dared to attempt.

One wellwisher who definitely hasn't lacked hardship or excitement in his life is a disabled Iraq war veteran in his 30s called Alex, who suffered chemical burns to his lungs. With his wife, Donna, and small children, Clarissa and Diego, Alex has been following my progress on my webpage since I left New York the first time, in January. They live in Virginia and had been trying to track us down for two days when finally they caught up with us on the road. Donna was overjoyed and said, 'Oh my God, I'm going to cry!' The children, who reminded me of Brooke and Dillon when they were little, presented me with big coloured pictures they had drawn and which I've pinned on the wall of my van. Despite his disability, which he refused even to mention, Alex ran with me for almost 2 kilometres and kept up well. At the end, we hugged. Alex told me that this was the first time he had run a mile since 1997 when he was in the Marine Corps.

Despite all the goodwill people have shown us, I so wish we could get more donations. The amount of money we have raised in Australia and over here, not yet $100,000 in total, remains far short of what I'd hoped to have at this stage of the proceedings.

The weather is sultry and matches the idea I've always had from movies of what it is like in the south of the United States. The temperature, in the high 30s, and the tropical terrain remind me a little of Cairns in north Queensland, except instead of sugar cane there are fields of corn. Every night, following intense humidity, the heavens open in spectacular storms, with lightning that turns night into day and cracking, rolling thunder.

A good Samaritan named Kevin Chesnutt, a member of the Mt Hope fire brigade at Julian, saw me sweltering as I ran under the blazing sun at high noon today and took pity. He offered to cool me down by spraying me with his fire hose. I said, 'Go for it!' He flicked a switch in the fire engine, and a huge gush of water shot 50 metres into the air and drenched me where I stood in the middle of a field like a bedraggled scarecrow. It cooled me right down, and it was a lot of fun!

The stench of dead animals on the roadside is even more overpowering and nauseating in the heat. I am attacked by the flies that buzz around the carcasses. On many occasions, I have nearly become roadkill myself, narrowly missing being swiped by the trucks, cars and caravans that scream past me. Often, their side mirrors, which can extend almost a metre from the vehicle, come close to bashing my shoulder. If I get hit by a mirror on a vehicle travelling that fast, I'm badly hurt or dead. These are possibilities you come to live with on the road.

JUNE 29

A day of terrible heat and relentless media demands that saw me stopping frequently to talk to reporters or do phone interviews. The heat really knocked me around, and, to make things worse, in the afternoon, with just 15 kilometres to go for the day, there was a deluge of biblical proportions. It was a horrific thunderstorm, possibly the worst I have ever run in, with enormously loud thunder cracks and lightning flashing all around me. I saw a number of strikes. I was wet to the skin and very scared that I'd be struck by a bolt of lightning.

I made a decision. The film crew had gone to Charlotte to organise shoots for tomorrow that we have set up with the Red Cross, triathletes' clubs and TV stations, so I insisted that the rest of us—Bernie, Katie, Emma, Brooke and Dillon—have an early dinner. I turned in right after I'd eaten, hoping the storm would pass by 2 am or so, and I could complete the remaining 15 kilometres then. My plan worked. At 2.10 am, I dragged myself and Bernie out of bed, and I ran down

A box of goodies and I'm anyone's.

the road in the mist and humidity that followed the rain, with Bernie following behind in the van with headlights blazing. Katie will catch us up in the morning at the Charlotte TV station.

After I'd completed the 15 kilometres I stopped and returned to bed for an hour's sleep before setting off again, well before the sun rose. By tonight, I will have run 100 kilometres in one day. I know this is too much—100 kilometres is *much* too far for a single day—but I can't afford to slacken.

JUNE 30

I did three TV interviews today in Charlotte. At every one, I was asked why an Australian was running through the United States to raise money for the Red Cross. I replied that I am a citizen of the world and that suffering is universal. Americans get it. Like we do in Australia, they have to cope with savage weather, fires and floods. I am continually struck by the people I meet who thank me for going to their town. I tell them that it's my privilege.

Today was one of the few days that I haven't completed 85 kilometres. It wasn't just the stop–start media schedule; I'm feeling wasted, tired and sore. For the first time, I admitted to the others that I'm human. I'm not feeling happy. I'm not always able to talk about my vulnerabilities. I don't like to acknowledge them even to myself, and I don't want the team to think I'm faltering. But, after all, I'm only human, and I feel *very* human today. The forces of nature are still very much in control.

The visit to New Orleans has been imposed on me by the Red Cross because the place is still recovering from Hurricane Katrina and Red Cross funds are needed there. But it will add 420 kilometres to my route. This is not an athletic venture; it is a fundraiser for the Red Cross, so to a degree I'm in their hands. But I can't allow commitments to make me late for the hop to the South Pole. I'm trying to do the right thing by the Red Cross, pushing an almost impossible schedule even further.

Leaving Charlotte, I was joined by a group of 30 or so young female runners known as 'Girls on the Run'. This is an organisation set

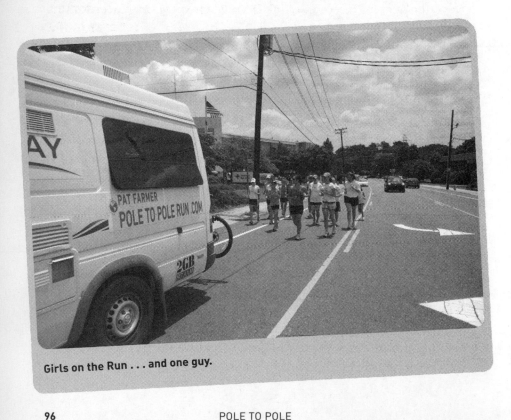

Girls on the Run . . . and one guy.

POLE TO POLE

up by an ex-triathlete named Molly Barker who saw running together as a way to help young women build self-esteem and self-awareness and to cope with life's challenges. At the end of that jog, Brooke and I plunged into the river and had a swim, which worked wonders loosening up my legs.

Tonight, we're camping at a beautiful spot: a man-made lake called Lake Wylie, on the Catawba River, in North Carolina. The Buster Boyd Bridge spans the lake; cross the bridge and you enter South Carolina, which we will do tomorrow. It's always exciting to leave one state and find yourself in another.

On Lake Wylie there's a marina, and we've seen people wakeboarding and waterskiing. I did an interview with the *Today* show for Channel Nine. I tried to be upbeat, though I was buggered; it's been a long, tough day. A local man saw me and raced home and asked his wife to whip up a cherry pie for me. It was delicious and greatly appreciated. Southern hospitality is not a myth.

I sat by the water with Brooke and Dillon, all of us aware that our time together is growing short. Brooke observed how special it is to be sitting here in the south of the United States, seeing places for real that we've only seen in movies such as *Gone with the Wind* or on TV, or that we've read about in books. Dillon was more impressed that we could see Michael Jordan's home, which is right by the lake. Dillon's a basketball fan and Jordan is one of his heroes.

I'm looking forward to Atlanta and being the guest of the Atlanta Braves baseball team at their big Fourth of July game against the Colorado Rockies at the Turner Field. There'll be 70,000 fans, fireworks and a military display. They're going to flash the details of my run on the giant electronic scoreboard and invite donations. This is a coup: we're all beside ourselves with excitement. It's a very big deal for us.

Judging by such invitations and the way we've been embraced by the people and the media, word about what I'm doing is definitely spreading. Sadly, I keep hearing from Greg Quail that there is little interest in my run in my homeland. In Australia, so far only about $35,000 has been raised, and $10,000 of that I contributed myself. The Nine Network, 2GB and my other sponsors are doing what they can, but the message is not translating into donations to the Red Cross. This is bitterly disappointing. The fundraising in the United States is very sophisticated: this is reflected in the large amounts of money

I came off second best when I took on the gi-normous Fat Boy Burger.

they raise and pour into projects. The Red Cross has a text number that people can call to make a donation. Apparently, there's some government red tape in Australia that doesn't allow such a facility. But this run is about providing much-needed money to desperate people. Surely the law can be changed to make that happen more effectively? There has been little coverage of my run at home, and that breaks my heart. All day as I run, I rack my brain to devise ways to raise my journey's profile. Maybe there will be more response in Australia when I hit South America and the South Pole. I can only hope.

🌐 ONLY IN AMERICA 1

In North Carolina, I took on the notorious Fat Boy Burger . . . and came off second best. At Mac's Speed Shop—a beer, burger and bike hangout where we stopped for refreshments at Northend, just south of Charlotte—the Fat Boy is the specialty of the house. Kevin the 'pit master' threw down a challenge: if I could eat this monster burger he would refund the $45 it cost me. Well, some people, including Brooke and Dillon, have been saying I'm looking a little thin, so I figured, why not?

But not even my refusal to give up on anything was of help today. When you know what the Fat Boy comprises, perhaps you'll forgive me. They pile into a bread roll the size of a full loaf a grilled half-kilogram spicy sausage patty, a warmed-up half-kilogram of brisket, a quarter-kilogram of pimento cheese, a half-kilogram of pulled pork, a big cup of coleslaw, a dozen rashers of smoked bacon, two handfuls of fried pickles and ten huge fried onion rings, everything doused in Mac's patented Burnout Sauce, which is a spicy tomato concoction. Kevin said, 'If you can eat this, you don't have to pay for it, and we put your name on the Wall of Fame. If you can't, you have to pay the bill, and your name goes on the Wall of Shame, which is right by the men's room! Nobody has ever defeated the Fat Boy.'

It was almost bigger than me, a veritable brontosaurus burger. I gave what I couldn't eat, which was most of it, to the crew, and even nine of them could barely finish it. I paid the bill and left. Very slowly.

JULY 1

• •

I've been feeling the strain lately. I'm as thin as I've ever been in my adult life and weigh less than 60 kilograms, about 8 kilograms lighter than when I started. I know I'll need to bulk up later, to cope with the Antarctic cold. Here in the south, it's terribly hot and humid. Within minutes of beginning my run each day I'm dripping with perspiration. As well as my back, legs and neck aching, I've got a throat infection that is depleting my energy. My distress is exacerbated by not having a doctor on my team to prescribe treatment, including antibiotics. I know I should probably call in at a medical practice for a check-up in one of the towns I run through, but that would take time I don't have. So I run on. One step, one kilometre, one day, one week at a time. I try not to think about what's to come: the brutal and energy-sapping heat and humidity I'm running into as I head further into the deep south of the United States and, even scarier, the Darién Gap and Antarctica. Instead, I pull myself up and think of something else.

Today, as usual, I started running early, in the dark at around 4 am, so I'd have time up my sleeve to take a break from the midday heat. Over here, at least, I'm becoming a bit of an attraction. Some people asked if they could take photos of my legs. A guy named Rick who ran with me for a way called his wife and she baked a peach cobbler and brought it to me on the run.

JULY 2

Bernie briefed me today on our plans for the run through northern Mexico. It can be tricky travelling through that country because of the bandits, drug runners and illegal immigrants trying to enter the United States, and there have been shootings there in the past, so I'm glad Kim Beazley was able to pull strings to try to keep us safe.

We've decided to arrive at the border at the end of a day's run, camp just on the US side, then next day, bright and early, we'll send the crew ahead 80 kilometres to suss out a safe route, and I'll follow the route they've set. By the time I finish that day we should be clear of the danger zone, and after three days we'll be well away from trouble. That's the theory, anyway.

I'm wondering if the wonderful hospitality I've been experiencing will cease at the Mexican border. Down there and in South America, the language, the road signs, the culture, the political and civil situations will all be different from what we know.

JULY 4

Today was a highlight in my life. In years to come, when I'm looking back at this pole-to-pole run, I'll remember with a smile the day I was a guest of the Atlanta Braves at Turner Field. With Brooke and Dillon, Bernie and Katie at my side, the team made such a fuss of me. The huge crowd cheered when I was introduced and the announcer broadcast my quest, and the donation details went up on the scoreboard. The players honoured me by inviting me to run the four bases, and they didn't have to ask me twice. What an experience! Players and fans wanted their photos taken with me. Peter Moylan, a Perth boy whose fast ball of 160 kilometres per hour has made him a star pitcher with the Braves, signed a ball for Dillon.

We sat in prime seats in the grandstand to see the Braves beat the Colorado Rockies and increase their chances as contenders for the World Series. I perched up there above the brightly lit diamond and consumed two milkshakes, two ice-creams, a piece of cheesecake and two hot dogs. It was worth missing my sleep for.

Earlier today, when I ran into Atlanta, I was corralled for TV, radio and newspaper interviews and also visited the Red Cross. I recorded another interview for the *Today* show. I tried to perk up for the cameras and do my best to project high spirits and optimism, but inside I'm feeling wrecked. There are definitely two sides to Pat Farmer.

I have to say that, from what little I've seen of Atlanta, it seems a place where I could happily live. It's not as built-up or busy as other major US cities. It's quite laid-back, with lovely homes, parks and bicycle trails. The people have been so welcoming. It's come a long way since it was burned to the ground in the Civil War.

Outside Turner Field—off to the baseball on the Fourth of July.

JULY 7

I've run through Georgia and am now in Alabama, heart of the deep south. It's darned hot, and the roads are like shimmering black seas. They truly look liquid as the heat rises from them in spectacular mirages. I spent the day drenched in my own sweat. I'm drinking so much water that I'm in danger of springing a leak. It's more humid than I have ever experienced, even in far north Queensland. I can't cool down. There are no breezes, and the vans have no air-conditioning. In our haste to get the vans fitted, and always trying to spend as little money as possible, we simply overlooked the air-con. It's tough going: that's all there is to it.

Hurricane season is approaching, and we'll have to take the weather as it comes. It's out of my control. If we get caught in a hurricane, we'll just have to deal with it. As usual, I'll try to blend in rather than fight.

The roadkill has changed. Today, I've seen a lot of dead armadillos, weird 'missing link'–type creatures that resemble enormous armour-plated rats. The stench of them decaying makes me gasp. There are many turtles, too, that haven't made it safely from one side of the highway to the other. There are also dead deer and squirrels. The mighty trucks that rush by just centimetres away from me are deadlier than any polar bear. In dark moments, I imagine a semitrailer hitting me and leaving me lying among the armadillos.

The kids are having an education on the road. The experience hasn't brought us closer together, because we were already as close as we could get. They're seeing me as I am, as a runner. They run beside me and tell me things—jokes, bits of news, memories of Lisa when we were a family of four, not three—that lift my spirits when I'm hurting.

JULY 8

Today, Bernie and I did the sums and worked out that when I finish the United States I'll have covered almost one-third of the route.

A man stopped me and gave me some melons, and then another presented me with a plant in a pot to brighten up the cabin in the van. A family of eight went out of their way to wish me well and

DuWayne's shrine to the cowboy days of yore.

exhort me to keep running. I have been overwhelmed by the kindness of strangers.

I interrupted my run for a brief stop at Bridges Boot Outlet & Western store, just inside the Alabama border. The proprietor, a politician and member of the Alabama House of Representatives with the very southern name of DuWayne Bridges, sent word that he wanted to donate $100 to the cause. And that's not all DuWayne did. He's one of those typical larger-than-life southern gents with a booming voice and a heart as big as the state, and he wouldn't let me leave until he'd given me a pair of the most magnificent alligator-hide boots from his range of alligator, lizard-skin and even ostrich-hide cowboy boots, a cowboy shirt and jeans.

The store has to be seen to be believed. It's a cowboy's dream. As well as more than 3000 pairs of boots, there are saddles, spurs, rifles, ropes, wagon wheels, a mechanical bison that sings 'Home on the Range' and posters of Hopalong Cassidy, Roy Rogers and other old cowboy heroes. There's an 'ol' timey outhouse from Alabama', as DuWayne described it, and when he opened the door for me a mechanical prospector told me to hang on, he'd be finished in just a minute! A picture caught my eye with the beautifully scripted words 'When life gets too hard to stand . . . kneel.' It resonated. It made me think how many times on the road I haven't known if I can continue but then have said a prayer and pushed on.

Time off at the cowboy store apart, today was typical of this stage of the run. I started at 4.30 am and ran 35 kilometres. Then I had a break in the van for 30 minutes to get out of the blazing sun and try to reduce the heat in my body's core. I was burning up, my face was beetroot-red and I had the shakes. At over 40 degrees and in my state of fatigue, sweating is not enough to reduce core temperature. If the body overheats, serious damage to the brain and vital organs can result. I cooled down by sitting in the full blast of a fan, poured cold water on my head and put my feet in a bucket of ice. I had some tea and toast and honey. I ran for another 25 kilometres, then broke for lunch. After I'd eaten I ran on until I finished my 85 kilometres for the day. I'm finding the stretch between 60 and 70 kilometres particularly hard. It drags on and feels like

Heat waves shimmer like liquid on the Alabama roads.

30 kilometres instead of 10. My body and mind scream at me to stop running. I ignore them.

My knee, the one that I banged in the Arctic, really gave me grief today. I got severe shooting pains in it, and a few times it gave out on me and I stumbled. I have to find a physiotherapist, fast. I also fear I may have nerve damage in my neck, back and butt. I'm thinking that I've lost so much weight that fat and muscle there have wasted away and there's just bone rubbing on bone. I'm literally running on the bones of my arse.

I wish we had more money. Each of the three vans has had to be serviced three times since we started, at $2000 a go. And it seems that every time we have a van serviced, in the following days a bunch of new mechanical problems arise with it. I was under the van in the pitch-dark the other night, trying to fix the generator.

> There are very few fields nowadays where you can still be the first person to achieve a goal . . . think about it: Everything's been done, but no one [has] ever attempted anything like this . . . It's really extraordinary. It's a real test of human endurance. But it's also a reminder of what the human body's capable of . . . People come out and run little stints, 3 or 6 miles, with me. People are looking to participate and they want to get involved . . . They understand. There's not much explanation needed, especially down here, down South, because you guys know better than anybody about the tornadoes and the effects that they can have on people's lives.
> Pat Farmer, quoted in 'Pole-to-pole runner passes through Lee County', *Opelika–Auburn News*, July 9, 2011

JULY 10

It's Dillon's birthday. He had let it be known that he was hoping for a birthday feast of ribs, so finding a suitable restaurant on the route was added to the crew's tasks for the day. We didn't find a ribs restaurant, but we came across a casino in the town of Atmore and took over half the restaurant there. The steaks were delicious. In the end, the food didn't matter. We put the difficulties of the run aside for an hour or two and let our hair down for Dillon's special day. And we gave the one-armed bandits a wide berth. Money is too scarce to be throwing it away.

JULY 12
••

We camped outside Atmore last night and, with everyone telling me how skinny I'm looking, I thought I'd load up on calories with a hearty breakfast at the Chevron service station cafe, where a big fellow who looked like he'd been sampling his own cooking for the past 20 years knocked me up a sumptuous feast of scrambled eggs and what he called 'The Pork Trifecta': bacon, sausage and pork patties, all deep-fried in pork fat. He topped it off with stone ground hominy corn grits with melted cheese. Nutritionists will frown, but it was delicious, and at least, I figured, with all of this on board, I didn't have to worry about my calorie intake for the rest of the day. I ran off bursting with energy.

Soon after, the blue sky turned dark purple as thick, ominous clouds descended. They seemed to be low enough for me to reach up and touch them. A warning came over the radio in the van: 'A dangerous storm is approaching,' crackled the voice of the announcer. 'If you are in its path prepare immediately for damaging winds, destructive hail and deadly cloud-to-ground lightning. People outside should move to a shelter, preferably inside a strong building but away from windows.' Within half an hour the rain was bucketing down, but thankfully the hail and lightning spared us. I ran on through the downpour and periodic deluges of water sprayed from the wheels of passing semitrailers, glad of the relief from the searing heat of recent days. We crossed the border from Alabama into Mississippi this afternoon.

Tomorrow, my brother Chris is arriving. He'll be with us for a few months. Like Bernie, he's a good man in a crisis. I'm sad, though, because the kids go home in two days. They'll be driven to the airport in New Orleans while I run my 85 kilometres. So tonight's dinner was our 'last supper'. It was a happy meal, though tinged with sadness because it was the last time that Brooke, Dillon and I will eat together until they return in the next school holidays, in September. By that time, God willing, I'll be in South America. We ate at a restaurant on the road. And Dillon finally got his ribs, a full set that was bigger than his plate. The watermelon juice was a treat, as were the beers.

No longer a lonely highway: Brooke keeps me company.

Brooke and Dillon's time with me has gone so quickly. We've been through six states since they arrived. It's been good. They've seen me giving everything I have as a runner, and we've had fun. There've been singalongs, and they've run with me and ridden the bicycle alongside me. They've kept my spirits high even when my body was suffering. The visit to the baseball will always be special to us.

Before they went to bed, I told Brooke and Dillon how much I love them. There are dangerous times ahead for me, and I want nothing left unsaid. When my dad died, when I was 14, I told my mum that I wished I'd told him I loved him more often. She said I shouldn't worry, because he knew how I felt about him. But I still believe that if you feel something, you should say it. You may not get the chance later. One day, my wife left for work, and I never saw her alive again. Her death taught me not to hold things inside, not to put things off, to tell my loved ones that I love them, and not to waste a second of this life.

JULY 14

Today I ran through Mobile, Alabama, and on into Pascagoula in Mississippi. I'm already missing Brooke and Dillon. I kissed them goodbye this morning, we said our last farewells, and I ran off into the darkness. Without them, I feel so alone.

Tomorrow I'll be in New Orleans. There are media commitments for me there, but I've just been advised that the arrangement that was set up for me to run with the mayor and meet some of the people who have reconstructed the city after Hurricane Katrina has been cancelled. We're not sure why yet. New Orleans is 420 kilometres out of my way, so I could have saved myself the extra distance had I known earlier. It's very disappointing.

We've decided that our major priority for the next few weeks is to connect with the Australian media and try to get coverage back home so people there will donate. I've spoken to Robert Tickner, chief executive of the Australian Red Cross, and told him I hope the fundraising gets into swing. We both believe there will be a rush of donations when I'm nearing the South Pole and people see that I will achieve this quest, but we need the money now. Robert told me the Red Cross is trying to establish a water project in Timor to give clean water and sanitary conditions to a village there, as well as a school and a medical centre. If I can somehow drum up the money, it will make it easier for the Red Cross to get started. I don't know how I will find the funds, but I'll give it my best.

My right leg—the one with the crook knee—is giving me hell. The shooting pains have not gone away. I'll just have to ignore it until I can track down a proper physiotherapist or masseur who can work out what the problem is and rectify it.

I have been receiving emails from Eric Philips, my North Pole guide, about his guiding me through Antarctica. He says if he's going to join me he'll be requiring his money soon, by August 1. I will definitely need him, or another guide who is as good. Whoever leads me through Antarctica will cost a heap of money. I have to find it somehow. Eric's being in contact shows that he has faith that I am going to make it to the South Pole. That makes two of us. Still, I'm a bit disappointed with his attitude that this is purely a business transaction. He has to cover his costs and make a living—I understand that.

Heading for New Orleans: doing it hard in the Big Easy.

JULY 15

One of my sponsors, David Hazlett of Hazcorp, which is based in Narellan, near Sydney, is in Texas on business, and today he made a 500-kilometre journey to rendezvous with me in the town of Hammond, Louisiana, just north of New Orleans. Our meeting was necessarily short, because I had a long way to run in the heat, but it was good to see David, and I told him how much I appreciated his financial and moral support.

The shooting pains in my butt and right knee are killing me. One minute it's fine, and the next the pain sends me through the roof. There was a chance of seeing a physio today, but he was 100 kilometres out of my way, and of course I'd have to run the 100 kilometres back to get on course, so I said no. Just too much lost time. I'll grin and bear it. Thank God for Nurofen . . . This event is about being in agony.

Even so, I'd prefer pain any day to the endless irritation of the sand flies. There are thousands of them in this swampy country, and they travel in swarms and sting like hell. I've been ripping branches from trees and using them as swatters.

I'm so skinny! I looked at myself in the van's mirror and got a shock. I'd be surprised if I'm more than 55 kilograms. I simply can't eat enough calories to balance the energy I'm expending, running 85 kilometres a day in blistering heat and 100 per cent humidity. Chris, my brother, is already earning his keep. He rustled me up a terrific dinner of fish, steak and vegies followed by delicious mangoes, my favourite fruit, which I've been devouring every day here in the south. I was ravenous.

Chris is a smart cookie. Emma will be leaving us soon, and Chris will take on her duties of cooking, washing and doing anything else that crops up. He's also a good mechanic and an excellent bloke. He can think on his feet and has a calm head in a crisis. Nothing is too much trouble. That's important. He's here for me, not just enjoying the trip. He's good fun, like Bernie and Katie, and together they help me to wind down. I'm feeling deflated since the children left, and I'm getting bored by the United States and want to get to Mexico. We're due to cross the border at the end of the month.

There was a lovely interlude on the road today. I came upon a group of people crabbing and fishing, and stopped for a moment to chat. They were pulling crab after crab out of the water, using chunks of turkey neck as bait. Later they were planning to boil and eat them. I had a go, ever the keen fisherman, and landed a crab. One woman asked me what I was doing and I told her, and she hugged me and said, 'We lost everything in Katrina, and the Red Cross helped us. God bless you for what you are doing.' I'll never forget her. Another bloke came up and wanted to donate a $20 note. I thanked him and asked him to do it via the Red Cross website. My aches and pains didn't bother me so much after those encounters.

Tonight I pulled off my right big toenail with a pair of pliers. It was loose and giving me hell. I'd had enough and had no other way to get rid of it, so I yanked it off. There was blood, but it soon stopped. I've put some artificial skin over the wound and bandaged it. The nail became loose because when my running shoes get wet they expand, and my feet slide around inside, and my toe has been rubbing against the shoe. The others were grossed out. It was a bit gory, but didn't worry me. I've pulled off toenails before and no doubt will do so again.

JULY 17

● ●

I had qualms about New Orleans. I don't have them anymore. As I ran into this port city, I was immediately struck by the defiant spirit of the place. The people here are soldiering on. What they endured from Hurricane Katrina in 2005 defies belief. Katrina was the sixth-strongest hurricane in recorded history, and the United States' third-strongest. The blasting winds topped 225 kilometres per hour. The storm surges, or tidal waves, were 6 metres high, and the poorly constructed levees were no match. The city was flooded in quick time, with 80 per cent under water that was 7 metres deep in some places. The death toll was 1836, and more than a million people in Louisiana and Mississippi had their homes destroyed. The city still has not been repaired. The residents are determined to restore their lives and their city to pre-Katrina conditions.

What a wonderful New Orleans welcome I received. As I ran into the beautiful, ravaged, historic city, the spiritual home of American jazz, blues and gospel music, I was greeted by a Dixieland jazz band playing 'You Are My Sunshine'. This was kind of ironic, because it was 40 degrees in the shade. The local Red Cross workers, led by Kay Wilkins, the chief executive of Red Cross Southeast Louisiana, all came out and danced to the music right there in Canal Street. I was honoured and touched that they'd go to such trouble.

I told them, with perhaps a little hyperbole, 'People across America and indeed across the world are making a big deal about this run, a simple little Australian who's putting one foot in front of the other, running from one polar ice cap to the other. But I have to tell you, I go through a little bit of pain on the road, and there are times when I question my reasons for doing what I'm doing, especially when I'm running alone and there is no band to play for me like there is today, and no welcoming crowds, no one from the Red Cross, no fanfare. I wonder why on earth I'm doing this. But at times like this, I know exactly why I'm pushing on. So on behalf of the people of the world, thanks to you all for turning up today. When you're working at your Red Cross desk and you think no one cares what you are doing, let me say that they do care and they appreciate the wonderful work you do. Never think that you are alone.'

Kay Wilkins then stepped up and did something very special,

Strike up the band—a New Orleans welcome.

something that I will remember until I die. She told each of her staff members to speak out loud their name, 'because,' she said, 'I want those names to go right here'—she pointed to my heart—'and when you don't have the band, or the people around, I want our names to give you strength because all of us have been affected by Katrina. We've lost homes, we've lost family, we've lost friends, and for the last six years we have been working to rebuild our community. I want you to hear these names.' And one by one the staff members called out: Sheila Spring . . . Thomas North . . . Darlene Embury . . . Al Hamilton . . . Bucky Sanchez . . . Joyce Bruce. And then everyone recommenced dancing in the street, to 'When the Saints Go Marching In'.

As I set off again, Kay called out to me, 'South Pole, here we come! We're going to run a little way with you, Pat!' And they did just that. As we were running, Kay said to me, 'What an amazing opportunity to run with you and get to know a little of the man behind the reputation . . . You have taught us, we who thought we had been taught lots of things, the value of heart, and that heart stretches across oceans. So good luck to you, Pat, and come back to New Orleans, because I want

Meeting the mayor, Mitch Landrieu, a running mate.

to show you some good places to eat!' At that moment, images of the local specialties of po-boy, gumbo and jambalaya danced before my eyes, but I put them out of my mind and ran on.

I also met with the mayor of New Orleans, Mitch Landrieu, who happens to be a keen runner, in his office at City Hall, and I presented him with a shirt.

I was so moved by the people in New Orleans. They are resilient and they never give up. So many were battered and smashed by Katrina, not to mention other hurricanes and tornadoes, and no one would have blamed them if they'd moved away to a safer part of the United States, but instead they picked themselves up and have stuck it out.

Finally, tonight I had some physiotherapy. A wonderful physio caught up with us and went to work, loosening up my legs. They have arranged for another physio to give me a session tomorrow.

Looking at my battered running shoes, I think I'll be moving on to my seventh pair tomorrow.

Back when Brooke and Dillon were running with me, I did a

phone interview with a reporter named Meghan M. Hicks from America's *Snowshoe* magazine. I've just been sent a copy. I told Meghan that while I travelled at a pace that allowed me to experience the towns through which I run, getting to see, feel, smell, and be a part of everyday life, I was also experiencing that which extends beyond my personal experience. I said, 'I want to inspire. I want others to do big things because they see me doing something I've dreamt about. Most importantly, though, this is more than an athletic feat. I want people to support the Red Cross and its worldwide efforts. That's what this is really about.'

JULY 20

The only news I get from home is what I see on the internet before I fall asleep at night. The arguments over the carbon tax and asylum seekers, the football results—the daily comings and goings that preoccupy me when I'm at home—seem distant to me, as if they are happening on another planet.

Emma and Anthony have left us. Greg is looking to replace them with Mexicans who, apart from being good film men, are resourceful and can speak the language. We need people who know how to drive, where to park, how to get the right food.

In Basile, Louisiana, I stepped briefly into Redlich's City Cash, a boudin sausage shop, and watched an elderly French-speaking Cajun man named George make this delicacy. He boiled up a kilogram of fatty pork meat and some pork liver and ground it all up into mince in a meat grinder. He stirred in rice and onions, salt, pepper and Cajun spices, then he loaded it into a stuffer, from which the mixture was stuffed into sausage casing. The sausages were then steamed. When they were ready, George showed me how to bite the end off and squeeze the meat into my mouth. It tastes more delicious than it sounds.

I had an excellent physio session this evening with Brenna and Chris, from an organisation called Anatomix. They needled me using a kind of acupuncture, and I felt like a porcupine. The needles released the pressure in my muscles and immediately I felt better.

I've run across so many bridges. Today I crossed a bridge that traversed 6 kilometres of swampland.

As I write this, I'm chomping on one of the most delicious mangoes

I've ever had, even better than the boudin sausage. The tropical fruit here in the south is luscious. I'm a sticky sweet mess.

We cross the border into Texas tomorrow.

JULY 22

Today was Pat Farmer Day in Houston, Texas. Wow! At a function at the City Hall, Mayor Annise Parker presented me with a framed document that read:

> Whereas the city of Houston honours Pat Farmer for his amazing strength, dedication and stamina on his extraordinary humanitarian mission and inspiration to all, I, Annise Parker, Mayor of the city of Houston, hereby declare July 22, 2011, Pat Farmer Day.

It was a solemn occasion staged in front of a number of dignitaries as well as my team, but while honoured, and I was appreciative,

Pat Farmer Day in Houston—what an honour for a boy from western Sydney.

I'm afraid I can't take such honours all that seriously. I just couldn't help it: I broke up. 'Hmmm,' I said. 'Pat Farmer Day. That's interesting! I want everyone in Australia to know how important I am—so important that I've been given a whole day to myself here in Houston, and that I expect the same thing when I get home to Sydney.' You'd think someone so special would get the afternoon off, but no such luck. The plaque went into the van and off I ran. I still had 20 kilometres to do to finish my day's distance.

JULY 23

The temperature was well into the 40s, and to demonstrate how hot the road was I put a frying pan on the bitumen and in a minute it was hot enough to fry an egg, which is exactly what I did. I cracked the egg, dropped it into the pan; immediately, it sizzled and cooked through. It was delicious.

I've met a nice guy, a Houston councillor named Steve Costello, an iron man and marathon runner. He invited us to dinner at his home

The hot Texas road fried this egg—as well as my feet.

outside Houston last night. At the dinner, I met a woman named Leslie and her daughter, Kate, both keen runners, and we chatted. The conversation turned to running shoes, and I mentioned that I'm wearing mine out at a rapid rate and that I'm not sponsored for shoes. Steve asked what size I take, and, without thinking why he'd ask such a question, I told him. Today, Leslie and Kate pulled up in their car and asked me to have a look in the boot. I did so: they had bought me seven new pairs of running shoes. I was overcome by their kindness and wept. Those shoes cost $200 a pair, and they and Steve, along with some of their friends, had chipped in. They also gave me three mangoes and a box of herbal tea, which I had mentioned that I enjoy. Theirs truly was a donation with heart.

JULY 24

We're in Corpus Christi, nearing the end of the United States sector of my run. Two Aussies from Brisbane called Scott and Michelle pulled over today and said hello, and some other people ran with me for a

The running shoe angels, Kate and Leslie.

bit in the searing heat. I certainly know I'm alive, and I'm grateful for that.

Bernie's van blew two tyres while I was running, and we got separated. As he and Chris were doing the repairs, Katie strapped on a backpack with bottles of water in it and ran to find me. She knew I would need water, and fast, because the temperature on the road was 48 degrees and I would soon dehydrate. When I realised the van was not bringing up the rear, I found a clump of trees and stood in the shade. I could have caused serious damage to myself if I'd run on being as parched as I was.

Katie didn't have a clue where I was, but she kept on running down the highway. A car pulled up behind her and the driver called out, 'Hey, do you know where I can find a bloke named Pat Farmer? He's an ultra-runner and I heard he's in these parts.' Katie couldn't believe it. She'd been corresponding with this guy, whose name was Juan, on Facebook as he stayed in touch with the run. She told him who she was and what had happened, and he told her to get in. They soon caught me up.

A few minutes later, Bernie and Chris, the van tyres repaired, joined us. A potentially terrible day turned into a great one. Brooke told me a guardian angel is looking after me, and, right now, I believe she's onto something.

The only thing spoiling my mood is that the generator in my van has broken down and inside it's 40 degrees, even nearing midnight. I'm bone-weary, but the heat is too intense for sleeping. We've left the door open tonight but won't be able to do that in Mexico, for fear of being robbed or attacked. Maybe the money Leslie and Kate saved me on running shoes can buy a new generator.

JULY 26

I can tell we're nearing Mexico, because the road signs and advertising hoardings are increasingly in Spanish. It's still very much Texas, though, as the 10-gallon hats, bull horns on the front of cars and sheer number of gun shops that we see attest. Guns are clearly too easy to buy in some parts of the world, and this state of affairs hit home today, as we learned of the July 23 massacre in Norway. Thank goodness, I thought, that we have strong gun control back home.

A good friend and one of the sponsors of the run, Martin Frost

Some friendly company on the run is always welcome.

of Alphapharm, is in the United States on business. Today, he flew to Houston, hired a car and drove to where I was. We ran together for two hours. He is going to pass a message to Tony Abbott inviting him to come and run with me too.

Out of the blue came a storm: the very end of Hurricane Don. I was running in the wet, and my feet were sliding around in my shoes. I'll be using my trusty needle and thread on the blisters later.

I'm not in terrific shape. The old spasms and aches are there in spades, and adding insult to injury is the fact that I'm burned to a crisp. I've been wearing a hat and sunscreen, but they're not enough to ward off the blazing heat.

My mental approach is poor because, frankly, I'm over the United States. The people here have been incredibly kind, and the scenery has been awesome, but it's been a long time—I've been running through the US for 50 days, around 4000 kilometres (or more, to accommodate detours and diversions), and now I need to experience new lands. I'll be in Mexico for 21 days, then the next five countries, being so small, will take me only a week or less apiece to run through. I'll feel like I'm really making headway. In this vast country, it has seemed as if I've been running on the spot. Since the kids went home, I've found it hard to motivate myself, though the people who are showing up have been great for my heart and mind. I'm finding the 85 kilometres every day a tall order. I need to recover physically and mentally, but I don't have that luxury. It's remorseless. I'm hoping the impending change of scenery will mentally, if not physically, refresh me.

I appreciate that I've done well to run so far, but I, and others, expect nothing less than for me to complete the run and make lots of money for the poor.

JULY 29

We are in Brownsville, and the Mexican border is just 30 minutes' run away. My plan is to get a good night's sleep here, be up at 5 am tomorrow and cross the border at 6 am. Meanwhile, the boys in the vans will be driving to a safe spot 80 kilometres into the new country.

Greg Quail is in Matamoros, just over the border in Mexico, liaising with the police and army to afford me protection as I run. Thanks to the efforts of Greg and Kim Beazley, I will have an armed escort of soldiers travelling with me, in eight vehicles. The Mexican government is desperate to kickstart tourism, and an international incident in which an elite Australian athlete and former politician falls foul of drug lords or bandits is the last thing the country needs. Me either, for that matter.

STAGE 4
CENTRAL AMERICA

July 30 to September 24

 DISTANCE TO COVER: Approximately 4200 kilometres

 TERRAIN: Mountain ranges, volcanoes, forests, plains, rivers, valleys, tropical rainforests, black sand beaches, towns and villages, farmland and sugar cane and coffee plantations

 TYPICAL WEATHER CONDITIONS: Fine days and rainy days, cool, mild and hot days, high humidity

 HAZARDS: An out-of-control truck, drug warriors, my aching legs, feet, neck and back, haemorrhoids, burned lips, blistered feet, infected toes, diarrhoea, the world's most reckless drivers, leeches, bandits and machete-wielding drunks, an incontinent cow, extortionist police, mosquitoes, crocodiles, snakes, spiders, dogs that chase and bite me, falling rocks and landslides

 KEY EQUIPMENT: Cap, T-shirt, shorts, running shoes, sunscreen, zinc cream, needle for puncturing blisters, hypobaric chamber, rubdown table, camera gear, Nurofen, food and water, vitamins

 PERSONNEL: Bernie Farmer, Katie Walsh, my brothers Chris and Tony Farmer, cameramen, technicians and interpreters Gustavo Garza, Javier Trujillo and Juan Femet, police and army escorts

# MEXICO

JULY 30

I set out from Brownsville at dawn this steamy morning and ran to the US–Mexico border. Between the two nations is no-man's-land, a nondescript patch illuminated by fierce lights. There were guards everywhere, determined to stop those who try to enter the United States illegally. Greg and Bernie had cleared my way, and I ran straight through the barriers with minimal paperwork. Suddenly, I was in Mexico, in Tamaulipas, one of the country's 32 federal entities, or states. I joined my security escort, which was waiting there for me, and after a quick greeting I began to run. The escort comprises eight utes with four machinegun-armed guards in each. Four travel ahead of me, and four bring up the rear. They keep an eye out for bandits and members of drug cartels who may kidnap me and then demand a ransom for my release. It has been organised for me to sleep in army or police compounds at night. I'll mark with paint the point on the road where I stop running in the evening, and return the next day to start again from that spot. I realise this flies in the face of my never taking a backward step or leaving the van at night, but I simply have no choice. My movements and the route that I run have all been set out for me by the Mexican government.

This is a place I can't wait to experience. It's famous for Aztec ruins, Corona beer, chillies, masked wrestlers and drug wars. The latter 'attraction' brings me to my security. If I make it safely through Mexico, I'll have many people to thank, not least the governor of Tamaulipas, Egidio Torre Cantú, and Mexico's minister for Tourism, Gloria Guevara. The same protection that Cantú has provided will be offered by the governors of all the states I run through. After Cantú had been advised of my run by Australia's ambassador to Mexico, Katrina Cooper, who in turn had been briefed by Kim Beazley, he threw his resources at me

Some of my Mexican escort—making sure I would come to no harm.

to ensure that I enjoy a strife-free run. 'I will guarantee Pat's safety,' he said. Minister Guevara, quite simply, wants tourists to return to Mexico and does not want an international incident in which an Australian athlete running for charity comes to harm.

The vans have gone on ahead, and in them, along with Katie, Bernie and Chris, are our newcomers, the Mexicans Gustavo Garza, Javier Trujillo and Juan Femet. Their job will be to handle the filming and technical aspects of the media coverage as well as carrying out general duties. Most importantly, they speak the language, and I have a feeling they'll be worth their weight in gold pesos before we part ways in South America.

The government and the army are in charge of Mexico by day, but the drug lords control it at night, so I've been told I need to start running after the sun rises and finish before it sets. Apart from the possibility that I will be kidnapped, the authorities worry that if I run at night or enter an unsafe area and in so doing interrupt a drug deal I could be gunned down without a qualm.

I'm grateful for the protection. Another bonus is that, because

Mexico is so influential through Central America right down to Panama, the high profile I've been given here will set me in good stead in the other countries. We will receive as much support in them as here, if not more.

AUGUST 1

Sitting here in the compound after a good day's run, and coming from a relatively law-abiding country such as Australia, it's hard for me to get my head around the fact that Mexico is in the grip of a drug war. Rival cartels, keen to control the growing of drugs in their region and their supply to the United States, fight to the death against each other. They are also at war with government forces. These cartels supply most of the illicit drugs that find their way into the United States, so the gangsters here are unbelievably powerful and wealthy. It's thought that the profits from drugs in the United States are as high as $US48 billion.

The blokes in my escort are taking their work very seriously. Today, when I stopped at a public loo, they surrounded the block and

It's not often I have the police on my tail.

prevented anyone from coming in until I was finished. I felt rather sheepish as I emerged. They, and others who saw me run by, gave me the big thumbs up and cheery grins.

I'm nearly 250 kilometres into Mexico, which means that I've notched up over 6300 kilometres since I left the North Pole. At Matamoros, where I entered Mexico, the country all around me was parched dry and brown, but today I ran over a mountain range and found myself in a world where everything is green: the hills, the paddocks, the forests. The sun, however, is just as hot.

AUGUST 3

I'm grateful for my armed escort, and it's kind of glamorous to run in this machinegun cavalcade, but the vehicles put a lot of stress on me to keep up with them. I find I'm running faster than I should be. Quite frankly, I'm in bad shape. The constant pounding on the road is taking a toll on my legs and has made my left shin and ankle swollen and painful, and I have an excruciating haemorrhoid on my backside. I've been applying cream to it, but that hasn't helped. I should stop at a hospital and have it banded, but I just don't have time. I'll keep running and hope the haemorrhoid goes away. It had better, and soon, because it is depleting my energy, and it rubs painfully as I take each step. I'm also getting back spasms and headaches, and pains in my feet, legs, shoulders and neck. My feet are covered in blisters. My nipples bleed from rubbing against my sweat-salty shirt as I run. I looked in the mirror last night and got a shock: I look wasted and drawn. The joys of the ultrarunner! I'm in a right mess. But I'll say it again: I'll die before I quit this run.

The scenery here is beautiful; it is so green and rustic. The sky is a perfect blue with little billowy white clouds. I can see mountains in the distance. The midday heat is ferocious, though. I can understand why they have siestas over here. Hopefully, there'll be relief at Veracruz, which is on the coast, about four days away.

People have been gathering to cheer me on as I run through their towns. They carry Mexican flags and wear T-shirts with 'Pat' scrawled on the front. One family who had been following my progress on TV news broadcasts and Facebook were wearing T-shirts painted with the words 'Go Pat Go!' The people have been flocking to me to shake

The support of the people warms my heart and spurs me on.

my hand, not at all deterred by the presence of the machinegunners. Weapons are commonplace here.

Ciudad Victoria, the capital city of Tamaulipas, is a US-style town with wide roads and a big retail and business district, but most of the towns we've seen so far have been small and quaint, just a few brightly painted wooden buildings clustered around a *cantina*. I took a photo today of a man riding his donkey along the side of the road, and another of a man working his fields with a horse-drawn plough, just like in ancient times. These Mexicans work hard. Some farmers have modern machinery, but most are poor and do not.

The scary-looking escort means that I'm not being bothered by cars and trucks speeding by too close. When drivers catch sight of those machineguns, they slow right down and give me the widest of berths.

AUGUST 5

More bad news came today from the Australian donation front. The money we've raised is pathetic, little more than $35,000, including, as I've said, my own $10,000 kick-start donation. I could make more money sitting at home and calling my corporate friends to chip in. My disposition wasn't helped by my flaming-red haemorrhoid, which is causing me tremendous pain. Then Bernie told me the latest news of the fighting, starvation and thousands of deaths occurring every day in Somalia, one of the stricken African regions this run will aid, and I told myself to pull my head in and keep running.

AUGUST 7

This evening, I had a massage from a masseur at a soccer club we passed on the road. He was happy to join us at day's end and give me a workover. At one point in the massage, he stopped rubbing and twisting, and, obviously stunned by how tight my muscles were, he asked, 'Pat, how often do you have massages?' I told him this was my fourth in over 6000 kilometres. He gasped and said, 'I'll say a prayer for you.'

I have to keep running at this intensity. If I slacken, I'll never finish. I have more than 15,000 kilometres still to run. Probably the most difficult conditions are ahead of me. But I have no fallback strategy: I have to complete this pole-to-pole run. I have burned my bridges: I have no job or home back in Australia; I sold my home to pay for this run. Unless I finish, and can parlay the event into funds for the Red Cross, a documentary, book, speaking engagements and product endorsements and other opportunities in years to come, I will be broke and my children and I will have no financial future. The kids support me, but I often worry that I have short-changed them in trying to realise this dream of saving lives in the third world.

Dillon is making things even tougher. He hasn't settled back into life in Australia since returning there from the United States a few weeks ago. He is calling me frequently, saying he is desperately unhappy. I can do nothing to help him. All I can say to my son is that he should hang on until I return, in February or March next year. Then we can have a heart-to-heart. I can't help thinking that my not being with him is making his life harder. He is, after all, just 14 years old. He wants what the other kids have. He doesn't understand that if I fail we will be skint. Brooke, who is two years older, knows we all have to stay positive.

I liken this run to a prison sentence, albeit a self-imposed one. I'm stuck here until I finish this journey; I have to serve my time. People say, 'Pat, you're being dramatic. You can stop running and go home any time you like.' But I can't. Apart from having burned personal bridges, to give up would be burning the bridges of all those without clean water who will have it only if I finish what I've started. Robert Tickner, chief of Red Cross Australia, has told me that there's a well ready to be built in Timor, but no funds to build it. I told him I'd raise the funds. I will, too.

AUGUST 9

Today, I ran down out of the mountains in the state of Veracruz, the second Mexican state I've traversed, and hit the Mexican Gulf, on the east coast, 170 kilometres north of the city of Veracruz. I halted by the wide blue sea, stood on the black sand and let the waves wash gently over my legs. It was wonderfully invigorating. Whether in reality or just wishful thinking, for the short time I stood there the water seemed to take away the pain. I closed my eyes and imagined I was back home at Bronte Beach with Brooke and Dillon, and it made me cry. God, this is a hard road I've chosen.

Now it's time for my regular roadkill report! What I'm seeing on the road here are the flattened shells of enormous crabs. The carcasses cook on the blisteringly hot asphalt. Even before they tangled with whatever truck or car ran them over and squashed them to twice their size, they were big fellas, easily the size of dinner plates. There are plenty of live crabs, too, scuttling along the sand and pathways. Today, I saw a dead monkey on the road. It was sad. I was told by a local yesterday that police have locked in a cell a spider monkey that was terrorising villages around these parts, because monkeys can carry rabies.

The terrain here is tropical, with an abundance of banana trees on the hills; it reminds me of Coffs Harbour on the New South Wales north coast. There are little cafes and *cantinas* everywhere, some simple lean-tos under sheltering palms, and this reminds me of Bali, where my family has had happy holidays.

The guards remain with me. The eight-vehicle escort has been downgraded to four, and comprises only federal police. My guards, however, are still packing machineguns; that hasn't changed, because there continues to be a threat that I may be targeted by drug lords. The police cars with their flashing red and blue lights are like something out of *Mad Max*. I suppose some people see all this protection as over the top, but I have been told in no uncertain terms that the drug cartels are out to disrupt people's lives as a means to gain their evil ends, so I would be mad to dispense with the guards.

Also part of my entourage is a Red Cross van, which trundles along behind the police vehicles. I find its presence a little unsettling, because it brings to mind the sweeper vehicle that follows the runners in an ultrarace, collecting the competitors who fall over from fatigue.

My bloody haemorrhoid is still hurting like blazes.

AUGUST 11

A doctor who we found to give me physiotherapy yesterday told me he was amazed that I was still churning out so many kilometres a day, and he thinks there's something freakish about me. As I've said, my body is like everyone else's; it's my mind that sets me apart from people who

The Pied Piper of Mexico.

choose not to do what I do. I understand the great City2Surf run is on in Sydney this coming weekend. Well, to put what I'm doing in perspective, every single day I run *six* City2Surfs.

I'm embarrassed at the enthusiasm I'm receiving from the Mexican people. I know I'm not a superstar, but they are making me feel like one. The mayor of every town I've run through has been on the road to welcome me, and the crowds wave at me and cheer. They take my photo and want my autograph. (I hope it's not because they're intimidated by my armed escort!) The publicity here has been good, and word is passing along the route. The excitement is the greatest I've experienced on this run. Sadly, though, there is no real mechanism to direct donations to the Mexican Red Cross. Email, phone and the Red Cross website are rudimentary and unreliable.

Entering the city of Tampico, I ran under the big 'Bienvenido' sign that stretches across the highway. Some people ran with me to the Red Cross headquarters, where, in front of a phalanx of TV cameras, one of the officials declared, 'The money you have raised for the International Red Cross, Pat, will help the Mexican Red Cross and its citizens, especially those who have less. This noble action of running thousands of kilometres for the Red Cross is something worth recognising, and the people of Tampico welcome you in our city.'

We had a big setback this week: we've lost the sponsorship of the SOC Exchange. They had paid one $75,000 instalment of their total commitment of $300,000. There won't be any more support from them. They pulled the plug because they were disappointed that I didn't mention them in every interview. I simply couldn't: newspapers and magazines cut plugs from their interviews. Losing the SOC Exchange plays on my mind; we certainly could have used their money. But there's nothing I can do about it. Onwards and upwards.

AUGUST 12

I reached the city of Veracruz today. Nowadays, Veracruz is a busy port with cars, trucks and industry, but it has a romantic past. Hernán Cortés landed here in 1519 and plundered the gold of the region. Pirates, also attracted by the gold, have made nuisances of themselves here through the centuries. Veracruz has also been attacked by France and the United States, and there is a western film called *Vera Cruz*, about a bunch of cowboys caught up in the Mexican rebellion of 1866, that was set here and filmed in 1954, starring Burt Lancaster and Gary Cooper.

We were guests of the Red Cross in Veracruz. They treated us all to a superb breakfast, then they made speeches of thanks, and so did I. It's an admirable organisation: the Veracruz Red Cross has built a hospital and nursing home, established an ambulance service and provided training for doctors. Officials from the Australian consulate joined us. Then I was swamped by the Mexican TV networks while I took a tour of the town. In some places, the streets were lined with cheering people. Quite a welcome for a runner.

I spoke to Brooke and Dillon today, and they'll be here again during the next school holidays, in September. So I'll see them in Panama before I tackle the Darién Gap. That's important to me.

I've received an email from the Australian Red Cross that has made me very happy, as it gave me a chance to make a difference. It read:

> Congratulations Pat on reaching another milestone and I hope you're getting some respite from the heat. Just getting back to you with some detail on a potential project in East Timor that could be funded by the money you've raised for the Australian Red Cross. The project connects a school, health post and a group of villages to a fresh water spring and latrines. Also included is delivery of hygiene promotion training to reduce the incidence of malaria and diarrhoea which plagues the community. Community mothers will be invited to participate in mothers groups where topics that benefit the health of infants and small children will be shared. This will deliver an activity for village-based women and improve health outcomes for current and future infants and children. The project is ready to go. This cuts out the usual process of evaluation and negotiation with the community, which can take up to six months before a project can start. This project is in a remote area—Com, in the Lautem District—and is the most remote area from Dili, taking around 8 hours driving to reach. However, it is in close proximity to another ongoing project and therefore staff and equipment are already in the area. Our Water and Sanitation team believe the project is a good fit with your objectives, being

focused on a school and a clinic. It is estimated that the total budget for this project is around AUD$60,000 but we expect to receive a final budget within the next few days. If you think this is a suitable project, please let me know and we can get the ball rolling.

I could think of no more apt project to help to fund, and I replied, saying, 'Let's do it, and do it now.'

AUGUST 13

In Alvarado today, about 80 kilometres south of Veracruz and still on the east coast, I realised I was more than a third of the way into my run, the run they said I would never complete. I feel pretty weary and sore, and I keep having to tell myself that when you have run as far as you think you possibly can, you have only gone half as far as you are capable of running. I thought today of the approaching Darién Gap, between Panama and Colombia, which Bernie has assured me—and

Grit and petrol fumes enveloped me in Mexican towns.

I'm tending to agree—is a bigger obstacle than the poles. Bandits and hostage takers, swamps, killer wildlife. The most dangerous place on earth. My crew is dealing with the Colombian government, trying to persuade it to provide some kind of armed escort. I know the vans won't be able to accompany me; when I run through that hell hole I'll be pretty much on my own, apart from, I hope, a squad of armed soldiers or police. I don't know what distance I'll be able to cover a day through that 150-odd kilometres of forbidding terrain, but it won't be anything like 85 kilometres.

Chris Smith of Radio 2GB rang to interview me today and said there's a fellow named Grover Logan walking from Albury to Canberra as part of an anti–carbon dioxide tax rally, and his feet are covered in blisters. Chris asked me what he should do about them. I told him to tell Grover firstly to get his head right and to understand that, while blisters are undoubtedly painful, nobody ever died of one. He has to walk through the discomfort. That's the harsh reality. I advised him to rub moisturiser into his feet at night, and I gave him details of my needle treatment. I also wished Grover all the best. Anyone who puts themselves through pain for a cause has my vote.

AUGUST 14

Today, I left the Gulf of Mexico and started running towards the west coast of this remarkable country. My route will take me across the rugged Sierra Madre (Mother Range) mountains to the coast, and then I'll head past Acapulco and carry on south-east to the border with Guatemala. It's a distance of about 1000 kilometres.

Mexico continues to delight me. With its gently flowing rivers, black sand beaches, palm trees, lush deep greens, primary-colour foliage and exotic animals, it's a tropical oasis, not the parched and barren desert with cacti and buzzards I was expecting. Its many little roadside stalls offer those who pass by a rich bounty of pineapples and coconuts, the best bananas I have ever tasted, fresh limes and lemons, and of course ice-cold fresh fruit juices. As I run, kids hold out to me coconuts with the tops chopped off, ready for me to take a deep drink of milk. Delicious. You can't get any fresher than that! We've also been able to feast on fresh fish and crabs, lobsters and shrimp: the seafood in Veracruz was the best I've ever had.

AUGUST 15

I had to change my route today, because recent floods had washed out a bridge that I was due to run across. I had to detour about 30 kilometres out of my way. We'd had no prior notice that the bridge had ceased to exist. These things happen; I take them in my stride.

Mexico has been a pleasant surprise. Well-meaning people caring only for my welfare have been constantly telling me, 'Watch out for this . . . watch out for that,' but so far everything has gone smoothly; the country is beautiful and so are the people. Carloads of families have been stopping and giving me fresh fruit and bread, and asking to have their photo taken with me. I always oblige. I know I have an escort, and I wouldn't have been given one if there was no danger, but, by and large, from what I've seen Mexico is safe.

I did a live cross with Karl Stefanovic on the *Today* show this morning, and he asked me how my body is holding up. I told him and all the viewers back home, 'I'd be lying if I said my body wasn't giving me grief. My legs are sore; the knee I cracked in the Arctic remains painful and I reckon I've chipped a bone, but I'll put up with the pain until I finish the run. I'm still going strong. We've got the North Pole done, Canada done, the United States done, and here we are in Mexico. Bloody hell . . . sometimes I have to pinch myself.'

AUGUST 18

I'm standing by the Pacific Ocean on the west coast of Mexico, just three days away from Guatemala.

The Sierra Madre mountains, which have taken three days to cross, form a daunting range that guards the west coast. The sheer beauty of the place took my mind off the gruelling run. The striking terrain comprises 3000-metre-high mountains, much of which are covered in pine oak forests, and plunging canyons. Tribes of indigenous people, who speak Uto-Aztecan languages, live there. I'm not sure if this was the setting for the classic Humphrey Bogart movie *The Treasure of the Sierra Madre*, because there are *five* Sierra Madre ranges in Mexico: the Sierra Madre Del Sur, which I traversed, the Sierra Madre Oriental, the Sierra Madre de Oaxaca, the Sierra Madre Occidental and the Sierra Madre de Chiapas. But I'm happy to believe I ran in Bogie's footsteps.

I've been as sick as a dog with diarrhoea. I don't know what the culprit was. I've been careful to drink sterilised water where possible and not to eat anything that looks dodgy from a stall, preferring to stick with fresh fruit. But a bug definitely got into something I ate. For the past two days, I've had to stop every 5 kilometres or so. It's been so bloody uncomfortable, and a huge bore to the motorcade—the vans and the escort vehicles—which of course have to pull up while I relieve myself.

I've found it difficult having to stop running every night and be driven to the police or army compound to sleep in safe quarters, and then be driven back to the place I stopped running in the morning for the new day's run to begin. At the end of each run, Chris sprays in white a big 'P to P' on the road to mark the spot; in this case, graffiti is encouraged! For the past week, for some reason, the compounds have been about 50 or 60 kilometres off my route, so I rise at four o'clock, travel to the road on which I'm to run, and because of red tape and formalities with the police, and checking our maps, I sometimes don't get going until seven o'clock or even later. It's hard under these

Chilling out in a police compound. It's not Coogee, but it's not bad.

circumstances to maintain my 85 kilometres a day, but I'm doing it, most days anyway.

On the sides of the roads are crosses, little makeshift memorials to those killed there. There have been scores of them along the way. I'm not surprised: the roads are dreadful. Mexico is a poor country. The edges have been washed away by the heavy rains and not repaired. One slip, and you could find yourself free-falling into a deep ravine. And this is the wet season: every day there is torrential rain, thunder and lightning, and the roads are literally falling apart before my eyes.

AUGUST 19

I woke up today thinking that this was going to be a day like any other. A bit blasé, perhaps, but the days all meld into each other. However, it turned out to be one I will never forget. Today, I came as close to death as I have been since I began this run, and probably as close as I have been in my life. It happened on an innocuous stretch of Highway 200.

We were at the 25-kilometre mark, and all day we had been on roads that had been ravaged by the recent heavy rains. The potholes and half-hearted attempts at repair by road crews were making driving hard for us and others on the road, and I was aware of some drivers being distracted, angry and impatient. I was running easily and steadily. Bernie in his Winnebago was directly behind me, and following him were two escort vehicles, while the other two were up ahead. Suddenly, I heard a screech of brakes and turned round to see a dirty big semitrailer smash into the front left corner of Bernie's Winnebago. The semi somehow came off worse: it careened off course. The driver over-corrected, and suddenly it was airborne, then sliding on its side down the road, heading at great speed in my direction. Sparks were flying, and the noise of metal on bitumen was terrible. My reflexes kicked in, and I dived headlong into a gully and landed hard. The out-of-control semi missed me by a metre or so and powered on for another 60 metres, then came to a stop on its side, like a wounded dinosaur, blocking both lanes of the road. The smell of smoke and dust and fuel filled the air. I climbed out of the gully and ran to where the semi was, hoping the fuel tanks would not explode. Bernie, badly shaken like me, but unhurt, ran to the semi too. To our astonishment, the driver emerged from the cabin with only a few cuts and bruises.

Brush with death—Bernie and I count our blessings after the truck smash.

He could have been killed. We all could have been killed.

There was only superficial damage to our van. Bernie and the guards remained on the scene and waited for local police to come and take details, and for tractors and cranes to remove the semitrailer from the road. There was nothing else I could do there, so I continued running, Katie following me on a pushbike with food and water. Some hours later, when the accident had been cleared up, Bernie caught up with us. I lost only half an hour from the run.

One of the cops, according to Bernie, wanted to know how he could donate to the run.

Life is balanced in such a fragile way. I thought about the shortness of our existence on earth and the poem 'The Dash', about making the most of the time we are given today, because we may not be here tomorrow.

Katie, who was badly shaken by the prang, has written down her impression of the near-calamity as she experienced it from inside the Winnebago, so I've included it here. It brings home the horror of the near-miss.

The truck accident was indeed a hardcore reality check for the three of us as to where we are, what we are doing and most importantly that no matter how much preparation and 'worst case scenarios' we try to predict we have very little control over how each day, hour, minute, even second plays out. Sometimes it works out but more often than not it is an up-hill battle.

I was sitting at the table drafting an email when I was jolted by the usual random spurt in the accelerator when an overtaking car gets a little too close. Immediately following was a screeching of brakes to the left of me but it was not until the entire RV was struck with a body-jarring crash that I looked up from the keyboard and saw the draws, cupboards, dishes and anything that was left unsecured on the benches flying across the vehicle, but the strangest was that when I looked to see where Pat was all I could see was a truck that was mid-air and from what I could tell had hit us and was flipped when it hit our RV. It was landing right in front of our vehicle and scraping the tarmac as it was still travelling forward when I realised I could not see Pat anywhere. I yelled to Uncle Bernie, 'Where's Pat?' I don't think I got a response but I was already out the side door in the grass that met the side of the road looking for him. Thankfully he emerged from a space where he had dived into, I saw blood on his face and shirt but was surprised because it was barely a paper cut. When I asked him if he was okay, did he get hit, etc., he said, 'No, this is just from jumping in the bushes.'

Uncle Bernie was out with us by then, not a couple of seconds after me, and we were all completely dumbfounded at the sight of this overturned truck in front of us blocking the entire road. The driver of the truck climbed out onto the driver's side door, which was now facing the sky, without a scratch and still trying to process what had just occurred. Amazingly the only damage our Winnebago had suffered was a hole no larger than the size of my palm where the truck had collided with the front driver's side not a metre from where Uncle Bernie was sitting.

We took photos and I tried interviewing Uncle Pat and Uncle Bernie because I knew how important it was to document such a close call but once we began replaying it over and over again among ourselves and with bystanders and the police I realised that the first jolt I felt of acceleration was the difference between a close call and a tragedy. Uncle Bernie has sped up just in time to intercept the truck so that it didn't hit Uncle Pat! It was so surreal to have that in my mind while I was packing supplies in a backpack and readying myself to ride the bike next to Uncle Pat so we could continue to cover the day's distance while the police tried to clear the wreckage from the road. No cars were getting through that road for hours and traffic was backed up as far as the eye could see.

After about an hour of cycling next to Uncle Pat and trying to get our minds off what had just happened, Andres, the federal police officer travelling with us that day, had caught up to us and had the driver of the truck from the accident in the passenger seat. He checked to see if we were okay and let us know that they were hoping to clear the road in the next 30 minutes. We asked if the truck driver was okay and he gave us a thumbs up which I couldn't help but notice was not accompanied with the usual carefree smile, but a hollow and frightened stare. Andres then proceeded to ask me if I could email him the photos that I took at the scene of the crash, which is when it really struck home that we are definitely NOT in Australia anymore. Andres told the passenger—the very same truck driver who had just collided with our Winnie after speeding past three police vehicles behind us and ignoring their directions to slow down, who had flipped his truck and missed Uncle Pat by no more than a foot was now being instructed by the federal police officer—to take the steering wheel of the police vehicle while Andres found a piece of paper and pen then proceeded to write down his contact details for me, all the while not looking up to glance at the road once. I could not help but laugh in disbelief!

AUGUST 20

We're about 65 kilometres from the border separating Mexico and Guatemala. Another country conquered. I'll be glad to get Mexico behind me, because it means I'm that much closer to the finish and because the remaining countries of Central America that I'm going to be running through—Guatemala, El Salvador, Honduras, Nicaragua,

Costa Rica and Panama—are geographically small, in comparison to Canada, the United States and Mexico; this will help me mentally, as I will be going through them much faster.

Good things came in the shape of my brother Tony, who joined us today and will be with us for a few weeks. Like Bernie, he's reliable, practical and calm in a crisis.

I started running late today, which I always hate, because it's hard to pull back the time. I felt very sluggish and weak in the legs. I had no energy and felt constipated, but I knew that this would be my last day in Mexico so I persevered with it. Tony saddled up the push bike and kept me company. We talked about the building trade in Australia and started designing a home for when I get this run over and done with. When I ran across the United States in 1993, I designed my whole home at Catherine Field in my head, right down to which way the doors would swing. Such thoughts help to pass the long, lonely hours.

Thirty kilometres into the run today, the camera crew received an urgent message from Greg Quail that we had to film a commercial for our sponsor Blackmores, and that it had to be done by the end of

Farewell to Mexico.

the day. This killed ninety minutes of my day and made things much more difficult, but I did it anyway. Then, as we were approaching the border, a message came through that six of the Mexican national running team wanted to run the last 20 kilometres out of Mexico with me. It was good, but it was bad. The Mexican runners were fresh, and I was tired, and because we all have a competitive streak it turned into a race, of course. I did well, but I was wrecked at the end.

As I ended my run in Mexico and neared the border with Guatemala, I found myself running down a hill. At the bottom was the river that divides Mexico from the republic of Guatemala. Right there, I saw the biggest flag I have ever seen, the Mexican flag. As it flapped in the breeze high above my head it blocked out the sun.

Finally, I reached the border, and there was much fanfare from the Mexican press saying goodbye and wanting my thoughts on their nation. Having simply run through the place, I was no expert, but I was happy to talk to them about my abiding personal memories of their land. There were many Mexican highlights, such as my swim in the Gulf of Mexico with my little brother Chris. The water had been cool and fresh, and a big moon had been shining brightly. I'd told Chris that this was a special moment for me, and he said it was for him too, because who'd have thought two kids from Sydney's west could ever experience such a thing? I'd marvelled at the vivid lime-greens and orange paint jobs on the houses we passed, the tropical jungles, the exotic fruits—pineapples, mangoes, lychees, coconuts—and the enormous wind farms on the Pacific side of the country. This has been another country of rivers and bridges. It's been dangerous more in terms of washed-out roads and precarious cliffs on which one trip could have seen me fall into a ravine than in terms of Mexican drug cartels. I have never seen so many guns. I haven't felt threatened at any stage, though, and I probably didn't need my heavily armed army and police escort. Still, who knows? If I hadn't had an escort, perhaps the drug bandits and kidnappers would have felt bold enough to attack me. Best I don't know.

GUATEMALA

AUGUST 22

The border crossing yesterday went smoothly, and for the next 10 kilo-metres, until we reached our resting destination, the streets were lined with people clapping and cheering as I ran past. I have not seen anything like this before. I hope I can justify their support in me by finishing this run.

We slept high on a mountaintop and woke this morning envel-oped in a blanket of cloud that extended to cover the jungle valley below. I thought we had all died and were in heaven.

Guatemala has many volcanoes, and I will be running over a number of them throughout the week that we will be here. I will need legs of steel and a heart as big as Phar Lap's to get through this, but the scenery will make it easier.

The Red Cross is going to chaperone me through this country as well, an official in a van watching my every step. Tonight, we'll be stay-ing in a nice hotel arranged for us by the police, who prefer us to be in lodgings rather than the vans because they can stay there too and keep an eye on us. Just like the Mexicans, nobody in Guatemala wants an international incident, and the government is aware that my run is being observed by the world's media. The government has assigned a policeman named Anghill to be my minder-bodyguard. He is with the tourist branch of the police and studied self-defence in Israel on a government scholarship. Anghill confided to me that there is a huge castle on the hill opposite tonight's hotel, and that it belonged to a drug baron before he was locked away. His family now lives there. There's obviously BIG money in drugs here.

Guatemalan Red Cross officials endorsed my efforts.

AUGUST 23
● ●

To sum up today in a word, I would say 'Accidents'. I made a 55-kilometre climb into the hills, then the heavens opened and a tropical downpour drenched me. Within the next 15 kilometres, I saw three horrific semi-trailer smashes. I thought that after the first one, with the rain pouring down, trucks would drive more slowly, but they actually went faster to make up lost time. So there followed two more prangs with the big vehicles slipping on the terrible road and careening off the bitumen down steep embankments. I don't know for sure, but it seems impossible that anyone walked away from those crashes. The only thing worse than the truck drivers in Guatemala are the bus drivers, who are cowboys getting their kicks by pushing the limits. Mechanics, smash repairers and tyre fitters must do really well out of these guys.

I had a terrible shock today when I picked up a newspaper and read that the Matamoros sports director Wilfrido Campos-Gonzalez, whom I met as I entered Mexico, had been shot dead. He was a cheery, dark-haired man in his 40s or 50s who enthusiastically welcomed me and held his own as we ran together for a few kilometres. If I ever needed reminding that life is cheap in Central America, Wilfrido's death rammed it home. The article told how Wilfrido was shot dead after getting into an argument with men at a club not far from where he worked at City Hall. One paragraph in the article made my blood run cold: 'Campos-Gonzalez was last shown on *Action 4 News* during a report about an Australian man running from the North Pole to the South but who made a pit stop in Matamoros.'

AUGUST 24

The Guatemalan flag includes two vertical blocks of blue flanking a block of white. The blue is for the ocean that borders Guatamala's south and part of its east, and the white represents peace. They have a program here through which international travellers can have a government tour guide assigned to them to ensure their safety and patronage. The government realises how important the tourist dollar is. The system works well. So if you're trekking to the crater of one of the volcanoes or surfing the coastline or even just running through, it pays to contact the government tourist board first.

A bridge was washed out by yesterday's torrential rain, which resulted in a 10-kilometre detour along a dirt road filled with potholes that has for now become the major highway to El Salvador; it was mayhem. It's doing my head in, constantly battling the semitrailers.

In the canopy of trees above, the orchids are spectacular. The lizards here are beautiful, big and bright green. The predominant roadkill, though, is snakes. I've seen many a squashed python on the road.

Children and the elderly wait at the sides of the roads with shovels and buckets: they fill in the potholes and hope that drivers will reward them with a small gratuity so they can buy food. I cannot understand why the United Nations does not concentrate its lending and expertise on infrastructure. All of Central America could really benefit and even profit from a good rail system for freight and passengers, to take a huge load off the roads and make the countries more productive.

For the past five days, I've been hugging Guatemala's south coast and often coming close to the Pacific Ocean. Communications have been a disaster: nothing has worked—no phones, emails, TV or radio crosses. It's a small country. I've covered around 300 kilometres since crossing the border, and already I'm only 17 kilometres from the border with El Salvador. But this small land has given me big and lasting memories. With its lush, tropical forests, many rivers and rolling countryside, Guatemala is probably the most beautiful country I've run through so far on this trek, and that's saying something. It's a land of volcanoes. It has 37, and four remain active. Today, on a detour inland to Guatemala City, I was 5 kilometres away from one called Pacaya, and smoke was belching out. Pacaya erupted in May 2010, causing fatalities and showering Guatemala City and the surrounding area with ash. Like so many other potentially dangerous threats on this journey, however, Pacaya left me alone.

Guatemala has a tragic history of political upheaval and civil

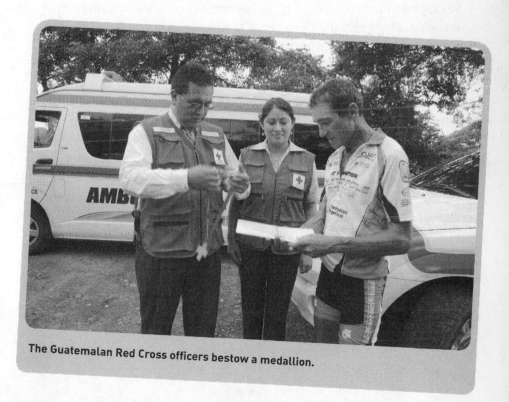

The Guatemalan Red Cross officers bestow a medallion.

war, and it has been smashed by such natural disasters as erupting volcanoes, hurricanes—such as 2005's Hurricane Stan, which killed 1500 people—and earthquakes, including a 7.5 quake in 1976 that killed 25,000 Guatemalans. Incredibly, having gone through all this, and despite the poverty that I'm seeing everywhere, the people smile a lot and are very tactile, throwing their arms around me and grasping my hand as I run past. In some villages, they had obviously heard of my run and emerged from their homes to line the streets and welcome me.

Guatemala City was built near and unfortunately in places right on top of the ruins of the ancient Mayan city of Kaminaljuyu, which was occupied until around 1200 BC. When I reached the city, the Guatemalan Red Cross said g'day and gave me T-shirts, and a medallion honouring my run was placed around my neck.

A far bigger danger to me than the volcanoes and occasional earthquakes that jolt Guatemala City is the traffic. I have *never* seen worse drivers. Whoever hands out licences to the blokes who drive the buses, usually multicoloured old rattlers like the one the Partridge Family used to ride around in, needs to have a look at their set-up. I ran past a big red Partridge Family bus and was transported back to when I was young and would watch that show on TV with my brothers and sisters. I always liked Danny Bonaduce, the red-headed kid, the best. Or maybe the bus drivers get their licences out of their cereal packets in the morning. Utes careened by us, weaving crazily all over the road, crammed with workers in the back who were hanging on for dear life. Exacerbating the chaos and danger are the roads themselves, which are all badly potholed, with pits so big I swear you'd have trouble climbing out if you fell in.

An official from the Guatemalan tourism office has joined the crew. In Mexico I needed help with security, but in Guatemala I'm being assisted with traffic management. A major cause of the motorised mayhem is that after six in the evening trucks are not allowed into the metropolis, so it's absolute madness as the laden vehicles rush to reach their destinations and unload. I narrowly missed being hit by trucks travelling at what must have been more than 120 kilometres per hour, sometimes screaming on two wheels around blind corners. Consequently, we have shortened our days in Guatemala, starting early but packing it in at five. Disappointingly, each day's run has had

Trucks are a health hazard.

to be reduced to around 50 or 60 kilometres. I will have to try to make up the lost kilometres sometime when trucks aren't using me for target practice.

Killer trucks and buses aside, running in Guatemala is easier than in Mexico. There, because I was straining to keep pace with the escort vehicles, I felt stressed almost all of the time. I was pushing hard to keep up. I couldn't rest. You'll recall—or perhaps you've pushed the thought out of your mind—that I had diarrhoea there, and it was such a chore to get them to stop while I took a toilet break. I like to walk a little way while I'm eating, but with the escort setting the pace I was running flat out, trying not to spill my bowl of cereal or mug of tea.

I've been eating well. Coconuts (and coconut milk fresh from the shell, deftly sliced open by local kids with machetes—delicious, and not at all bad with a dash of Red Bull for energy), lychees, pineapples, mangoes, corn: all kinds of fruit and vegetables abound because of the hot, rainy climate and rich soil. I'm drinking 10 litres of water a day on the run, and a few more when I finish.

The days have a sameness to them: hot and humid until a tropical deluge in the afternoon. The rain, as in Mexico, washes away bridges and roads, and just yesterday I had to run 15 kilometres out of my way when a bridge I was planning to cross proved to be a pile of debris on the river bank. I've been reading how Hurricane Irene is wreaking havoc on the east coast of the United States, especially in such places as Manhattan and North Carolina, where I ran. I pray for those people there who were so kind to me and hope they'll be okay.

Right now, the team comprises my brothers Bernie, Chris and Tony, my niece Katie and the two Mexican cameramen (Javier Trujillo, the third, has left us), whose ability to speak the language here has pulled us out of many a hole. It's good to have my brother Tony with us. Just as Brooke, Dillon and Chris did when they turned up, Tony has created a positive vibe. We run together, and he and I talk about where I might live when I return to Australia, the beach, landscaping, houses, and the fish and chips we are going to devour together. He especially endeared himself to me when he arrived with ten blocks of dark chocolate in his bag.

Brooke and Dillon have been in touch and will be able to get out of

Just in case—my personal ambulance escort.

the last week of their school term so they can join me before I enter the Darién Gap, with Juan the cameraman and whatever security Greg can organise for me. He's scrambling to find some right now. It's important my kids and I are together before this, one of the most dangerous parts of the run.

AUGUST 27

Today, as I ran my last day in Guatemala, rivers flowed all around me, bringing life to the many village communities and coursing on into the sea. The people have little but hold their heads high. It occurred to me that they are as proud of the bananas, pineapples and melons that they grow in the fields around their wooden shanties and sell from makeshift roadside stalls as people in the first world are of their million-dollar homes and expensive cars.

The weather today was typical of what we've experienced in Guatemala, changing rapidly from hot sunshine to driving rain. I have made it through unscathed, and I haven't needed medical attention—a miracle, really, considering the drivers' demolition derby.

EL SALVADOR

AUGUST 28

There was a small but noisy group of Guatemalans on hand to say goodbye as I entered El Salvador. The border was a big letdown: just a narrow, muddy pathway lined with parked trucks. At least the trucks weren't speeding. After the crew and I had had our papers stamped and were allowed to enter this once war-torn country, I was forced to zigzag through the obstacle course of filthy old vehicles, whose drivers were dozing or smoking at the wheel or standing in groups talking. A cacophonous scream of police, ambulance or fire brigade sirens—or maybe all three—competed with the Central American folk music that blared from the radios in the trucks. When I asked a local what the story was with them, he told me there was a teachers' strike on, and the truckies were out in support.

When I cleared the ruck of vehicles, a few kilometres down a dilapidated road I ran past maybe the ugliest motel I have ever seen. Rundown and ancient, it looked to me to be in danger of collapse. Out the front was a hand-painted sign: 'Hotel California. *Banos Parqueo Y TV Con Cable* (bath and cable TV).' I'm sure it wasn't the Hotel California that the Eagles immortalised in their song.

It was a late night getting our Winnebagos over the border, which really taxed the crew, who were up until 3 am. Katie and Chris are absolutely bushed. This run is taking a toll on everyone, not just me. The most difficult thing is that there are no days off, even when we are sick. We are all putting in long hours, seven days a week. That's why it's nice to get visitors from time to time to help out.

We're being escorted through El Salvador by the Red Cross and the police, and, as in the other Central American countries, there are the usual Red Cross presentations and media commitments. It gets dark early in this part of the world, and, it being the wet season here now, most afternoons we are drenched by heavy rain for at least three hours.

🌐 HOW TO TELL A CLASSY HOTEL

From time to time we've been staying in a hotel if the police feel we are in a city or town that isn't safe. We have come to class a hotel over here as a good one if:

- the toilet has a seat
- there are cold *and* hot water taps in the bathroom
- the bedrooms have air conditioners
- bugs and water don't fly out of the air conditioners' vents when you turn them on
- the beds have cotton sheets, or at least plastic ones like they use in operating theatres.

Bandits beware! My El Salvadoran escort.

The republic of El Salvador is the smallest and most densely populated of the Central American countries I am running through. Since independence, its major primary industry has been coffee-growing. Tragically, throughout its history it has been torn asunder by government corruption, armed insurrection and coups d'état. Thousands died in the civil war that was waged from 1980 to 1992 between left-wing and communist guerrilla groups and the right-wing, US-backed Salvadoran government. The war ended when the government agreed to give its political opponents a say in the running of the republic and to rein in the brutal police and military. Although the civil war is over and El Salvador is embracing industry and tourism, it remains a lawless land, with a high murder rate and gang activity. It pays to keep your wits about you. I'm grateful for our police escort.

Because of its location smack-dab on the Pacific Ring of Fire, El Salvador has suffered numerous earthquakes, one in 1986 causing

Volcanoes and maize are defining features of El Salvador.

1500 deaths and leaving 100,000 homeless. It has also been assailed by both floods and droughts.

The first major city in El Salvador I'm running through, Ahuachapán, has bustling, crazy, crowded, haphazard streets, with hordes of pedestrians defying death by blithely crossing the road in the face of wild-eyed drivers. The teeming markets were riots of sights and smells I've never encountered before. People at the thrown-together stalls were selling fruit and vegies, watches, straw hats, cheap musical instruments, T-shirts and work pants, colourful dresses, ice-cream, meat and fish. Stews comprising God knows what bubbled in big metal pots over open fires. The aroma was delicious, but I didn't go near them; another dose of diarrhoea is the last thing I need. I resisted the cries from the people stirring them that I should try some.

Leaving Ahuachapán and entering the rural regions is like stepping back in time. The side of the roads are spread thick and wide with maize which has been left there by the growers to dry in the blazing sun. I saw a wooden cart which had to be centuries old being pulled along by an ox. The beast, and the bloke driving the cart, seemed to

The towns rushed by in a blur.

be hundreds of years old as well. As in Mexico and Guatemala, the countryside is a rich green. As I ran along a road carved in the mountainside, the cliff faces on either side of me were strewn with thick, hanging ferns and vines. I passed fig trees growing 50 metres above my head, with vines dangling all the way to the road. I couldn't help but think that the inspiration for the movie *Avatar* must have come from a place just like this.

Clean, fresh, running water pours down the mountainsides. I often stopped today to drink and to soak my hot and weary body in the cool springs. It was as good as a magic elixir! It reminded me again that clean water is the reason I have embarked on this momentous journey.

The humidity is incredible, and within 20 minutes of starting running my clothes were sweat-soaked. I cut small slits into my hat to allow some ventilation. That was a good and a bad idea: it certainly cooled me down by letting in the air, but it also let in a leech. The slimy little beast attached itself to my scalp and started sucking. I didn't feel anything until the blood began to run down my face. I removed my hat and grabbed the leech, which by that point was engorged with my blood and the size of my finger. One of the many hazards of jungle areas is that, whether you're asleep or running full pelt, there is always a bug or grub trying to gnaw on you.

There are many road tunnels in El Salvador, which seem like gateways from one region to the next. You can be travelling over mountains and across rivers, enter a tunnel, and emerge onto a flat plain. I ran through one today, and, when I exited it, stretching before me was the Pacific Ocean. Wow. The view, looking out over dramatic cliffs that plunged straight down to palm-fringed black sand beaches and on to the raging sea, took my breath away. On this run, I get a thrill every time I encounter the Pacific. That mighty ocean always reminds me of home; it comforts me to know that on the other side of it lies Australia. It makes me feel a little bit closer to my loved ones and helps me to forget for a moment my aches and pains.

Of course, I had a swim, and Chris and Tony joined me. Although the sand is volcanic and black, the ocean is clear and clean, with great waves for surfing. It's good for my range of movement to stretch out in the water and have a swim, and better than a massage because the salt water also helps to heal my blisters and wounds. Chris and Tony will be flying home tomorrow. My brothers have been a help with their

My beloved Pacific Ocean. On the other side lies Australia.

sensible, practical, but cheery ways, and I'll miss them. Our party for the next sector will be me, Katie, Bernie and the Mexican film men.

El Salvador is a blink-and-you-miss it country. My route through it has been just 220 kilometres long. No sooner, it seems, did I enter it than I've reached the other side. If all goes to plan, I'll be crossing the border into Honduras after dark on August 31, and in that country I'll have an even shorter distance to run, around 100 kilometres, across the lower corner. And then it's Nicaragua.

AUGUST 31

The roads are far better in El Salvador than the potholed death traps of Guatemala. This is because El Salvador is the recipient of US government aid. Likewise, the US Red Cross pours funds into the Salvadoran Red Cross, and there is a lot to spend them on. I have to say, the food in El Salvador has been first-class. As in all of Central America, the local produce is terrific, but in this country it's cooked in an American or Italian style, because, thanks to US money, El Salvador is more prosperous than other Central American countries, and people can afford to eat out more.

The beer is very cheap—75 cents a can—so I've been rewarding myself with one at the end of each day's run. It has a refreshingly different taste from the sweet and isotonic drinks I have during the day. Carbs such as rice and pasta are my staple food, but I've been livening up my palate with fresh fruit from the side of the road, like coconut milk, mangoes, pineapples, rambutans, paw paws, oranges and limes.

Red tape at the border entering Honduras earlier tonight cost me precious hours, but I stayed calm as the annoyingly pedantic bureaucrats processed me. Then, when they finally allowed me through, as if they were doing me a huge favour, I was swamped by a crowd of media folk, including newspaper reporters and three TV news crews. Everyone was speaking at once in a language I couldn't understand. The Mexican film guys helped out where they could. It was bedlam.

All the while as I was being interviewed I was smiling and friendly, but inside I was furious because of the border hold-up and the media demands; I know they're necessary, but I just want to run.

HONDURAS

SEPTEMBER 1

My alarm went off at four o'clock this morning, and I spent the next hour and a half preparing my body for the stresses ahead. I am struggling at the moment. In the mornings, I'm stiff and rigid, like a robot. It's taking longer and longer to loosen up each day; I need a massage or physio but there's none available. There is no other way to say it: my body is a mess. I am at the stage where I have multiple injuries, and I don't know which one is going to cause the most problems each day. Sometimes it's my toe, sometimes my knee, sometimes my hip. My right knee, which I banged at the North Pole, is giving me tremendous pain. My feet are in terrible shape. The nails on three toes of my right foot, including that of my big toe, and two toes on my left foot are bruised, black and bleeding. I'll lose them all soon. My big toe is expelling large quantities of pus, which sounds awful, but it's good because it's relieving the pressure and making the pain less. At the end of each day's run, I take off my shoes, peel off my bloody socks and dress my wounds. Next morning, I pull on a clean pair of socks and ease my feet into my shoes. It hurts when I run, but pain has become a companion. One look at my feet today told me that my toes were going to be causing me grief, so I cut the toe box out of my shoes.

Yesterday I was so happy, and I was on schedule, but today the whole lot fell apart. I started at sunrise in torrential rain, running through water that was up to 8 centimetres deep on the road. I could barely see a metre ahead through the downpour. The lights on Bernie's van and the police escort were but a dim glow through the rain.

And then we got lost. One of the cops in our police escort gave us a bum steer, and I took the wrong track up a mountain. I ran to the top, realised I was off course and had to run all the way down to the bottom again. It cost me seven hours and 70 kilometres. Added to that,

The support of dedicated Red Cross people has been a constant from country to country.

it was a very dangerous area to be running in. There are bandits in these parts, and the terrain was wet and slippery; I fell over on rough, moss-covered ground and hurt my shoulder badly when I hit the road.

It's been one of the toughest days. I'm drenched, exhausted, angry, and my shoulder is hurting like hell, along with my legs, feet and back. Today's misfortune rammed home to me that this run is being conducted on a knife's edge: I've only got to stuff up once and lose time or hurt myself and the entire project could be put in jeopardy.

This country, like so many Central American countries, has been smashed by war, both civil and with neighbouring nations, as well as by natural disasters such as floods, earthquakes and hurricanes. In the 1980s, there was ferocious fighting as the left-wing Honduran government battled against the right-wing, US-backed Contra guerrillas; and, in 1998, Hurricane Mitch laid waste to much of the land, destroying 70 per cent of all crops and 80 per cent of the transport infrastructure. Some 33,000 houses were razed, and 5000 Hondurans perished.

It's such a striking land. Mountain ranges and coastal plains, thick jungle and rainforests with astonishingly vivid flora, including brightly coloured orchids, and a vast variety of fauna: mammals, reptiles, amphibians and birds you find nowhere else edge right up to some of the roads.

One of the police officers decided he was going to run the last 40 kilometres with me to the Nicaraguan border. He lasted just 15 kilometres in the heat and humidity.

 NICARAGUA

SEPTEMBER 2

I entered Nicaragua and ran down the west coast's wide, fertile plains—ash from the volcanoes in the region makes for good soil—alongside beautiful wide lakes that are home to the world's only freshwater sharks. Beauty, however, is only skin deep: it didn't take long for reality to set in. The poverty in the republic of Nicaragua, the largest Central American country, with a population of 6 million, is the worst I have ever seen. Nearly half the population lives below the poverty line, and, with a basic staple diet of corn, rice and beans, nearly 30 per cent of

Welcome to Nicaragua, a troubled and dangerous country.

the people are under-nourished. Obviously, the government has not found a way to distribute the wealth from exports of fish, tobacco, sugar, coffee and beef to those who produce them. Maybe the Red Cross can send some of the money I raise in my run to these poor folk.

Nicaragua has a tragic past. There have been the usual earthquakes and erupting volcanoes, along with a bloody revolution in 1979 in which the left-wing Sandinista National Liberation Front rebels violently ousted the oppressive right-wing Somoza regime, which had been in power since the 1930s. In turn, there was severe fighting between the right-wing Contras, who were funded by both the United States and drug barons, and the new government. After the Sandinista–Contras war, inflation gripped the nation, rising to a ruinous 13,000 per cent in 1988. Today, Nicaragua is classified as a recovering economy. The current president, Daniel Ortega, was a powerful and ruthless leader of the Sandinistas.

It broke my heart today to see the malnourished kids who sat along the road in their rags, hunched and downcast, begging for food or money. Their parents were begging too, often aggressively and with the menace that a machete can bring to any negotiation. Skinny dogs and cats prowled the alleys of the villages looking for scraps. There were large gangs of unemployed, drunken young men hanging about—some too drunk to even stand—and as I ran past them they mocked me. I didn't react in any way. I am scared here, and it's affecting the way I run. As the day wore on and the men became more drunk, the taunting grew more vicious. They were hoping I would react so they could attack me. Street crime, as in most poverty-stricken places, is rife here. People flared at each other in the streets. I was constantly looking around, my radar on full alert, trying to identify dangerous people or situations and then avoid them. I am standing out too much here.

The border towns reminded me of that bar scene in *Star Wars* with all the weird and scary monsters. There were some decidedly odd-looking customers around, carrying the ubiquitous machetes, which are used for work in the fields during the day, but as weapons after-hours. I feel like my life is at risk here, more so than it was in Mexico, or anywhere else on this run. We'll be locking our vans tightly at night, and our police escort has told us that running at dusk or in the dark is forbidden. I haven't argued. I'll set off at four in the morning

Kids watching from the roadside.

and make sure I'm back in the van with Bernie, Katie and the team by around five each evening.

I wish all I had to do was run. Unfortunately, after finishing 85 kilometres, I'm thrust back into the logistics of my journey. If I don't find new sponsors to pay for guides and vehicles and flights and equipment, I may not be able to afford to go to the South Pole. I spend my nights writing emails to companies, begging them to back me. Just getting myself across the Darién Gap and into Colombia in South America will set us back many thousands of dollars. We have to pay for the vehicles and crew to be shipped through the canal and on to Colombia. I am preoccupied by the dangers of the Darién rainforest, with its bandits, paramilitary thugs and wild animals. I'm thinking that if I survive all that I stand a chance of finishing the run, but only if we can then somehow raise the money needed to get in and out of the Antarctic. I have no clue where that money is going to come from; I just have a strong faith that it will turn up.

I learned today from the Australian Red Cross that the East Timor clean water project is underway, funded in part by donations I've raised from this run. That's a tangible benefit and makes me happy. Things are looking up.

SEPTEMBER 3

I ran into the capital city, Managua, today. It felt as though I'd been climbing all day, and it wasn't until I had completed 76 kilometres that I could finally see the lights of the city, and from there it was all downhill.

On the road, I saw vultures feeding from a dead cow's carcass. While it's easy to see these birds as morbid opportunists, they do play a vital role in cleaning up the environment.

SEPTEMBER 5

I was running well when a truck full of cows brushed by me at the precise moment when one cow decided to relieve itself. At first, I thought it was a cooling rain shower; then I realised it was another kind of shower—of cow urine. I spent all day stinking, until a thunderstorm, with real rain this time, gave me a wash.

SEPTEMBER 6

First thing today, I started pushing up a very steep hill, not knowing that this was the start of a mountain range that would climb for the next 22 kilometres with a gradient of 30 degrees. Up and up and up I ran. It was a tough and unrelenting grind. There were no flat sections. I knew that I had to reach the top eventually, but every time I rounded a corner or reached what I thought was the peak that damned mountain road kept climbing. I was exhausted by the time I reached the top. The view was spectacular, but I'm not sure the effort was worth it. The ordeal meant I've finished late to squeeze in my allotted number of kilometres. I'm paying for it tonight.

I've had to remind myself yet again that this run is all about the mind being more powerful than the body. My body was in bad shape when I got off the ice of the Arctic, and it hasn't really improved much since then. It's my attitude and flat-out refusal to quit that have got me almost to the halfway point of my run. When I face a steep hill, or when I take a wrong turn, like I did coming out of El Salvador, I have to be philosophical and accept that these things are going to happen. Tomorrow is another day.

We stripped the American Red Cross decals off our vehicles today after we learned how much Nicaraguans hate the United States. We don't want to be mistaken for Americans and attacked.

SEPTEMBER 7

Nicaragua has no rival as the worst place I have run through. There is a nastiness in the air, and people seem to be on the verge of violence. I am genuinely concerned for my safety. In other Central American countries, much to my surprise, the police have been helpful and honest. In Nicaragua, they have been unfriendly and openly corrupt. I've seen them stop motorists and demand money on many occasions. Their method is to book a driver for some imaginary defect on their car and then offer to let them off if they fork out some cash. Another giveaway that there are serious problems with Nicaraguan cops is

Into the Third World.

that they are terrible litterers. Papers, bottles: all kinds of garbage is blithely heaved out of the squad car window onto the road. Even our own escort does it: when we gave them drinks they downed them and then tossed the bottles on the ground. They are looking after me, but they are grubs. They haven't asked me for a bribe yet, but I think it may be only a matter of time before they do.

Today, I saw an appalling sight. Stock animals roam freely here and often get hit by cars and trucks, and there was a dead white horse lying on the road. Passers-by were just ignoring the carcass, not even trying to remove it from the road, which would have at least given the poor beast a tiny bit of dignity. I wanted to shift the horse myself, but Bernie talked me out of it, afraid that I might be attacked for sticking my nose into local affairs. For me, the Nicaraguans' callousness over the horse typified their lack of respect for life. I suppose I can understand it, though. They live in terrible poverty. Most live in mosquito-infested swamps in hovels comprising four bamboo poles stuck in the ground with black plastic wrapped around them as walls and palm fronds over the top as a roof. The townships reek of raw sewage. There is no sewerage system in rural Nicaragua, at least, not where I ran, and I saw people drinking from and washing in polluted creeks. I am embarrassed that our van has a shower, fridge and gas stove as well as four comfortable beds. No wonder people look amazed when we drive past.

 COSTA RICA

SEPTEMBER 8

We're in Costa Rica, which is, in comparison with some other Central American countries, peaceful, and economically and technologically advanced. Coffee and bananas are among its major exports. Politically, Costa Rica is a stable democracy, and the economy is thriving. Consequently, the people here enjoy the highest standard of living in Central America; many people have replaced their traditional machetes with lawnmowers. Tourists flock to the country for its tropical beauty, rich history and panoramic landscapes, which include volcanoes and

Costa Rica—Central American paradise.

beaches. A quarter of this country is national park or protected area, and those parts teem with wildlife: although Costa Rica has just 0.5 per cent of the world's land mass, it is home to 5 per cent of its wildlife, including four species of monkey, big cats, turtles, tapirs, lizards, iguanas, rainbow-coloured toucans and two- and three-toed sloths. It's a nature lover's Garden of Eden.

A lot of schools in Australia are teaching their classes about the places where I've run by logging on to my website in class. The messages of support that have been pouring in from Aussie schoolkids have been heartening. They'll know of my enthusiasm for Costa Rica.

SEPTEMBER 9

Another arduous day in paradise. I'll never tire of the rivers or the ocean. The jungle melds into suburbia, and the monkeys use the high branches of trees as a superhighway far above my head as I run. There is colour everywhere; even the squirrels here have a more vibrant tone. The macaws seem puzzled by my journey.

As I ran along the roads lined with palm trees today, I passed truck after truck lying on its side after careening out of control. Who'd have thought it? I was worried about polar bears and bandits before I started this trip, but it may turn out that the most terrifying thing I'll face is out-of-control trucks.

SEPTEMBER 10

I heard from Greg Quail today. He is pulling every string he can to round up some armed security for me when I am in the Darién Gap. Whether he succeeds or not, I'll be running through it. The Darién and the South Pole are the major (foreseeable) remaining obstacles.

The shoulder I damaged when I fell after I took that wrong turn is not good. Every step I take, it hurts. I am no doctor, but I reckon it will take two weeks to heal properly. I can add a sore shoulder to my lengthening list of aches and pains.

I'm not the only patient. Katie had to go to a local hospital last night to receive 2 litres of intravenous fluid. She had a migraine, was badly dehydrated, and her blood pressure was low. For the past few

Meeting friendly Aussies on hols.

days, she has not been eating, drinking or sleeping because she has felt too sick, and the lack of sustenance is worsening her condition. It's a vicious circle. She is feeling better today, and it's our mission to make sure she eats and drinks and doesn't get ill again.

We're three days in to Costa Rica, and will leave it in two. I am loving this place. I keep bumping into Australian and American surfers who come here for the testing waves and awesome beaches. We have no police escort and don't need one: it is safe here. We sleep by the side of the road without a qualm.

I am moved by how hard the Costa Rican people work, from dawn to dark and often with rudimentary tools. I asked the cameramen to take lots of photos of them. There was a tiny man, no more than 120 centimetres tall, and frail, and he was dragging a huge wagon full of farm produce. There were women, young and old, balancing fully laden baskets on their heads while carrying heavy packs on their backs. There were kids cutting grass with machetes. I've learned that many of the local people suffer respiratory problems, because they inhale the smoke from green wood burnt when they are cooking in

Above: The Mexican Government, concerned at the very real prospect that I would be kidnapped or attacked by drug cartel gangsters, assigned a protection squad.

Left: In turbulent Mexico, the Red Cross is always flat out.

Above: Lush vegetation in Mexico—it's much greener here than I expected.

Below: Protecting me was a priority for the Mexican government.

Above: Our not-so-trusty Winnebagos.

Below: Sweating it out in steamy Guatemala.

Above: I found my Partridge Family bus in Guatemala.

Below: Marking the spot at the end of the day in El Salvador.

Above: El Salvadoran shanties by the sea.

Below: Squalor and traffic in El Salvador.

Above: Another Costa Rican deluge.
Below: Running through Panama.

Above: Ready to tackle the Darién, 'the most dangerous place on Earth'.
Below: Braving the Darién jungle.

Above: I survived the Darién—many have not.

Left: Creeks can flood in a flash.

Below: My boots were doing it tough.

their mud-floored huts. Right now, I want to dedicate this book to the poor people on my route, doing the hardest of yards.

SEPTEMBER 14

This morning, Costa Rica presented me with a sight I'll never forget. At five-thirty, as I started my run, I crossed a bridge, looked down into the river below and saw five large crocodiles resting on the banks. I also received a fright. Some kilometres down the track, I went to take a pee in some bushes, heard a rustle and found myself face to face with another croc. Thankfully, at just 1.5 metres in length, he was smaller than his brothers and sisters down the river. Nevertheless, I finished my business and shot through.

SEPTEMBER 15

Another five o'clock start. Just 20 minutes into the run, as usual, my shirt was wet with sweat. The humidity makes breathing difficult. I feel

My guard has dwindled in peaceful Costa Rica.

sure it will pour again later, because the air is so thick with vapour. The nearby ocean was tempting me, and I wanted to stop, take a detour and swim, but if I did I wouldn't complete my 85 kilometres, so I pushed on.

I have asked Bernie to go ahead tomorrow night to Panama and meet with a company which specialises in getting people through the Darién Gap. He also has to meet the ferry operators and arrange for the vans to be taken to Colombia. This will be no mean feat, and must happen before I emerge from the jungle so they can meet me on the other side. The logistics of this event were head-spinning when I first started planning it, and they still are.

SEPTEMBER 16

I woke with no energy, and things didn't improve. I wish I had a physio to put me through some stretches. It has rained heavily all day, and I ran wringing wet, and as a result I am badly chafed under the arms and around my groin. My fingers and feet look like prunes. I am worn out and tired, but I did 80 kilometres. I will make it into Panama tomorrow. I pray I will have some energy then. Costa Rica has been great, but I still have so far to run and I just haven't been able to enjoy most of it.

 **PANAMA**

SEPTEMBER 17

I'm afraid I know little about Panama, except for the canal and Panama hats. When we arrived, it was like emerging from the jungle into the space age. I feel good about Panama, apart from a glitch when it became clear that an experienced adventure guide named Javier, whom we had paid to organise a smooth passage through customs, had fixed nothing at all, and we had to wait for more than two hours to be processed by the officials. I have a theory that most of the world's shady characters lurk around border crossings.

I knew that Brooke and Dillon were flying into Panama City today, so as I ran I watched the skies, imagining that every plane I saw was delivering my children. Could that one be their plane . . . or that one?

At noon, I was caught in a terrific thunderstorm, which made my clothes heavy and added to my blister count as my feet slid around inside my shoes. As I ran through the province of Veraguas, I was swamped by the media: TV news teams, a newspaper journalist and photographer, and a radio broadcaster. I hear there will be around 100 people running with me in Panama City tomorrow. I don't know how I will cope with this, seeing as I am having problems with the five or six who are alongside me today. It's always difficult to maintain a steady pace when other runners fade in and out for short periods. They are fresh and always try to run faster than me. I shouldn't compete, but I can't help myself. My pride kicks in and I run at their pace or a bit quicker, and I pay the price at the end of the day. I desperately need a physiotherapist.

Suddenly, Brooke and Dillon showed up with Bernie and my old friend Rachael, who has come over with the kids. I shared my dream to run the length of this planet with her many years ago and

Seeing the kids again always cheers me up.

she always believed I had the ability. It was so very good to see them. After the usual hugs and tears and questions of 'How have you been?' they presented me with a big bag of assorted chocolates from my favourite store in Sydney, Darrell Lea. Despite their jet lag, Brooke ran 15 kilometres with me, Rachael ran 20, and Dillon rode 5 on the bike.

Another visitor today was a fellow named Marco, whom we have hired to organise my trek through the Darién. He has brought some maps and a wealth of knowledge about the area. He sees security issues and the fact that we are running through the jungle in the rainy season as the major hurdles. He told me that it's easy to get caught in a flash flood at this time of year. Sixteen people have lost their lives recently in deluges in the region.

SEPTEMBER 18

Running into Panama City was an unforgettable experience. Apart from it being pretty much the exact halfway mark of my run, it is a city of futuristic skyscrapers clustered around the canal. Greg Quail and the Red Cross had done their advance publicity well, and children and adults, including local entertainers and Red Cross folk, came out to run with me. I was given the signal honour of being allowed, with a police escort, to run over the bridge that spans the Panama Canal; it being a traffic-only bridge, it's a privilege only rarely extended to runners.

The 77-kilometre-long Panama Canal was cut and constructed between 1904 and 1914 to allow shipping to pass from the Pacific to the Atlantic Ocean. Before the canal was constructed, ships had to sail about 10,000 kilometres further, around Cape Horn. The canal was largely paid for by the United States, and for more than 60 years they held sovereignty over it.

I took a short break in Panama City's Balboa Park, named after the 16th-century Spanish adventurer and first European to see the Pacific Ocean, Vasco Núñez de Balboa. There is a statue of Balboa in the park; he stands proudly brandishing a sword in his right hand and a Spanish flag in his left. Around him, Panamanians were ambling through the

The modern city of Panama.

Standing under the statue of Balboa, with Dillon, Brooke and Rachael.

palm trees, gardens and waterways and buying the wares of local artisans. It was a nice place to decompress.

I ran down a thoroughfare named Martyrs' Avenue and asked a fellow runner what significance it had. He told me the story. Each January 9, Martyrs' Day, Panamanians commemorate riots that broke out in the city on that date in 1964 over the sovereignty of the Panama Canal Zone. When Panamanian students demanded the right to fly the Panama flag alongside the American flag in the zone, they were attacked by police officers sympathetic to the Americans. The students' flag was torn in the melee, which took place in Balboa High School, and fighting escalated all over the city. The US army was sent in, and, after three days of pitched battles, 21 Panamanians and four American soldiers were dead. Two monuments in the city—one on the site of the high school and one in the forecourt of the Legislative Assembly depicting students climbing a lamppost to raise their flag—are testimony to the locals' defiance. In 1977, the United States ceded control of the canal zone to Panama.

There were close to 100 people jogging beside me in Panama City and the surrounding suburbs. A couple stopped me on the side of the road and introduced themselves as South African Australians. They live in Queensland and so had heard of me and my exploits, and they run a monkey refuge in Panama, just 15 kilometres down the road from where we were. They invited us to visit. I was keen but still had 50 kilometres to run, so Katie and the film crew went. Katie was thrilled: she adores monkeys, and she got to hold some, including a two-month-old baby.

In two days' time, Bernie will be flying home to Canberra for a week. He'll be celebrating his 35th wedding anniversary and trying to raise money to fund the rest of the run, including the expensive Antarctic sector. Greg has had some recent success raising money. The South Pole logistics are complex. My guide, Eric Philips, and Greg are trying to persuade me to take a six-wheel-drive support vehicle onto the ice. The vehicle will cost me around $350,000 to hire for 20 days. I haven't got anything like that kind of money. I told Greg that the idea is ludicrous, even if it would make the trek easier for Eric and the cameramen. I would prefer to have three motorised scooters for the crew, while I run alongside. I can rent skidoos for $100,000. The major issue, though, is getting to Tierra del Fuego in time to get to the Antarctic, run to the pole and then rendezvous with the last regular flight back to civilisation. If I miss that plane, I'll have to charter my own aircraft, and how the hell will I pay for that? My goal is to be back in Australia to celebrate Brooke's 17th birthday on January 24 and Australia Day on January 26. We'll see. It's going to be tight.

SEPTEMBER 19

I had a huge thrill today when a video message was beamed through to me from the steps of the Sydney Opera House from some men I respect enormously. The Sydney Marathon was in full swing, and sending me a big cheerio call were Aussie long-distance running greats Pat Carroll, Lee Troop and Steve Moneghetti. Pat called me a maniac—I'm not going to disagree with that!—then he told me that he was in awe of what I was doing and that I was making my countrymen very proud.

Steve said, 'Hope you're holding up okay. It must be unbelievably tough physically, but I know how mentally tough you are, and if anyone can run pole to pole, it's you. Hang in there; we're all running with you in spirit.'

Lee said, 'You've set the highest bar for us all in the past, and this is just another step up, mate. Best of luck!'

Then the crowd of spectators all yelled their support as the video ended. Their words and cheers had the same effect on me as if I'd been fitted with superchargers.

SEPTEMBER 21

Three days into Panama and two to go. The Darién approaches and takes up all my thoughts, but I am running well and am ahead of schedule. I have to be at the entrance to the Darién Gap on September 23, so have cut my daily run back to 70 kilometres for the past two days so I don't arrive early. I will set off into the jungle on September 24, with an armed guard, Juan the cameraman, a couple of locals to carry the gear, and a Red Cross official. We will all be on foot as there are no roads. I haven't a clue how far I'll be able to run each day in the 144-kilometre-long, 50-kilometre-wide gap of undeveloped thick and forbidding rainforest, which has no roads, just vine-entangled tracks. No doubt I'll be travelling only as fast as the slowest member of the group. I'm hoping to be able to make it through in four days, covering 36 kilometres a day, but that is in the lap of the gods.

Most inhabitants of the Darién, that I know of, at least, are local Indians. More worrying are the Marxist Revolutionary Armed Forces of Colombia (FARC), which have committed a number of human rights

Panama is a country of jungles and rivers.

violations, including murders and kidnappings, during their long war with the Colombian government.

According to one internet blogger who survived the Darién, it is

a forbidding mountainous jungle on the Panama side; full of swamps, guerrillas, drug traffickers and kidnappers on the Colombian side, making travel through the area not just a struggle against a hostile environment but also a maze of bribing the right people for passage and ducking bullets.

The dangers to be faced there include 'tough nasty jungle with plenty of disagreeable wildlife; impenetrable swamps; crazed drug traffickers; pissed-off guerrillas; greedy kidnappers (all of the guys mentioned above); paranoid government police; no marked trails'. *National Geographic Adventure* contributing editor Robert Young Pelton, who with two backpackers was held captive by guerrillas for ten days in 2003, adds his two bobs' worth:

It was a relief to meet my armed guard for the Darién.

The Darién Gap is one of the last—not only unexplored—but one of the last places people really hesitate to venture to . . . It's also one of the most rugged places. The basic problem of the Darién Gap is that it's one of the toughest hikes there is. It's an absolute pristine jungle but it's got some nasty sections with thorns, wasps, snakes, thieves, criminals, you name it. Everything that's bad for you is in there.

Katie, Brooke, Dillon, Rachael and our other cameraman will be ferried, with the Winnebagos, up the Panama Canal and into Colombia. We'll rendezvous at a town called Turbo, on the coast.

SEPTEMBER 23

I don't mind telling you that, one day away from the Darién Gap, I'm feeling very nervous. I have run through the Arctic Circle and nine countries to get here, but, for all that, what the Darién has in store for me is a mystery. I've heard about the bandits, the guerrillas with guns, the kidnappers, the snakes and spiders and panthers and jaguars and whatever else, but I still don't know quite what to expect. I expected to have one guard, or maybe no guard at all, but to my enormous surprise and relief, I have a guard of 17 armed soldiers in camouflage gear. At first light, I'll be getting into a boat and, with my guards and cameraman, I'll be entering the jungle, one of the most dangerous places on earth. I am really concerned about this section. In my mind, I have divided the run into six parts: the North Pole, Canada and North America, Central America, the Darién, South America and the South Pole. The Darién gets its own stage simply because it is so dangerous.

SEPTEMBER 24

I am finally face to face with my nemesis, the Darién. Earlier today, I stood on the bank of the river leading into the Darién doing a final check of my bag before stepping into the canoe that would take me into the jungle. I ran 10 kilometres to that point this morning, which gave me a lot of time to imagine scenarios that I may encounter. At about the 7-kilometre mark today, on a rubble-strewn track to the river, I fell over again. I suffered just a few cuts and bruises, but it was

Crossing the river into the unknown.

a big reality check for me. I have to be careful that I don't injure myself so badly that I can't keep running. I have all the logistics rummaging around in my brain and am delighted that Brooke, Dillon and Rachael are here, but I simply can't allow my mind to wander from the task at hand, because one lapse of concentration is all it would take to bring me, and the entire run, crashing down.

Brooke, Dillon and Rachael gathered around for one last hug goodbye before I set off on this next big challenge. My team is scared for me. The kids have been spooked by the machineguns my guards are carrying. The sight of the heavily armed soldiers rammed home to them that I am about to undertake possibly the most dangerous part of my journey. If there was no need for an armed guard, there wouldn't be one. I can't wait to come out the other side next week and tell them all about my experiences in the jungle.

Suddenly, one of the guards started singing, in a sweet, low voice, a folksong about the delights of Panama. It was truly surreal: being serenaded as I was about to enter the most dangerous place on earth. It has been a hot, still day. The river was murky, and the jungle on the mountains ahead looked black-green and thick. I pulled on the sturdy hiking boots with extra strong heel grips that I'm going to be wearing through this section, climbed into the canoe with my protectors and cameraman, and set off up the river into the Darién jungle.

STAGE 5
SOUTH AMERICA

September 24 to December 28

Distance to cover: Approximately 10,000 kilometres

Terrain: Jungle, mountain ranges, volcanoes, cliffs, rainforests, plains, rivers, valleys, barren deserts, towns, cities and fishing villages, vineyards and coffee plantations

Typical weather conditions: Hot days (growing cooler as we move south), cold nights

Hazards: Flooded rivers, FARC, giant mosquitoes, snakes and spiders, our higgledly-piggledy planning, my battered body (especially my ruined feet), bad drivers, debris on the road, rats and biting dogs, thieves

Key equipment: Cap with protective legionnaire-style flap at back, T-shirt, shorts, running shoes, warm jacket for nights, extra supplies of water and food for desert runs, sunscreen, zinc cream, needle for puncturing blisters, camera gear, Nurofen, vitamins

Personnel: Me, logistics man and chief back-up driver Bernie Farmer, assistant and running mate Katie Walsh, cameramen, technicians and interpreters Gustavo Garza, Juan Femet and Ming d'Arcy, police and army escorts and a 17-man armed army guard to protect me in the Darién, my children Brooke and Dillon

🌐 DARIÉN GAP

SEPTEMBER 24

My first day in the Darién is over. My guide is Luis Puleio, and it is evident that he is very comfortable here. Juan the cameraman and I are also being accompanied by 17 members of the Panamanian military armed with machineguns, pistols and knives. They are under orders to stay with us in the Darién to protect us from the notorious Marxist Revolutionary Armed Forces of Colombia, or FARC—anti-government guerrillas who have been responsible for the murders and kidnappings in this area.

The soldiers have usurped the role of the crew hired by a local man called Marco—who has organised this part of the run—and who were originally going to take me through the Darién. At first, there looked like being a nasty clash of interests, so I called Marco on his cell phone and told him we had a stand-off between his men and the army. He said that the army called the shots and that I should do exactly as they said. 'We have got to live with them long after you've moved on,' he explained.

Marco has warned me that we are going in during the wet season, and that this holds added dangers. Such is the force of the daily rain that in just 20 minutes a trickle of a stream can become a 2-metre-deep raging white-water torrent, carrying along with it uprooted trees and boulders. Many people have drowned after being caught unawares; others have spent days perched high in the branches of trees as the river coursed below. We crossed three rivers today, and I had mud up to my knees every step I took.

One guard, Sergeant Villa, a skilful sniper with a high-powered rifle, literally has not left my side all day, not even when nature called. The guards look terrifying, but they are the nicest guys. Doing the Darién without them would be a lot more life-threatening and arduous.

Crossing the many rivers is tiring, not to mention dangerous.

The guard is split into two groups: fast and slow. The faster men stay close to me, carrying just their machineguns and a pack of provisions and emergency medical equipment; the others bring up the rear with the heavy camping gear.

Unbeknown to me, Nick the cameraman and Greg Quail, believing that I may not be able to survive the Darién and also fearing that any delay here will derail the rest of the run, hired a helicopter and gave the pilot instructions to collect me and Juan today—after just one day. I believe they wanted some dramatic footage for the documentary they are making. When the helicopter arrived, I was furious. I sent it away.

Then, Juan fell ill—a combination of stress, excitement, fatigue from tramping through the knee-deep mud, heat, and not eating or drinking well or enough. He was fainting and vomiting. He told me he wanted to quit; he wanted the helicopter back. I told him no: there are a whole lot of people all over the world counting on me to finish this run, and I was not about to let him destroy my dream just because he'd failed to prepare for this challenge. I sent him ahead upriver, in a dugout canoe with a couple of guards, to the village called Canaan where we are camping tonight. I told him to get stuck into the food and drinks, and down potassium and magnesium tablets, get a good night's sleep and decide whether he's staying with the expedition or returning to Panama in the canoe. I was a hard case with Juan but felt justified. This journey needs no embellishment for drama's sake—it's dramatic enough. And, besides, I haven't sacrificed everything I have and forgone seeing my kids for ages just to give up in the Darién sector.

SEPTEMBER 25

The Darién Gap comprises thick tropical jungle and rainforest. There are few defined tracks, so we're carrying machetes to hack pathways through the undergrowth. There are tall hills and deep ravines. Every plant and tree seems to have needles and spikes—inbuilt protection mechanisms in this unforgiving place. It's a natural instinct to reach out and grasp a branch or vine when you lose your footing, and doing so has left my hands puffed and infected after being punctured by spikes. Even the grass in the Darién has razor-sharp edges! It's very

Even the trees have weapons.

humid under the canopy of trees, and there is a thick, muggy mist always hanging in the air. So far, it has rained almost constantly.

To his credit, Juan woke today feeling much better and pressed on. We got off to a good start from Canaan and covered the first 25 kilometres very quickly. We run, scramble, climb—whatever the terrain dictates. I think the message has got through to the soldiers that as well as safety we need speed. The mud was thick and slushy after heavy rain last night. There were many river crossings today, and I fell into the fast-moving water twice. Eventually, though, we left the mud behind for a riverside path to the mountains.

We're trekking from the southern, Pacific side of Panama towards the Caribbean Sea section of the Atlantic, on the northern coast. The indigenous people, including the Embera-Wounaan and Kuna tribes, have villages deep in the jungle. The native people of the Darién don't grow hair on their arms, legs or faces, so have no need for razors. They wear colourful traditional garb and headdresses as bright as the plumage of the jungle birds. We've been told that they are welcoming but that there is an element of danger in visiting their camps, because guerrillas often hole up in them. They have ingratiated themselves with the indigenous people by helping them to defend their villages against opposing tribes, so villagers may do the FARC's bidding, including being accomplices in kidnappings. My guards, who see their major role as forming good relationships with the villagers and flushing out the criminal element, go out of their way to befriend the locals in the hope that they may be allies against the FARC, whose members are sworn to do anything they can to disrupt the government.

I've been encouraged to wear a Panama Red Cross T-shirt, because the US shirts may make me a target. I'm also wearing long pants to ward off bites from the Darién's mosquitoes, which look to me the size of bats!

Dinner tonight was fresh-caught fish and wild rice.

SEPTEMBER 26

I woke to the horrendous screams of howler monkeys. It's good to be away from the highways and the noise of passing vehicles. All I can hear in the Darién are the sounds of monkeys, birds, frogs, crickets, an occasional wild boar and the rush of water.

The Darién can be divided into four sections—swamps, rivers, mountains and coast. Today was all about river crossings and mountains. We had flash floods, and the rain did not stop.

At one point, I heard loud gunfire, and, fearing there was a firefight between my soldiers and FARC guerrillas, I investigated. A short way ahead I found the bullet-riddled carcass of a large snake. Two soldiers had passed it and it had left them alone, but when a third soldier had walked by, the snake had reared up savagely, hissing and snapping its fangs. The soldier drew, aimed and blasted the critter.

We camped on a steep slope, because our original camp spot beside the river was flooded; I spent all night pushing my tent back up the hill. My feet are badly swollen, and my hands are sore from the spikes and prickles of the bush. Every time I sit down, some insect or other jungle creature bites me on the arse. I'm spending a lot of time standing up.

SEPTEMBER 27

It's raining heavily again. Today we crossed the mountains, and we are now on the northern, Caribbean Sea side of Panama. We are following a river to the beach. I'm hoping that the rain doesn't get any heavier, certainly not as heavy as yesterday, because if the river swells and overflows again it will cost me time and maybe my life. The water charges down the mountain like an out-of-control train. I've been saying prayers as I listen to the thunder.

Everything is wet. Tonight I am cold and shivering and very, very tired. The soldiers wanted to take it easier, but I stressed that this is a race, and I drove them on. Like it was on the ice, it is hard for people around me to understand the urgency.

The Darién is home to spider monkeys, white-faced monkeys and howler monkeys, which bellow like gorillas and yell at us through huge sharp teeth as we pass. I've seen masses of brilliantly hued macaws and toucans. There are also many venomous snakes.

My special bodyguard, Sergeant Villa, and another officer, Lieutenant Pirez, continue to stay close. They're still nearby as I write this, and they constantly ask if I am okay. These people are great.

Another soldier in the group reminds me of my brother Tony. Every chance he gets, he wets a fishing line in the river and usually catches a

Enjoying the hospitality of the local tribespeople.

fish, which we cook for dinner on the open camp fire. He calls himself a 'survivor'—I guess he's referring to the TV show. There's another bloke who is just like the comedian Eddie Murphy. He's constantly cracking jokes and clowning around, especially when the camera's rolling.

Today I dipped my feet in the Caribbean Sea, and I will sleep on the dirt floor of a hut of a welcoming, kind and very curious local tribe. They cooked me rice and noodle soup for dinner.

SEPTEMBER 28

I slept for only a couple of hours last night, because my mind was racing ahead of my body to the Colombian border. I was wondering what will greet me there. I've heard stories about murderous drug cartels. But, first things first, I told myself: there were still 35 kilometres—a full day's run in this terrain—to go. So far, thanks to my guard, I have stayed safe in the Darién, but there is still time for plenty to go wrong on this, my last day in the notorious rainforest. As I started running, my clothes and shoes were still drenched from yesterday.

And what a day it has been! We started at five o'clock at what is surely one of the most picturesque places on earth: the shore of the Caribbean Sea, in the village of Carreto. From there we made our way through the jungle; the guard won't travel along the beach for fear of being an easy target for terrorists.

We put our backpacks in an army boat and sent it on ahead towards the border, so that we could move faster. But we still had to carry enough guns and ammunition to wage a small war. We plucked bananas and coconuts from the trees we passed and ate them on the run. I believe you could easily survive in the Darién without taking in a scrap of food. There are cacao trees (the soldiers have shown me how to rip off the leaves, break the leaf pod against a tree and eat the flesh inside), limes, coconuts, bananas, pineapples, wild rice, avocados, and fruit that I have never laid eyes on before.

It rained again, as usual. But, although we were wet through, nothing could dampen our spirits today. We are camping in the forest at the very edge of the Darién.

SEPTEMBER 29

I've survived the Darién! I've beaten the bastard. I was in the rainforest for five days, emerging from it yesterday, but haven't a clue how far I ran—or, rather, stumbled, hacking my way with a machete the whole way—because the terrible terrain of thick jungle and knee-deep mud meant we had to keep zigzagging. I'm in great spirits. I was so worried about making it through, because it was a huge unknown, with the well-justified reputation as the most dangerous place on earth.

When we all emerged safely from the rainforest, and just before the guard handed me over to the safekeeping of the Colombian police for the next section of the run, they gave me a shirt which all of them had signed, then they hugged me and wished me well. Many were close to tears. Now, I'm sitting in the town of Turbo, on the Colombian side of the rainforest, waiting to rendezvous with Katie and the vans.

As I've said, I have to reach Tierra del Fuego in time to get to the Antarctic. Right now, the plan is for me, Brooke and Dillon to record a Christmas segment for Channel Nine on December 25, and then soon after for me to fly to the Antarctic for the final race to the South Pole.

 COLOMBIA

OCTOBER 1

I've bumped up my progress to 90 kilometres a day, in spite of a couple of steep 25-kilometre hills today which put terrible pressure on my knees and aching feet, and gave me a burning butt. I punished my knees going down the mountain as well, but I wanted to pull back some time. I have to cover this extra territory to have any hope of reaching Tierra del Fuego in time to depart for the South Pole.

With all my fears about the Darién behind me, I'm on a high and running well, starting in the dark between four and five o'clock and finishing long after the sun has set and it's too dark to see my way. There was a problem encountered, and solved, in getting the ferry company to release our vehicles—the usual red-tape hassles. It cost me two days, during which I nearly went out of my mind with frustration. But, at last, Juan and I have reunited with Katie and the other Mexican cameraman, Gustavo. (Bernie is still in Australia.) It was good to see them. Katie, who enjoyed her few days off—her first since she joined the run—told me that being on the road together again was like coming home.

Tonight, we are 1150 kilometres from the border with Ecuador: that's thirteen days at my current rate. I'll feel good when I cross the border. It's only a small country, and I'll run through it in a week, leaving just Peru, Chile and Argentina before the final hurdle—the South Pole. I'm mentally tired. I'm over this run. Really over it.

OCTOBER 2

There was a beautiful church just across the road from where I started my run this morning, so I went in and said a few prayers. I prayed that I would not let down the people who have supported me, I prayed for strength to overcome the many obstacles along the way, and I prayed that I might have the ability to deal with the pain I am feeling.

My feet are the worst they have ever been and feel like minced meat. I'm still running in the hiking boots I used in the Darién, because the Winnebago with my running shoes in it is still at the border, waiting for Bernie to arrive from Australia and catch up with us. The heat is affecting me badly, and I fainted twice today, once at the 50-kilometre mark and then again at the finish. My body is covered in salt from sweat.

The countryside is lush and green, and the villages and towns seem as though they are in carnival mode every night. The streets are mad with motorcycles. There is no accommodation, so tonight we are sleeping in the van in the grounds of the police station.

OCTOBER 3

Mountain after mountain after mountain. Today, all I could achieve by dark was 81 kilometres, and it took me 15 hours. I was aiming for 90 kilometres. Doubts are starting to enter my mind over whether I can

Colombia would have to be a mountainous country.

make it to Tierra del Fuego in time. My feet are a bloody mess. I feel almost broken. God help me. I've got to get out of these boots.

So the days are getting tougher, and my body is breaking down more. But the cheers and support from people I pass on the road spur me on.

OCTOBER 4

Much to the delight of the crew, today I started late, setting out at seven o'clock instead of five. I needed a long recovery sleep after yesterday's gruelling trek. The truth is, my legs ached all night, and I didn't get much sleep. When we did start, the road led me straight up another mountain.

I was delayed after we witnessed a motorcycle accident just outside the city of Medellín. The rider suffered no serious injuries, just some cuts and bruises. I kept running and left Katie and Gustavo to tell the police what they saw. It didn't take long, and they soon caught up.

Medellín is a large, bustling city that has been home to notorious drug cartels, some of which were run by the late drug baron Pablo Escobar, who was shot dead by police in 1993. The Colombian government has put a halt to the activities of many of the cartels, but they still exist, and kidnapping and murders continue to take place. We met a colonel from the US army whose job is to work with the Colombian army to flush out the drug gangs and guerrillas. Tourists are now returning to this beautiful land, and the coffee trade is booming.

Katie adores the country and said to me that, while she has never really considered living anywhere other than Australia, she might make an exception for Colombia. I asked her why, and she said that the place has such appeal: its friendly people, beautiful countryside, colourful wildlife and sheer exotic nature. I think I know what she's talking about.

Medellín was crazy with erratic traffic, but after 15 kilometres of stopping and starting and ducking and weaving I made it through and climbed another 25-kilometre mountain, accompanied by a Red Cross and police escort. When I reached the top, my butt was burning again. We were above the clouds; the views took my breath away. I hurt my knees by going quickly down the mountain, but again I wanted to make up some time.

Running through Medellín.

OCTOBER 5

There were times today when I wished I could stop running and call in to one of the small churches I passed for a little quiet reflection. Sure, I get plenty of time to think on the road, but reflecting while sitting or even kneeling is preferable. I followed a river course for most of the day, and, although it is winding, the terrain is much flatter than anything I have experienced for several weeks. My legs feel like they are encased in heavy steel callipers. Never again will I take for granted my ability to put one foot in front of the other and run.

I hope Bernie returns soon from visiting his family in Australia, because we need the Winnebago and all the gear in it, not least my running shoes. I've had to buy an emergency pair. Hurry up, brother.

OCTOBER 6

I've now run over 10,000 kilometres. That leaves me with the little matter of running another 10,000 kilometres between now and Christmas:

87 kilometres per day, every day. So far, I've gone through one pair of snowshoes, 15 pairs of joggers and the pair of hiking boots that I wore in the Darién. I have a sore shoulder from my fall on the mossy road when I got lost in El Salvador, and my right knee, which I hurt seemingly a lifetime ago in the ice of the North Pole, still gives me hell. The pain in my knee is increased by the camber of the road, always running at an angle.

🌐 COLOMBIA

As I've run through Colombia, I've had no sense of the turbulent history of this country. It has hosted the usual revolutions, insurrections and civil disturbances; and, in the past two decades, drug cartels, notably those led by Pablo Escobar, have waged a terror campaign against the government and the police, manifesting in brutal kidnappings and executions. Guerrilla outfits like the FARC, who inhabit the Darién Gap, have also caused bloody mayhem. President Alvaro Uribe, with the support of the US government, curbed the violence, although hostage taking and murders continue and will do so for as long as the terror outfits exist.

Slowly, though, tourists are daring to discover the delights of Colombia again: its quaint historic cities and towns, national parks, beaches, fields of flowers, and fauna including toucans, manatees, alligators, snapping turtles, spectacled bears, jaguars, anteaters and armadillos. When I met with the Colombian ambassador in Canberra in 2009, he mentioned to me that the common perception of Colombia as bristling with murderous drug lords is an image from the past. Today, he said, Colombia is focusing on being a tourism destination with excellent hotels, good roads, friendly people and the most beautiful churches and landscapes. It also has adventure sports like hang-gliding. I can only agree, because since I've been here I've seen all of that. I've run past many people hang-gliding from the mountain tops to the valleys. The coffee is the best I have ever tasted, and when you see the rich hillsides where it's grown and experience the climate, you can understand why. I've run through a number of old towns and have noticed that the churches are always the main attraction, with beautifully rendered and painted steeples.

Beware, however, the snakes of Colombia: anacondas, boa constrictors and the deadly *Bothrops atrox*, also known as the lancehead, for obvious reasons.

OCTOBER 7

I've run along Highway 62 from where the Darién ended, at Turbo, on the shores of the Caribbean Sea in the north, down to Medellín, and now I'm running down Highway 25 towards the Ecuadoran border, a distance of around 1250 kilometres.

Colombia is a Garden of Eden. It's a crying shame that drugs and greed have kept the country in the dark ages for so long. Colombian tourism now has a slogan: 'Once you visit you won't want to leave.' As far as I'm concerned, that's true. But I must leave. I have to get to Ecuador as soon as possible to maintain my terrible schedule. I hope my body can withstand this pressure.

The coffee plantations of Colombia line the hills.

OCTOBER 10

A Red Cross doctor and three nurses examined my foot on the road today and told me I had to do something about my left big toe, which is very badly infected. My feet are in crook shape because of the daily pounding they are taking, but making the problem worse is the fungal infection I picked up in the Darién through my wet boots. I've started trying to roll my feet as I run, to keep the pressure off my infected toes, but this is causing my calves to cramp. I told the medicos I didn't have time for them to treat me, but they insisted and said that if they didn't I mightn't be able to run at all. They found a motel, plonked me on a bed, gave me a massage, then got down to their excruciating work. Squeamish readers should turn the page now. The doctor plunged a needle into the middle of the infection. There was no anaesthetic. I screamed in pain and writhed like I'd been electrocuted. The puncture released a stream of pus and fluid. More howls of pain from me. Then . . . sweet relief. My toe still hurts when I run, but not nearly so much as before the pressure was released.

The countryside in this region of Colombia is rocky, dry and mountainous. There was a section of the run yesterday called the Coffee Road, which ran through coffee plantations stretching as far as you could see. I stopped at a roadside stall and had the best cup of coffee I've ever had, bar none. It was a short black from heaven. Today, instead of coffee plantations, I passed through sugarcane fields, and the father of my police guard, who runs a stall, gave me some thick, rich sugar syrup after his son told me it was good for boosting energy. I can't attest to that, but it tasted terrific.

Our Mexican cameraman Gustavo had a thrill when he rode in a police car and was allowed to pose with a large bag of marijuana that the police had confiscated. It was bound for a secret location, where it would be burned. The police told us they had to do the burning behind locked gates in case locals got wind of it and came rushing to inhale the marijuana smoke.

Roadkill report: Foxes, iguanas and lizards come to grief frequently here.

Gustavo with the confiscated marijuana. He had to return it!

OCTOBER 11

Bernie has not shown up yet, and my fear is that we will be through Colombia and into Ecuador before he arrives. His Winnebago has all our fresh clothing and gear in it. This run is a huge logistics exercise, dealing with customs, immigration, the Australian consulate, the consulates of the countries we are going into and out of, police, army, Red Cross, media and so on, and at the moment all conducted in a foreign language.

If I am to make the plane to the South Pole, I will have to maintain absolute discipline with the distance I run every day, no matter how bad my injuries are. I am constantly in pain. If it's not my knee, it's my feet, or arms, or back, or something else. I feel like a piece of metal that has been overworked and is showing fracture signs. I just need to hold it together for three more months.

OCTOBER 12

I didn't sleep last night, so my mood was not good when we were held up for a one-hour TV interview that I was promised would take five minutes. A magazine reporter arrived as soon as filming ended, and the delay went on and on. That's why the run ended at close to eleven o'clock tonight. I am really under the pump to get my kilometres done.

OCTOBER 13

Falling rocks. The roads all through the mountains are very dangerous, due not just to traffic but also to rock slides. Boulders sit in the middle of the road, causing vehicles, including ours, to swerve wildly to miss them. I have been hit by small falling rocks while I've been running. Thankfully, the bigger rocks and boulders make a bit more noise as they crash down the mountain, so I can hear them coming in time to duck out of their path. I am not listening to my iPod through this region, because I need to be alert to the danger.

OCTOBER 14

Bernie has returned from Australia, and, while it's good to have the van with all our gear and my running shoes, it's even better to have him back on board. I rely on his wisdom and practical ways, and his inability to get flustered no matter what befalls us. Another of Bernie's traits is his honesty: he is totally straight with me and tells me what he believes, not what he thinks I want to hear. He is the coolest person in a crisis I know, and I'm blessed that he's with me. Today we had a heart-to-heart, and he pulled no punches. He told me what I already know but try not to think about: that it is going to be tight making it to Tierra del Fuego by Christmas in time to get to Punta Arenas for the flight to the Antarctic that gives me enough time to trek the 1100 kilometres to the South Pole (at around 40 kilometres a day for 30 days) and catch a plane back out by the mid-January deadline. Around January 19 is, we've been told from the start, the last date on which planes fly out before conditions deteriorate. To reach Tierra del Fuego by Christmas, I need to run more than 100 kilometres a day, and that is going to be horrific.

So, in Australia, Bernie approached the Red Cross and people such as Dick Smith to try to organise a mid-February departure from the South Pole. He's waiting to hear if his pleas have been successful. There may be extra flights to the Antarctic this year, because December 2011 marks the centenary of the Norwegian explorer Roald Amundsen and his party becoming the first men to reach the South Pole, and a month later comes the centenary of the great British explorer Robert Falcon Scott reaching the pole; sadly, of course, he then perished with his party on the Ross Ice Shelf on March 29, 1912.

Meanwhile, all I can do is assume that the original deadline remains in place and bump up my distances. I have no idea what the rest of the road in South America will hold for me. Up ahead, there are mountains, and the high altitude there can play havoc with a runner. In Chile and Argentina there are mudslides that can obliterate a road in a flash, which will mean a detour that might take me many kilometres away from my route, and Argentina also has a bewildering and ever-changing road system. We won't know what conditions will be until we are on the spot. I am paying the price for all those media

Colombia is a very vibrant country, with lots of colourful rituals.

appearances and detours to places such as New Orleans. It's not that such appointments haven't helped to raise good money for the Red Cross, but we've made it tough for ourselves.

Bernie confided to me that he's over the adventure side of our event now and sees it as a bloody hard task that he must accomplish. The novelty of travelling through different countries has worn thin for him, as it has for me, especially since all of our focus is on running, and kilometres achieved, which leaves little time to delight in our surroundings.

Sometimes, I underestimate the great work that my crew does. Like Bernie, Katie has been so strong for me. They have a lot to do: planning the route so I don't have to run a single kilometre further than necessary, dealing with the police, the army and the Red Cross, driving in blizzards and torrential rain, cooking, raising donations and sponsorship, responding to emails and Facebook messages, juggling the budget, dealing with the 1001 problems that arise from being in strange lands. And, yes, putting up with me.

I've never denied that I'm difficult, and Bernie took the opportunity today to remind me that we're a team. 'We all have a job to do,' he said. 'Yours is to run. That's all you have to do. None of us can do that, and you can't handle our responsibilities. Forget about everything else but running those kilometres every day. Don't encroach on our territory, or the camera guys'. All it takes is for you to lose concentration and it could be disaster. Death is not out of the question.

'You're bloody difficult. You often run off ahead of us because you get frustrated when we take time setting up for the day. And if there are two roads to be taken, you'll always take the wrong one; then we have to scramble to find you, and you give us both barrels as if it's our fault.

'We know you have your moods; you sometimes even feed on your despair and anger as motivation to run and forget about your pain, and that's okay. We love you and are with you 100 per cent. We know that ten minutes after you've acted like a goose and we've walked away and left you with your thoughts, you'll be all smiles again. We don't take it personally.'

He's a special brother, and I'm lucky to have him. He is also a fine motivator. I was in an event in Australia some years ago, and I was running towards Cooma in the middle of winter. Bern was backing up in a vehicle. It was freezing, and I was buggered and fell. He stopped the car and ran to my side to find me in tears, saying I couldn't run another step. He offered to run alongside me for a while. As we ran, he reminded me of the great days when we were kids, fishing with our other siblings and our dad at Bermagui, on the south coast of New South Wales. We shared wonderful memories, and I realised after a bit that I'd run another 20 kilometres. All I needed was my mind taken off the run: I felt no weariness, no cold, no pain, as Bern and I relived our halcyon childhood. He knew exactly what he was doing. I powered on to Cooma.

Bernie worries that I always need a new challenge and is wondering what I will do when this event is over. How will I ever top it? He is a man who is satisfied with his life and feels no need to constantly test himself. I'm not built that way. I wonder too.

Bernie ended our little chat by telling me to get treatment for my sunburned bottom lip, which, for some time now, because of my daily exposure to the elements, has been bleeding constantly and refuses to heal. 'You're not Superman, Pat. You'll end up with bloody skin cancer!'

I'll cross into Ecuador tomorrow. As I've run through Colombia I've seen swampland, tropical forest, impenetrable jungle, low plains and photogenic mountains. I ran through banana and coffee plantations. I saw no violent incidents and didn't feel threatened at any stage. Nor, although Colombia is on the Ring of Fire, did I experience earthquakes or volcanic eruptions. It's been a pleasure to run through.

ECUADOR

OCTOBER 17

I crossed into Ecuador a couple of days ago and have been running steadily south towards Quito, the capital. Another late finish tonight, after eleven o'clock—a fitting end to a shitty couple of days. Two days ago, Bernie was driving the Winnebago when an oncoming truck veered into his lane, causing him to swerve, and he wiped out a section of his undercarriage on the gutter. The vehicle was still drivable, but last night when he went on ahead to scout for somewhere for us to buy food for dinner, he was behind a truck going down a steep hill

Ecuador is just as mountainous as Colombia.

when the truck braked suddenly. Bernie hit his anchors, burned out his brakes and blew two tyres. So tonight Bernie is about 100 kilometres back on the road with Juan, trying to get the Winnebago repaired. It's going to cost us the Ecuadorian equivalent of a few thousand dollars. I hope they catch us up before we hit the Peruvian border, in a few days.

To make matters worse, today, while Bernie was away, I got lost. The guys in the other Winnebago were using Google Maps, and the roads that we were making for turned out not to exist. That cost me three hours. Luckily, the Red Cross turned up and guided us to the right route.

Through Colombia, and now in Ecuador, I seem to have been climbing at a 45-degree angle the whole way. Soon I'll start descending to the coast, and I'll stick to it as much as I can, taking in rejuvenating glimpses of the mighty Pacific. It will be good to get out of the mountains; they've been taking a toll on my body. It's not just that they're steep: I'm up so high that the altitude has played havoc with my breathing. I take lots of short, sharp breaths to keep the oxygen flowing. What are really killing me, though, are the fumes and smoke I'm inhaling from passing vehicles. Petrol is incredibly cheap here, just 30 cents a litre, but I don't think it's the best quality. There's a black petrol haze hanging in the air. Because petrol is affordable, there are a lot of vehicles on the roads. The natural air here is clean and fresh, but you'd never know.

OCTOBER 18

Ecuador is incredibly beautiful and diverse, with enormous snow-topped volcanoes soaring out of the plains. I'm running up in the clouds, 3000 metres above sea level. It's similar to Mount Kosciuszko, with short brown grass and snow patches, and not a lot else. Everywhere, we're seeing signs directing travellers to Inca ruins, but, guess what, I'm not even tempted. I have to keep running. One day I'll be a tourist in this country and see every Inca ruin there is. The photo boys have taken some terrific pictures of the gorgeous scenery but have to frame the mountains carefully so that they avoid photographing the litter on the ground. Rubbish, in the form of plastic bottles and food containers, discarded household goods and dead animals, is just tossed onto the ground and left to fester. No one gives a damn, and it makes me realise how the Clean Up Australia campaign worked wonders at home. It simply wouldn't occur to Australians to junk their country. Australia is so clean; since I've been running, only Canada has come close. Mexico, Central and South America and large parts of the United States? Forget it.

Because of the garbage, there is also a perpetual rat plague here. I see the rodents everywhere, many being squished on the road. And don't get me started about the dogs! It seems that everyone owns about three dogs, and they roam free. They're aggressive and bark at me, chasing me and snapping their jaws. I've been bitten on the legs a number of times.

Another unpleasant fact of life in South America, as we also found in parts of Central America, is drunkenness. I can't believe the number of drunk men I've come across. They drink themselves into a stupor and fall where they stand until they regain consciousness. There are blotto bodies strewn everywhere. The worry is that they are often, like the dogs, aggressive to me. The dogs have sharp teeth; the humans have machetes.

My lips, feet and knees are hurting badly. I don't have time to take

A huge volcano called Cotopaxi looms above me as I run south from Quito.

care of them, and they're not repairing naturally. I first damaged my lips on the ice, when I put on a frozen face mask and it stuck to my cheeks, nose and lips. By the time I got it off, it had burned my skin. On a more positive note, there is an abundance of fresh produce—coconuts, oranges, bananas—and they grow truly delicious coffee.

TODAY SHOW INTERVIEW, OCTOBER 19

Karl Stefanovic: Pat Farmer is pushing the limits of human endurance with his pole-to-pole run. He's covered 11,000 kilometres from the North Pole to Ecuador, and that's where I caught up with him a little earlier. Pat, how are you?

Pat Farmer: Karl, old mate, physically I'm a wreck, but mentally I'm very focused on the end goal, which is to get to the South Pole. I've had a pretty tough last month, when you consider the Darién and Colombia and some of the mountains of Colombia. It's been incredible. At an elevation of 3000 metres, it's been hard to breathe, let alone run competitively, but that's exactly what I've had to do to stay on schedule.

KS: Pat, physically are you able to hold up? Are you able to keep going? I mean, what have been the biggest problems physically?

PF: It's just fatigue on my body, that's all there is to it. I'm managing as best I can, looking after myself at night, rubbing the right creams into my legs every night and taking in vitamins, but you have to understand that I've run 11,000 kilometres to this point through some of the most extreme temperatures and environments on earth.

KS: Are you worried that this might do your body harm long term?

PF: I'm not concerned about that. I've always been a person who lives for the moment, and this is the moment. Apart from my children and family, this run is all that matters to me on earth at this point in time. I have to make this run a success. I have to finish this thing. I have been renowned for finishing what I start, and this will be no different. The Darién rainforest really took its toll. We were running through mud up to our knees, day after day, and there was torrential rain and flooding. The soggy conditions caused a toe infection and other bits and pieces. The Darién was a bloody tough gig.

KS: Does it get any easier in the next few weeks?

PF: I'm looking forward to Peru next. I'll be running close to the west coast, so I'll be near my beloved Pacific Ocean. I'll be away from the high altitudes I've been running in.

KS: Keep charging, my friend.

OCTOBER 21
• •

Greg Quail and Bernie have devised a schedule for the end of my trek. The plan now, although it could always change, is that on December 29 I will fly to the ice from Punta Arenas, in the south of Chile. Brooke and Dillon are arriving on December 10 and will spend Christmas with me before I depart. The Nine Network is planning to film us as part of a Christmas Day special. I must be at the South Pole by January 18 and will fly back out on January 19. That will get me home by around January 22 or 23, just before Brooke's birthday on January 24 and Australia Day on January 26. Those two dates mean the world to me. That's why I must run 90 kilometres a day now and a daunting 50 kilometres a day on the Antarctic ice.

Reading back over this, I worry that I'm sounding repetitive, but repetition is my lot. I run, I sleep, I run . . . There is no time to do anything else except deal with the pain.

Only one more day's running to go in Ecuador and then we're in Peru!

PERU

OCTOBER 24

I'm over 100 kilometres into Peru, at a place called Piura, the capital of the Piura region. It was founded by the Spaniard Francisco Pizarro in 1532. The coast of Piura has some good surfing beaches. The seafood is the best in Peru, the locals say, and after trying some I'll take them at their word. I've been joined by a good mate, Tony Collins, who is running with me for a few days. He can keep up, too, because Tony is an ultramarathon runner, and we competed in Westfield Sydney to Melbourne runs years ago. These days, Tony's a dentist on the central coast of New South Wales, and to support me he has detoured to Peru during a trip over here.

Piura is nice, but so far my impressions of Peru are mixed. The road I'm running along, the Pan-American Highway, was bounded today on the east by a vast barren desert with not even a cactus growing there, and on the west by green, fertile agricultural land. The reason for this is that the Peruvian government drilled bores on the west side of the road, and now sugar cane and rice grow thickly in the lush green fields. What a contrast. Again, it made me realise how water can magically transform the most unproductive land. Water, after all, is what my run is all about.

Sadly, people in this region are poor. They live in shanty towns as impoverished as any I saw in Soweto. Poverty, I'm sure, is the reason our Winnebago was robbed yesterday. They say bad luck comes in threes, and if so we should be fine for the rest of the run. Bernie returned from getting the Winnebago repaired after the prang, the burned brakes and the blown tyres, and he and Gustavo drove into a town called Tumbes, just 30 kilometres over the border, and stopped to do our washing at a laundromat. While they were inside, someone jimmied the lock on the van's driver's door and broke in. They stole all the cash from my wallet,

Running with Tony Collins, an old ultrarunning mate from home.

my bag, which contained clothes and precious letters from Brooke and Dillon, and my reading glasses. It's distressing to have been robbed, and losing the letters breaks my heart, but I'm philosophical about it. People here have nothing. To them, our bashed-up old Winnebago was a luxury vehicle, and they wanted to help themselves to whatever was inside. It happens. I expected to be robbed in Mexico, El Salvador or Nicaragua, not in Peru, but there you go.

We have no police escort in this country, but the cops show up at the end of the day to make sure that we camp in a safe area. Last night we parked on the side of the road, but they told us to do so would be dangerous and made us move to outside the police station.

OCTOBER 25

Occasionally the road veers towards the coast, and I see the Pacific Ocean, which always does my heart good.

I learned today that Peruvians eat guinea pigs. Pork is also a favourite dish. In the towns, we've seen pig carcasses hanging from hooks in the street, and locals are allowed to come along with a knife and hack off a chunk of flesh, take it home to their shack and cook it over an open fire. Weirdly, for all the raw meat out in the sun, there are no flies.

Doing 90 kilometres a day is tough. I try to get 30 kilometres under my belt as early as possible, then have a short rest before launching out for a further 50, which I try to achieve by late afternoon. The final 10 or 15 kilometres are killers. Sometimes I eat dinner while running the final 5 kilometres, so I can crash as soon as I stop running, sleep for as long as possible and get up and do it all again the next day.

Greg is flying from his base in Los Angeles to meet me in Lima in ten days' time. We'll be having a crisis meeting over the South Pole transport. The organising company, ALE (Antarctic Logistics and Expeditions), guide Eric Philips and the cameraman are insisting that we have a big expensive six-wheel drive ice vehicle that they can follow me in as I run. It would undoubtedly make their life easier. The problem is that the particular vehicle they want will cost as much as $350,000 to rent, I've discovered. For God's sake—you can buy a Maserati for $350,000 . . . *and keep it!* My idea is to use skidoos, which will be hard work but cheaper and available in late December, when

I arrive after running 90 kilometres a day. The others will kick at the meeting, but I can't see any other solution.

OCTOBER 27

I ran through Chiclayo today, still on the Pan-American Highway. It was founded by Spanish missionaries in the 16th century, but now it's a gritty, commercial city with honking, revving, tyre-squealing trucks and buses, and heavy pollution. Apparently it's also home to witch doctors, and some of the stores I ran past were selling 'magical' herbs and potions and various magic charms. If there was one that could make me run further and faster each day, take away my aches and pains and make Brooke and Dillon materialise before my eyes, I'd buy a truckload.

Peru is a country divided into the jungle of the Amazon Basin in the east, the astonishingly beautiful Andes in the centre, and the arid desert on the west coast. Guess where my route takes me? Through the desert, of course. It's just the way it has to be. My role is not sightseeing

A colonial building in Peru.

but getting from the top of Peru to the bottom as quickly as I can, and that is on the Pan-American Highway, which lines the west coast. I've ticked off Peru as another place I'll return to one day to get to know it, and its people, food, music and sights, properly.

OCTOBER 28

Today has been a disaster: I didn't even come close to reaching 90 kilometres. I was continuing through the Sechura desert, making good time in spite of a ripping headwind that was powering in off the Pacific, when a police car drove up and motioned for me and our vans to stop. The officer, conversing in Spanish with Gustavo and Juan, asked where we thought we'd be camping, and the boys told them we planned to stop by the side of the road. The policeman said that was out of the question. Apparently, in this part of Peru, there are criminals with guns who don't mind using them, and we'll be setting ourselves up for a robbery or something much worse if we camp in the open. It's far too dangerous. He told us that there have been numerous cases of bandits opening fire on and ramming passing motor vehicles and even bicycles. Many people have been robbed at gunpoint.

The officer ordered us to follow him, and we drove to the next town, Paiján, and are spending the night in a guarded garage. For the equivalent of $4, security men are keeping an eye on our vehicle, as well as other trucks, buses and travellers' cars whose owners have chosen not to court calamity. We may survive the night, but I was only able to run 76 kilometres, not nearly enough. The pressure to reach Tierra del Fuego in time to make it to the Antarctic mounts.

OCTOBER 29

The weather is mild, around the mid-20s. Apart from llamas and anteaters wandering everywhere, there wasn't much to see today, to be frank. There were no more crops growing on the west side of the highway; instead, there were sandy flats on either side of the road. The Pan-American Highway has brought us to the flat, brown Sechura desert. Early this evening it was a pleasure to run out of the desert for a while and into the town of Trujillo, about 550 kilometres north of the Peruvian capital of Lima. Somehow, a number of the old colonial streets, with their buildings and majestic churches that are hundreds of years old, have resisted the cheap office blocks, strip malls and apartment blocks that have engulfed the rest of the town. Trujillo has an interesting history: it was the first Peruvian city to break from Spain and become independent, and ever since it has been a place where revolutions and insurrections have been plotted.

After emerging from the town, there was again nothing to see apart from the vast expanse in which nothing, not even a cactus, grows. The day has been mild, but after leaving Trujillo I was running into a strong headwind of 60 kilometres per hour.

We have a major problem. Bernie has done the sums, and, running at my present rate of 90 kilometres a day, we will finish between 14 and 16 days too late for the flight to the South Pole. To make it on time to Tierra del Fuego, then get to Punta Arenas to meet up with Eric and fly to the Antarctic to start my final run to the South Pole, I would have to run 120 kilometres a day from now until December 29: two months. That would break me. I can't do it.

I have asked Greg to fly from his base in Los Angeles to Lima in about a week's time, for a face-to-face crisis meeting with Bernie and me. We need to thrash out some issues. I've tried countless times to have a phone meeting with Greg, but the communications are deplorable, and either I can't get through to him, or he can't reach me, and when he *is* on the line the connection invariably cuts out. (It's not just Greg suffering from communication breakdown: some of my planned live links with Channel Nine's *Today* show have also been unable to take place.) The only thing to do is meet in person; together we need to come up with solutions.

Sir Edmund Hillary faced terrible obstacles climbing Mount Everest, and he overcame them. I take strength and inspiration from that.

OCTOBER 30

I am now just 450 kilometres north of Lima, and, frankly, Peru has been disappointing. I expected a more exotic, colourful, friendly place. All I've experienced so far are the desert, which is forbidding and desolate except for the odd scraggly gum tree, and a threatening atmosphere. Again, guns and drunks are ubiquitous. I'm running for 16 hours every day, finishing after eleven o'clock. The highway is littered with dead

🌐 THE PROBLEMS

There are no commercial flights to Antarctica after the end of December and none out of Antarctica after mid-January. We'll be too late for these, so somehow we have to organise a later flight into and out of the Antarctic. We may have to pull strings, and after coming so far I'm not too proud to do that. Perhaps I'll have to prevail upon my contacts—Australian consuls and officials that I've met during my run, or Robert Tickner, the head of Red Cross Australia—to organise another airline or special charter flights for me.

I can't reach Tierra del Fuego until sometime between January 9 and 14, and, after taking 20 days to reach the South Pole, running 50-odd kilometres a day, I will then be ready to depart the pole in mid-February or thereabouts. This will mean that I'll miss out on my dream of celebrating Brooke's birthday and Australia Day in Sydney in January, but there will be plenty more times to enjoy these events in the future. My main priority must be to finish what I have started.

I've told Greg we have to explore every option. An absolute last resort may be to fly from southern Chile to the Antarctic, run to the South Pole and then fly back to where I ended up in South America to finish the run down to Tierra del Fuego. I will be going back on my vow never to take a backward step, but if I run every day and cover the territory I said I would, I can live with that. It's just that it's messy, and I resent that it's not me changing the plan, but forces out of my control.

Another problem, as I've said, is deciding whether to use the six-wheel drive in the Antarctic or skidoos. Greg and Eric want us to use the six-wheel drive. It's more comfortable for the crew coming with me, and better to film from. The downside, as I see it, is that it is ruinously expensive. Greg says he can pay for the vehicle by using Channel Nine's final sponsorship payment and getting more donations. Even so, I believe that using it would mean we will finish in the red. I prefer the skidoo option, because they can be there when we need them and they are far, far cheaper.

It's a dusty road and a difficult slog sometimes.

dogs and rats. I wasn't expecting to be running into a relentless head-wind, either, which has made my job all the more arduous.

To be honest, I'm struggling. This is a slog. I run in a trance, trying not to think of my ailments and crippling schedule. The wind blows dust and sand into my face, which stings, and is murder on my blis-tered and bleeding lips. The sand sticks to the sores.

My mate Tony has gone now, and I miss him. It was good to run with a close pal, and, more than that, he reminded me that I have a homeland, which I am missing badly. The crew now is down to Bernie, Katie, Gustavo and Juan. Katie and Bernie don't run with me anymore. They are too busy doing their jobs: driving, handling correspondence, liaising with the media and Greg Quail, dealing with the Red Cross and potential sponsors, buying and cooking our food, doing the washing, maintaining the vehicles . . .

I tried to work out today how many pairs of running shoes I've gone through—I can't pin it down exactly, but it's somewhere between 15 and 17. I kept my promise to those kind women, Leslie and her daughter, Kate, who gave me the precious gift of a stack of running shoes, and I wore the pair they autographed through Colombia and Ecuador. By the time I finished they were demolished, in shreds.

It's said that runners get a second wind in a race, but when the race goes for 21,000 kilometres it's a hell of a second wind that's needed. Every day I have so many ups and downs, but one thing that keeps me going is this belief in the second wind, the belief that, no matter how tired and sore I get, if I push through it I'll recover and be able to run even more strongly.

We've booked Brooke and Dillon's flights. They'll be flying out in December when school finishes, and will link up with me, wherever I am on the road, and stay with me until I fly to the Antarctic.

In Lima, as well as attending the meeting with Greg, I have to go to a function that the Australian embassy has organised for me. The Australian ambassador to Peru, John Woods, has invited prominent Australians living and working in Peru to come and say g'day and hear about my quest. I'm looking forward to it, but I'm hoping it will be brief.

OCTOBER 31
· ·

I did another live cross to Karl Stefanovic on the *Today* show today, standing in the most godforsaken place—the desert of northern Peru. My battered lips were smothered in zinc; seeing that must have been a treat for all the viewers back home. And if they weren't grossed out by my lips, I'll bet they were when I showed them the footage of me having my infected toe lanced. I'm 300 kilometres north of Lima. All around me are small, windswept, pointed hills, with sand blasting everywhere. It's *hot*. The sky is white. Karl reckoned it looked like I was standing on the surface of Mars.

To date, we've destroyed 12 tyres on the Winnebagos. The tyres explode on the hot roads. Conditions are very hard on anything that slaps the surface of the planet in this part of the world. Karl and his co-host Lisa Wilkinson were gobsmacked when I told them that I was planning to increase my distance from 85 or 90 kilometres a day to 95 kilometres and, who knows, maybe to 100 kilometres. I explained to them that the 5 or 10 extra kilometres a day mean that I have to work much harder in the day and get less sleep at night, but that the increased distance is crucial to me getting on that flight to the

Above: Trudging the endless highway through Colombian coffee plantations.

Left: Local farmers offer home-grown produce ... and it is gratefully accepted. Fresh fruit never tastes as good as when you're out on your feet.

Below: The ravishing Colombian scenery made me think I was running through a succession of postcards.

Above: Religion permeates everything in Colombia.

Right: Hot days and heavy rainfall produced misty mornings in northern Ecuador.

Below: Manuela Saenz, the lover of Simon Bolivar, is still a heroine in Ecuador. She saved the South American statesman and general from assassination in 1828.

Above: Impressive Ecuadoran volcano Cotopaxi smoulders in the distance.

Above: The scenery changed dramatically as I ran into the deserts of northern Peru.

Below: There's no time to stop at the picturesque fishing villages dotting the Peruvian coastline.

Above: The daytime heat makes it essential to keep fluids up.

Left: Sunset turns the forbidding desert into a thing of beauty.

Below: Goats look for food and somewhere to shelter from the blazing sun.

Above: Taking a well-earned, and very short, breather.

Above right: Resilient cacti flourish on the barren plains.

Below: Rough-hewn memorials to those who haven't made it—a constant on the roads of South America.

Above: Coastal breezes offer a welcome respite from the heat.

Below: In the distance the support vehicle: the road winds on forever.

Left: The Chilean flag: like me, this one looks a bit worse for wear.

Below left: The local farmers work hard for little reward.

Below right: Burned to a crisp—running in Chile is hard enough without a hole in the ozone layer making the sun even more treacherous.

Above left: I've had times of elation and times of foot-weary despair.

Above right: Eating on the run. Ming, our ace cameraman and part-time chef, helps me keep my calorie intake high.

Below: The lights of my life: Dillon and Brooke rejoin me in Chile.

Doing a live cross to *Today*'s Karl Stefanovic.

Antarctic on time. Karl gasped, 'How much of a legend is this bloke?' I don't know about that.

Later I ran through towns whose walls had been painted by the locals in brightly coloured religious scenes. Huge boulders had fallen from the sides of cliffs and littered the roads like the marbles of giants. They brought traffic, and me, to a standstill.

NOVEMBER 2

We've been robbed again, for the second time in Peru. I was sleeping in the Winnebago at two o'clock this morning when a noise woke me. I peered outside and saw a fellow cutting the straps on a gear basket which contained clothing and shoes. By the time I got up and gave chase, he had disappeared into the black night. Can't say that I'm enjoying Peru.

The festival of the Day of the Dead—Día de los Muertos—actually lasts for three days, from October 31 to November 2. It is a holiday during which people honour the memory of those who have passed away by wearing colourful skull masks, making elaborate altars and celebrating in their homes and in the cemeteries where their loved ones are buried. They eat local delicacies, including barbecued meats and a particular kind of bread that is known as *pan de muerto*, or 'bread of the dead'. I have run past many such gatherings in the last few days. The Peruvians also hold vigils by the roadside where traffic accidents have claimed those close to them. Considering the way people drive here, it comes as no surprise to me that I've seen hundreds of these memorials along my route. I've been bumped into by taxis on a few occasions here; the drivers seem to take offence that I'm running on their roads.

I'm on the outskirts of Lima, 79 kilometres from the city, and will arrive there tomorrow. I'm so close, but all around me are sugarcane fields, desolate slums and people living in poverty. Usually, this close to a capital city, I'd be seeing suburbs, high rise, industry, and a bit of wealth.

I'm still doing 90 kilometres a day; the only time I couldn't keep up this rate was when the cops made us stop early. As I've said, I'm planning to bump up my distance to 95 kilometres a day and maybe more if the conditions in Chile, the next country we enter, are favourable.

I was disappointed today to receive a text from Greg saying that he won't be able to make our meeting in Lima, although he says he'll be flying down soon afterwards. I'm aware that there's not much money left in the kitty. I pray for a donation or 50.

The best thing about today was the big plate of lasagne that Katie made me for dinner. It's weird and humbling to realise that no one in the history of the world has ever run as far as I am running every day for so many, many months.

NOVEMBER 4

We have spent the day in Lima, and what a busy day it's been. Getting into the city was the usual bunfight caused by madcap traffic—cars came at me like wild animals—and confusing streets. We made it to the Australian embassy, where I was guest speaker at the Australian Trade Commission's Australia Business Club function. Australian business leaders in Peru, from such companies as Qantas and BHP,

At Lima I met up with Peruvian Red Cross officials.

came to shake hands and wish me well for the remainder of the run. My crew and I were honoured to be a part of the evening, not just to chat to some fellow Aussies, but also to spread the word about the life-changing work that the International Red Cross does every day and to highlight our own mission. Today I fired off emails to the executives I met, saying that any financial support they could give me to pay for the mounting costs would be greatly appreciated.

NOVEMBER 5

Feeling good today. I've just had a Skype catch-up with Mum for her 79th birthday. After I'd wished her many happy returns, up on the screen came all the family who were there with her, sending their love and best wishes to me. Mum broke her wrist a few months ago, but it's mended well. She has made me a Christmas pudding and is saving it for my return. No pudding will ever taste so wonderful.

This morning before we left Lima we had breakfast with the officials of the Peruvian Red Cross. They told us about the good work they do with disaster relief, collecting blood and conducting education campaigns about what people should do if caught in a mud or sand slide or an earthquake. I have never seen such big sandhills as in Peru. I was very impressed and once more proud that my run is helping their efforts.

The running south of Lima is better than in the north of the country. I've left the lunar landscape and roaring headwinds and am closer to the Pacific Ocean and its cooling breezes. The sky is cloudless.

NOVEMBER 7

We're over 200 kilometres south of Lima, and I'm running 90-plus kilometres a day. I break the distance up into five-hour chunks, running 15 hours a day. Add meal breaks and media obligations onto that, and you'll understand why I'm sleeping only a few hours a night. I've been on an emotional downer after talking to Mum and the family. The only thing brightening my outlook is the arrival of my children next month.

The white road shows the chalky soil that lies just under the surface of the Nazca desert.

POLE TO POLE

NOVEMBER 9

Today I ran past one of the wonders of the world: the Nazca Lines, in southern Peru's Nazca desert, 400 kilometres south of Lima.

It's been an interesting week. I've received some fantastic supportive emails, including some photos and a video from a young primary school student in Sydney who went to a celebrity dress-up day at school dressed as me. She had bought a Pole to Pole T-shirt from the website and on big posters had traced my run. I was very chuffed.

THE NAZCA LINES

Created around 2000 years ago, the Nazca Lines are collections of geoglyphs extending over almost 500 square kilometres. They range from geometric designs to depictions of animals and birds—including a pelican, spiders, lizards, fish, sharks and monkeys—as well as trees and flowers. They are so big (the pelican is 285 metres wide) that the only way you can see them properly is from the air.

Goodness knows how the Nazca people created the images so accurately. It was an enormous logistical exercise to make the pictures, done by removing the red pebbles that cover the desert to expose the white sandy earth beneath. The legend, propounded by people who believe that the markings could not have been made without someone directing proceedings from the air, is that aliens made the markings. I thought as I ran that, if it's true, and they're still lurking around up there, it would be nice if they'd drop a couple of cool drinks down my way. It was bloody hot today.

I've been in Peru for 17 days, and just recently I've been knocking over 100 kilometres a day. I'm feeling and looking healthier and stronger. It must be that second wind. The last time Karl Stefanovic interviewed me, he said I was looking a whole lot better than I had been two weeks earlier, when he and his co-host Lisa Wilkinson had feared for my health. Perhaps that Bembo's burger had something to do with it. Someone from the Peruvian Red Cross dared me to stop at this famous fast food chain and try one of their 'Extreme' hamburgers, with meat, chicken, bacon, salad and Peruvian spices crammed into a huge roll. They said it was rare for anyone to finish the monster burger. Well, I finished one in quick time and then devoured another, much to my crew's shock and awe. That's the thing about running 100 kilometres a day: you can eat as much as you like and you don't put on a skerrick of weight.

PAT'S DAILY INTAKE

This is a list of a typical day's food and drink at the moment:

- 1 bowl of cereal with milk
- 10 pancakes with half a jar of strawberry jam and lashings of honey
- 2 fried eggs
- 1 bowl of chicken noodle soup with vegetables
- 1 piece of battered fish with vegetables
- 2 large bowls of boiled rice
- 2 bananas
- 5 dried apricots
- 5 bread rolls with butter
- 2 packets of potato chips
- 2 bowls of ice cream
- 1 ice block
- 550 grams of chocolate
- 3 litres of water
- ½ litre of cola
- 1½ litres of energy drink
- 2 cups of coffee
- 1 beer
- 7 vitamin tablets

I have no idea how many kilojoules is in that lot! All I know is that it's fuel and it keeps me running.

NOVEMBER 12

I have managed to pull back two days from the 16 I was behind schedule, but I'm still 14 days behind schedule. If I can keep up this rate, I will cross into Chile on November 17.

The scenery now is different from the flat, dull desert expanses north of Lima. I am running straight down the coastal highway, and the views in every direction are spectacular: wide blue ocean on my right and soaring white cliffs on my left. The closest Australian equivalent would be Victoria's Great Ocean Road. There are seals by the water and birds soaring everywhere. The predominant sounds are the crashing waves and the crying seagulls. Vultures perch on the rocks as I run

Eating on the run—the image of elegance.

by, peering impassively, though ominously, at me. Today I sheltered behind a sand dune to go to the toilet. As I was squatting there, two vultures came right up to me. They must have thought I was about to die. I was glad to disappoint them. I pulled my shorts back up and took off.

I've bumped into some Scottish tourists who I met back at the Nazca Lines—lovely people, keen to know why I am doing this crazy event and happy to be photographed with the madman from Down Under.

I was heartened to see that the *Sunday Telegraph* newspaper back home ran a two-page feature on me and the run, written by their journalist Nick Walshaw. I no longer get a buzz seeing my name in print, but I'm grateful to the paper and to Nick, because the feature, which made a point of running my website address, has resulted in more donations.

Tonight I feel optimistic about what lies ahead. I am determined to give the South Pole a red hot go. I want people to see what I achieve on that final 1100-kilometre leg and say 'Wow!' I am determined to cover between 50 and 65 kilometres per day, every day I'm on the ice. I want to show what I'm made of. When I finish this run I want nothing left in my tank.

NOVEMBER 13
• •

What a day. We decided to leave the Pan-American Highway at the 50-kilometre point in the day's run, at a town called Camana, and take the coast road to Islay. This will reduce the distance I have to cover between the towns from 200 kilometres to just 100 kilometres, saving around a day's travel. When we planned the run, we figured that for safety's sake we should stick to the highways, but now that we've acquired a little local knowledge I feel okay about getting off the main road. Also, we can send one vehicle ahead to scout the route and so be more precise and take into consideration traffic and terrain when we are planning the next day.

I passed through many little fishing villages hidden in the rocky coves, including a few where men were building boats by hand. It was good to see old-fashioned craftsmanship. On one beach, four men stripped off and waded out past the breakers with a drag net and then slowly pulled it in to reveal a catch of fish and crabs big enough to feed a whole village.

The crew went ahead to Quilca, to meet the guide who had been organised by the local police to show me the way tomorrow, necessary because the coast road we've taken as a shortcut is difficult to find in places. He was a local man who would ride his horse and direct me along the route. However, when I arrived in Quilca the crew told me that my guide had had a bad fall that very afternoon and had been rushed to hospital with a suspected broken collar bone. Now I have three choices for tomorrow: I find someone else, I go back 40 kilometres to the Pan-American Highway and lose another day, or I equip myself with a compass and backpack full of food and drinks for the next 80 kilometres, pick up the old track we were going to use and just get on with it. We've tried to find another guide, but no luck: this is a very small fishing village. Also, I hate going backwards. So the third option is my best bet. I will start at five o'clock, just on dawn, and hopefully meet my crew near Islay.

A fishing village on the coast.

NOVEMBER 14

More distance saved today, but it was arduous. I started at 4.45 am from the town of Quilca and finished at 11.30 pm after a rendezvous with the vans, which, unable to travel on the potholed back road, had taken the highway. I ended up running in the pitch dark, Bernie following my progress on the tracker on his phone. I repeatedly tripped over rocks, foliage and cacti, and my legs and hands were bruised and bleeding. At the end, I was weeping. Bernie put his arm around my shoulder and said, 'Good on you, mate.'

The road I took was no more than a bullock track running up and down sand dunes, cliffs and hills, and steep gorges that went right down to the sea.

Along the way, I found a different kind of roadkill from that which I've encountered so far: a human foot. When I later reported my find to Juan and Gustavo, saying that we should contact the police in case whoever once owned that foot was murdered, they said that piles of bones are common in these parts. In Peru, it's normal to bury

My gruesome roadside discovery.

people where they die—there are thousands of sad little shrines to the departed on the roadsides—and then vultures disturb the makeshift graves and attack the corpse, eating the flesh. The remains of their meal are left exposed in the sun. Hence the piles of bones I saw, and the foot.

NOVEMBER 16

I have been out-voted and my polar guide, Eric, and the cameraman will be accompanying me in Antarctica in the six-wheel drive vehicle rather than on the skidoos I had insisted upon. They have always said they need it, to be a base for us and to facilitate the filming. As I've said, the vehicle is very much more expensive than the skidoos, but Greg has raised the money to fund it. The other problem that I see with the six-wheel drive is that we are now locked in to a schedule. We have booked the vehicle from December 29 to January 26. We now have to fly from Punta Arenas in Chile to the northern tip of Antarctica on December 29, I must take no more than 28 days to reach the South Pole—that's

39 kilometres a day to cover the 1100 kilometres—and then we must fly out of the pole on January 26.

I'm going to flog my guts out to finish the South American leg but to do so will have to run between 105 and 110 kilometres a day. That may be beyond me. If it becomes obvious that I cannot do it, Greg says I must stop running wherever I am and fly to Punta Arenas to arrive there on December 29 to rendezvous with Eric, the cameraman and the vehicle and fly out. Then, after completing the Antarctica section, I must fly back to exactly the same spot at which I stopped running, which looks like being 2000 kilometres north of Tierra del Fuego, and finish the leg, 75 kilometres or so a day for around 22 days, to Ushuaia in Tierra del Fuego.

This plan makes me angry and frustrated, because it has been my aim to run from pole to pole continuously, without backtracking. It has been about moving forward every day, with no days off. But if this messy anticlimax is how it has to be, then so be it; I can only take solace in my original mission, which was to raise funds for clean water, which I'll have done, and to make Brooke and Dillon proud of their dad, and I will have accomplished this too.

What keeps me running are my dreams of having my life back, of being with my loved ones in my beautiful Australia . . . Coogee Beach, mango smoothies . . . of not having to run these insane distances every day, of reuniting with friends, of maybe reading a newspaper or watching TV, or enjoying some other simple pleasure that I once took for granted but never will again. But really, I just need my kids to be proud of me. It doesn't matter a damn what the rest of the world thinks.

I have no idea how much money I've raised. With the Red Cross offices that have received donations so disconnected and far-flung, I suspect I will never find out for sure.

I finished the day resting in the back of the van, listening to Cold Chisel with Bernie.

 **CHILE**

NOVEMBER 18

Today I crossed the border into Chile. Chile is a long (4300 kilometres), narrow (average 175 kilometres) country squeezed between the Pacific Ocean to the west, Bolivia to the north-east and the Andes and Argentina to the east.

After what seemed to be a never-ending trek in Peru, running through the relentless sandy desert and scrambling up and down sand dunes, we're all excited to pass another milestone. On the road I realised again that I am grateful for many things in life, and Peru, which in parts has terrible sanitation, showed me just how lucky I am to have access to clean water. Once more it has impressed upon me the fact that water is life. Even in Peru, one of the most arid countries I have ever been to, the few places with access to water have flourishing crops and animals and thriving communities.

I ran more than 100 kilometres again today. The scenery was similar to some of that in Peru, except I ran past picturesque fishing villages and a not-so-picturesque copper mine with a refinery that stank to the high heavens. I saw some squished hares on the road.

NOVEMBER 19

A successful day. I ran 90 kilometres, which reduced by a little the ground I have to make up in my probably hopeless quest to be in Punta Arenas by December 29. After the run, the crew and I sat around talking and laughing. Our spirits are high again after some time in the doldrums caused by the issues over the schedule and the six-wheel drive vehicle. We sat and looked up at the stars and were blown away by their brightness. They seemed so large. When I made out the familiar shape of the saucepan, I was transported back in my mind to wonderful times camping and fishing with my father at Bermagui on the south coast of New South Wales when my siblings and I were kids. The stars were vivid then, too, and over us in the deep-blue, unpolluted sky was the saucepan. My six brothers and sisters and I would lie on the beach around a fire, happy and tired after a day's fishing and swimming, and we would drift off to sleep, safe and secure in our father's love.

NOVEMBER 20

On this run there have been good days and there have been bad days— and today was one of the worst days. I stopped running at 11.30 pm. I am beyond exhausted and have been burned to a crisp after seemingly endless hours under a desert sun blazing out of a cloudless sky.

I began the day at 4.30 am and was feeling terrific. I was determined to save maybe 30 or 40 kilometres by leaving the highway and taking a shortcut across the desert. The bliss that lingered from last night's star gazing did not survive the first couple of hours of running.

I set off wearing an old fishing hat with protective flaps on the back and sides (I don't give a damn about how I look anymore) and scrambled for an hour and a half up a 1500-metre mountain to reach the desert plateau above. The terrain in this part of Chile is different from that of Peru: it is still desert, but instead of sand dunes there are mountain ranges of biblical proportions—the types of mountains Moses would have climbed to collect the Ten Commandments! When I reached the plateau, I began running.

The sun came up and I knew it was going to be terribly hot. I wasn't unduly concerned, though, because I would be rendezvousing with the crew in the vans on the highway after

No time for vanity.

about five hours, and in the meantime Juan was going to be bringing me litres and litres of water on a motor scooter we had acquired and mounted on the back of a Winnebago. Time passed—one hour, two hours, three and four hours—but no Juan. In the heat, which was over 40 degrees Celsius, I became dehydrated, I had no energy, and I was feeling woozy in the head and nauseous. What I later learned was that Juan had become disoriented in the uncharted desert and was riding in circles searching for me in vain. I refused to stop running; anyway, there was no shade. I was staggering and weaving crazily over the sand and mineral rocks that reflected the sun's heat back up at me. I tried too hard and wiped myself out.

To take my mind off my plight, I pictured myself standing at the South Pole beside the Red Cross flag that I had just plunged into the ice. A friend recently reminded me that the waves are still rolling onto Coogee Beach and will be waiting for me when I return, so I thought of taking Brooke and Dillon for a surf and then us all devouring mango smoothies at our favourite cafe.

Nearing lunchtime, I reached the highway, and there were Bernie, Katie, Gustavo and the new film guy, Ming d'Arcy, waiting for me. (Ming is a vastly experienced Sydney-based cinematographer and cameraman who specialises in shooting adventure documentaries. Apart from that he is a great guy who mucks in, doing anything required of him.) Juan was still lost. Then more despair when we consulted the map and discovered that, contrary to our planning, we had not made up any distance by my nearly killing myself in the desert.

After lunch I ran off, the others following and hoping Juan would catch up. After three hours he arrived on his scooter, sunburned and on the point of collapse.

Bernie and I had a talk and decided that there was still a chance to claw back some distance if I left the highway and ran in the desert again. It was the last thing I felt like doing, but if I can possibly run to Ushuaia, catch that flight from Punta Arenas on the 29th and avoid having to backtrack, I'm prepared to take risks to do it. To reach the desert meant that I had to clamber down the side of a 400-metre cliff face over loose rocks and thorn bushes, battle through the bush at the bottom of the ravine and then climb 500 metres up a cliff onto the desert plateau on top of the mountain. Unfortunately the plateau was scored by ravines, so I had to do that three times.

At nightfall we all met up again, and found that, because I'd lost my bearings during the afternoon, I had saved only a few kilometres. Ming later told me that they had seen me running in the wrong direction in the desert, but because it was too rugged for them to leave the road to fetch me and because there was no mobile phone coverage they'd had to watch helplessly as I ran like a rabbit out of sight.

Not one of my best days.

I sat on the step of the Winnebago to peel off my socks, which were filled with sand and pebbles, and was hit by a wave of despair. I need to pull back between 700 and 800 kilometres, but, no matter how hard I try, how much I push myself, I'm making no impression. I put my head in my hands and sat there for some time. Heartbroken. Right then, my despair was as profound as at any time on this damned run.

Then, as I always do, I pulled on my socks and shoes and started to run. I had managed only 50 kilometres today so far, and I would run 30 more if it killed me. Ming ran beside me, and that buoyed my spirits. We made the 30 kilometres.

My forehead, face, arms and legs are burned badly after today. I have blisters all over me, particularly nasty ones on my hands from clawing my way up the mountains. At least I remembered to plaster zinc cream on my lips, to prevent further sunburn to my bottom lip, which has been an open wound for months now. I am very worried that the sore will become cancerous.

Today has been hard on me, and hard on the crew. After such a happy day yesterday, morale is again low. They work so hard and are the best people, and when things go wrong they hurt. I'm lucky to have them. Tomorrow we will all head out again with a fresh and optimistic attitude.

The nothingness seems to go on forever.

NOVEMBER 22

Lots of nothingness . . . just like in the movie *The NeverEnding Story*, when the boy loses his ability to dream. I have been angry at the world but I need to get angry at me, so I tell myself, 'Shut up, Pat. Put your head down; do what you came here to do. Be content with what you're doing. This is what you do. So befriend the road and do it.'

To put you in the picture, below is recent email correspondence between Bernie and my South Pole guide, Eric Philips. I asked Bernie to beseech Eric to try to organise a later flight from Punta Arenas to the Antarctic. I've picked up a lot of time, but I still think making it to Punta Arenas by December 29 is beyond me. If only the plane could leave later, allowing me to finish the South American leg, and then fly me out of the South Pole a week or so later than planned, I wouldn't have to consider flying to Punta Arenas from wherever I am in Chile, then backtracking after the South Pole to continue running from where I left off. You'll see how my hopes have been dashed.

From: Bernie Farmer
To: Eric Philips
Hi Eric,
Just a quick update on our progress through Chile. It appears that we will be in Santiago on 10 December.

We are still hopeful that we may be able to pull back more time by going on off-road trails and alternative roads if the opportunity arises. We pulled back three days in Peru and are looking for opportunities here. Eric, ideally we would like to finish this event at the South Pole and not have to return to Argentina for a further week. What are the chances if required that you and the cameraman fly on 29 and if required [the Antarctic organisers] ALE find Pat a seat one week later? I ask this as a contingency as I want to ensure after coming this far that we don't fall at the last hurdle. Would it be okay for me to speak to ALE regarding this, or would you prefer to ask them on my behalf?
Kind regards,
Bernie

From: Eric Philips
To: Bernie Farmer
Hi Bernie,

How are things on the road? What an incredible journey for you all, to experience all those countries. Hope you can get the vans all the way to Punta (and Pat, of course!). I am sure you have pondered Pat's progress to Punta but can you please give some thought and forward planning to ensure his timely arrival in Punta Arenas on December 29 latest. It appears as though he won't be able to run all the way, so will you drive or fly the remainder? If you fly, it's a very busy time of the season for flights into Punta so you will need to book well in advance. If you drive in, then be sure that the route is passable as this cannot always be guaranteed in South America. I look forward to seeing you all in Punta.
Kind regards,
Eric

From: Bernie Farmer
To: Eric Philips
Hi Eric,

We have been running off-road to pull back some time and have had some success so far. Pat's main concern with leaving to go to the pole and come back to run the mainland is that if the flight is delayed, his continuous record is dead. He can't afford one day off. With this in mind, would ALE pick Pat up if he finished early? Also, if weather is a problem, could he get to a point where he could be guaranteed a flight out? This is his main worry with the current departure scenario. We are still looking for every distance saving to make the finish at Punta Arenas. Thanks for your help.
Kind regards,
Bernie

From: Eric Philips
To: Bernie Farmer
Hi Bernie,

Well done with the off-road plan. There is nothing we can do to predict flight delays; it is one of the great (or not so great) unknowns of Antarctica. We hope to stay on schedule but can never know what comes up. In regards to picking Pat up early, if you are referring to him reaching the pole early, no, they won't pick him up because we have paid for a shared flight, not a dedicated flight, which means teams gather at the South Pole until all have arrived and then we are all flown out. This is scheduled for January 26, but if all teams arrive early, and the ALE *Twin Otter* is not tasked for other flights, then, yes, they will come earlier. But bank on the 26th.

In the event of bad weather at Union Glacier, the only point that Pat could be guaranteed a flight out is from the South Pole itself by the Americans. But I think he has been down that path already a couple of times and their answer is usually a resounding 'no'. Besides, they only fly out to New Zealand and then Pat would need to fly back to Punta again or perhaps Puerto Montt.

Good luck with the rest of Chile; let's hope he can get into Punta in time. BTW, ALE have just replied that they will not change our flight date to January 5 because they believe that Pat is already at the absolute limit of completing the Antarctic leg in the time given, and I agree with that.

Kind regards,

Eric

NOVEMBER 24

I woke up the worse for wear today. Last night, running in the gloom, I tripped over some wires that were sticking out of a discarded truck tyre on the road. I crashed down and cut my knees and elbows and was badly shaken up. But I kept running, blood flowing down my arms and legs. I will do anything to finish this run before my flight to Antarctica on December 29. I desperately do not want to have to backtrack to finish up after I reach the South Pole. I know I'm taking chances and damaging my body to make up the time, and I know that getting there on time on foot may be beyond me, but I'm pushing on anyway.

I treated myself to a ten-minute haircut this morning in a little village on the road. I had no intention of stopping for anything, but then I saw the barber's shop and thought I'd give myself a little luxury. There are many media dates ahead, and I want to look as good as possible under the circumstances! I luxuriated in that big leather chair, having my hair washed and cut. I told the hairdresser about Pole to Pole while she was snipping away, and when I tried to pay her at the end she refused to take my money and insisted I accept her gift of a Chile national soccer team T-shirt. Just another instance of kindness on the road.

I am running nearly 130,000 steps per day every day to complete the 90 kilometres per day goal that I set myself after leaving the Darién Gap. My stride has shortened from 1 metre to around 70 centimetres.

NOVEMBER 27

There have been many close shaves on this run: I could easily have died in the Arctic ice; there was the time when Bernie and I narrowly missed death when the out-of-control truck literally flew past our heads; and there were the bandits, flash floods and predators of the Darién. In the past two days, though, I have come closer to dying than I have at any other point. What nearly claimed my life and that of my

The inhospitable desert, where death awaits the foolhardy.

crew member Juan was my ruthless determination to make up time, after reading the emails from Eric saying that the plane would be leaving on the scheduled date, and not a day later.

Two days ago, I decided I would save time by running across the desert again, rather than continuing to run on the Pan-American Highway. By doing so, I would cut off about 40 kilometres. In my desperate state of mind, I reckoned it was worth it. Once again, the vans could not accompany me, because the desert sand is soft and we couldn't risk them getting bogged. So the plan was that I would run across the desert, accompanied only by Juan on the motor scooter carrying water, food and fuel. The vans would travel down the highway but detour at a number of tributary roads that cross the desert. The vehicles would wait for me, Bernie would give me a drink of cold water and something to eat, then meet me again at the next tributary crossing. Bernie and I found the point on our map where the desert met up again with the Pan-American Highway and arranged to rendezvous there finally, late in the evening.

Things began going wrong almost immediately. Juan and I entered the desert without our mobile phones. We simply left them in the vans in our crazy rush to get going. We also failed to check the battery level on our GPS satellite navigation device and didn't check the fuel gauge on the motor scooter. The main contributor to the fiasco that ensued was something out of our control, however. Soon after we'd parted ways, the radiator hose on Bernie's Winnebago blew and the van broke down. The other van took Bernie to try to find a replacement part. Of course, this meant that when we arrived at the first tributary crossing, Bernie wasn't there. With no phone, I couldn't call him.

I decided to press on, hoping to meet Bernie at the next crossing. Of course, he wasn't there either. I cursed him—how could he let me down? I continued on, in a rage. By now, Juan's motor scooter was running low on fuel. We had also depleted our water and food supplies. The temperature was 42 degrees Celsius, all around us was empty desert, and, on the far southern horizon, the direction in which I was running, we could see a mountain range. What should we do? The batteries on the GPS were dead. We were lost. With no phone, we couldn't send a rescue call to Bernie. But we did know that south was the direction in which we should be travelling and that sooner or later we'd reach the Pan-American. The trouble was, with no replenishments along the way,

Juan, who shared my desert ordeal.

we would run out of fuel, water and food before we got there.

Juan and I agreed that he should take his water, turn around and hope to hell he had enough fuel to make it back to the highway at the point we'd left it, then get some fuel and come back with provisions to rescue me. In the meantime, thinking of nothing but making up time and kilometres, I decided to keep running. I took Juan's backpack: in it were 4 litres of water and some snacks.

By nightfall, Juan had not returned. I was down to half a litre of water and a chocolate bar. I reached the mountain range. I could either run around it to meet the highway, a distance of 90 kilometres, or I could go over the top and down the other side to the highway, a mere 75 kilometres. Running out of sustenance, I thought time was of the essence, so I started clambering up the mountain in my way. By the time I made it to the top, my hands were cut and blistered from climbing. I was exhausted, parched and hungry.

This, I knew for certain, had become a matter of life and death. Without liquid I would not survive the night. So I urinated into what remained of my water and sipped the liquid through the night. It tasted bloody awful—bitter and salty—but I didn't care. By midnight the temperature had plunged and I was freezing. I curled up as best I could under my backpack, although it only just covered my legs, and shivered through the night. I didn't sleep.

As I lay there in a crevice on the mountain, I reflected on the dire predicament in which I had found myself, and I had an epiphany. Believing that you are about to die tends to focus your thoughts. I became aware in a blinding flash that this project was not worth perishing for. Not worth it for me, and certainly not worth it for my crew. I have said many times that I would die before quitting, but I knew then that I was no longer prepared to pay the ultimate price to complete this run in the way I had promised. Raising money for the people of the developing world was my aim and my dream, but how could I help them further if I was dead? I loved life too much to risk it, and the prospect of never hugging my children again was unbearable. And there was my crew. I had no idea at this point if Juan had survived the desert. I felt terrible for him. Fair enough if I died, because the run was my gig, but I had a duty of care to the crew to keep them safe and sound. I took another sip of urine and water and prayed for survival.

At first light, I dragged myself to my feet, weakened, parched and dizzy. I now knew what it would be like to die of thirst. I struggled on for 50 kilometres and came to a road just after midday. Thank God. The Pan-American. But it wasn't: it was a minor road. I waited by the roadside under the scorching naked sun, hoping against hope that someone would happen along. After an hour, a truck came. The blokes on board were off to a mine. They responded to my broken Spanish pleas by letting me have a little of their water and food. They told me that the highway was 65 kilometres further on.

Looking for Pat.

Just then the most wonderful sight: a Winnebago approached and pulled up, and in it were Juan and Katie. They had been scouring the back roads for me. I hugged them. I was so glad to see my mates. I was safe and so was Juan. Inside, I showered and then collapsed onto my bunk and ate and drank my fill. They contacted Bernie and Gustavo, who were searching for me too, and they soon arrived in their van.

Juan told me his story. The bike's fuel had run out some kilometres before the highway. Unable to push the bike, he had left it in the desert and staggered back to the vans, badly sunburned and dehydrated. He frequently fell. He had also thought he was going to perish. Finally, he reached the road and waved down a vehicle that took him to a police station. It was two in the morning before he was able to contact Bernie and Gustavo on the police phone. They had repaired the van by then and came to collect him.

We slept there on the mine road last night.

This morning, before setting out again, I called a meeting. I told the crew the conclusions I had reached on the mountain. In future, safety will be everything. We will keep to the main roads, and there can be no more forgotten phones or half-arsed planning. No more recklessly courting danger. I confessed that I had lost touch with reality, that the pressure and exhaustion had blinkered me, and that this had led me to take risks with my own life and with theirs. This run is important, yes, but it's not worth a life. I will continue to bust a gut to finish the South American leg by December 29, but if it is beyond me to do so, I'll run the rest of the way later. I will still be running from pole to pole. I will still have raised money for the Red Cross.

Here we were, all together again. In terms of lessons learned, this has been the most important experience of the event. I take heart in the knowledge that in a few months I'll be home in Australia, and this is making me run all the harder to help those in the world living without clean water in places of poverty, violence and natural disasters.

NOVEMBER 28

Tonight we are 1340 kilometres north of Santiago. I am still shaking at the memory of my near-death experience in the desert. Somehow, the scare has lifted my spirits. I am more determined than ever to finish the run and to finish it in one piece. Run, Pat, run. It seems inevitable

Still shaken after my desert experience.

now that I'll have to backtrack to Chile or Argentina after I reach the South Pole, but I've been in touch with the Red Cross and I'm going to make the last eight days of the run a big media event, get all the newspapers, radio and TV stations to cover the dying days of Pole to Pole. Full speed ahead for Santiago, and Brooke and Dillon, who will arrive there on December 10.

NOVEMBER 29

Last night we camped 2 kilometres from a mountain pass. Just before dawn I got up, had a snack and lots of water, and ran. After I hit the top of the mountain, there was a big and beautiful 42-kilometre downhill stretch. I felt like I had wings. For the first time in a while, I was exhilarated by running.

It has been one of those freakish days when everything goes right. When I started running, in the dark at five o'clock, I looked up and there in the sky was the Southern Cross. It was the first time I'd seen it since I left Australia. I felt suddenly close to home and got a little

Today's run, mostly downhill, was exhilarating.

teary. Then there was the downhill run off the mountain and to the coast, through plains of wildflowers and cacti, and forest where birds were singing. The desert where I nearly died just a couple of days back seemed forever ago.

About 120 kilometres south of the town of Antofagasta, I passed the European Southern Observatory's Paranal Observatory, perched on a red earth mound. It is an awesome sight, and it's no wonder that it cost more than $1 billion to establish. Its main telescope is called, for reasons that are obvious when you see it, the Very Large Telescope.

At the end of the downhill run, I arrived at the town of Paposo, and then, after I'd run 90 kilometres, I found myself in Taltal, an idyllic fishing village with sandy beaches on one side and a high mountain range on the other. We parked for the night in a car park and, it still being light—which has been unheard of since I've been running 90 or 95 kilometres a day—we cruised the town. On the beach, fishermen were pulling fish out of the sea. I had a beer, which tasted very good. I ran strongly today.

DECEMBER 1

A rough, hot day. It began with a 45-kilometre climb into a strong headwind and finished with another 45 kilometres of winding roads, meandering east, west, north and occasionally south, around mountains. Those final 45 kilometres actually represented about 11 kilometres of forward progress. Much of the scenery, now that I'm back on the coast and out of the Atacama desert, is beautiful, but I'm just too buggered and preoccupied by the logistics of the South Pole to pay it much attention.

I don't want it to sound like I'm always whinging, but the fact is that running 90 kilometres every day is a hard and relentless slog, and the further I get towards the end, the more beat-up my body is, and the more difficult it gets. Please don't get me wrong: some days are diamonds. But I'm still fatigued by my day lost in the Atacama desert and night out in the cold. I'm sure that's why I lacked energy and felt dispirited today. That stuff-up in the desert was a terrifying experience. I don't think I'd have survived another day wandering lost in that heat.

We received an email today from a woman who works in the mine

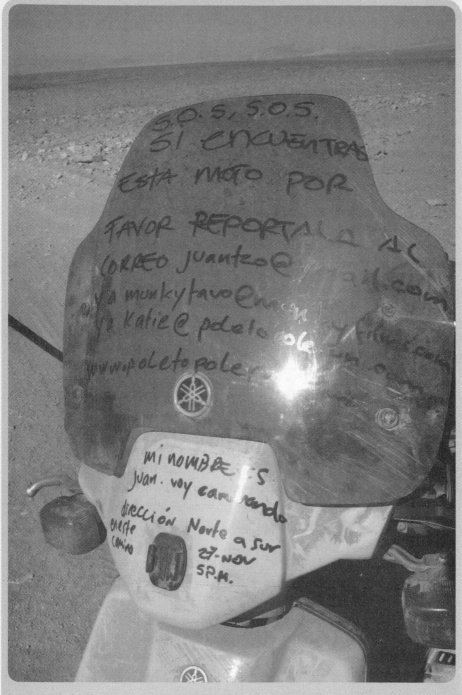

Juan's deserted scooter and his message to whoever found it.

POLE TO POLE

near to where Juan left his bike after it ran out of fuel. He had written his contact details on the windshield, along with an SOS.

The woman had found the bike and wanted to check that Juan was okay. We told her the bike was hers, and we hope she can make good use of it. It's no good to us anymore.

Brooke and Dillon will be here in 10 days. I miss them. I need my kids like I need oxygen. When they come we'll all feel better. They bring with them news of home and school and the world outside. Here on the run it's easy to think that we are the universe—we have to keep it going—and it's good when Brooke and Dillon remind us that we're not. I sometimes allow myself to think that in a little more than two months, God willing, I'll be home. The thought overwhelms me.

I learned today that the Atacama desert, which almost took my life, has soil similar to that found on Mars and in fact has been the setting for some science fiction movies about the Red Planet. NASA also uses it to simulate Mars missions. It was certainly almost *my* final frontier.

DECEMBER 3

Katie put up Christmas decorations in the van today. She is a wonderful crew member: she brings some sanity to my insane world. There's a Santa Claus hanging from the rear-vision mirror, stockings for each of us, a Frosty the Snowman, and some red and gold baubles. Very festive. She bought them in the little coastal town of Chañaral. We are a happy team. The desert experience has brought us all closer together.

I am pleased that the cameraman accompanying me to the Antarctic is Ming. He is also a runner, and he understands me better than most. Although he has not been to the Antarctic before, mentally he is the best person to handle the conditions. He is great to have on the team: nothing is ever too much trouble for him. He runs with me, cooks, cleans up and has done some terrific filming. He is also genuinely interested in the places we pass through and spends time on the internet gathering information and passing it on to us.

We are low on funds. We are waiting for the final cheque from Channel Nine to pay the salaries of the crew. On December 28, we'll sell or ditch the vans. We may get rid of one even sooner, to save money on fuel and maintenance. When I fly to Antarctica, the group will disband. Katie and Bernie will return to Australia with Brooke and Dillon, and Gustavo and Juan to Mexico. I'd like Bernie and Katie to return to be with me for the final running leg to the southern tip of South America in late January, but that will depend on whether I can afford to pay for their airfares back. I may have to hire a car and do the seven- or eight-day run with local Red Cross volunteers. We'll decide all that in the coming weeks. First I have to make it to the South Pole. That will be no mean feat. Many before me have tried and paid the ultimate price.

DECEMBER 4

In the past few days we've passed through some cities and towns—Copiapó, Vallenar, Coquimbo—then worked our way back into the desert. Happily, this desert is not as barren as the others I've run through recently, although there's still a very strong wind blowing, and I have to shield my face from the dust. Here, there are green shrubs, goats, wild donkeys and tiny villages of farm workers and miners. There are copper mines everywhere. The mines are a blessing, because they make serious money for the country, but the way the companies are allowed to dispose of residue, dumping it in the ocean, is a disgrace.

🌐 LUCKY 33

Some 45 kilometres north of Copiapó, in the Atacama desert, was the site of the mining accident of August 5, 2010, when 33 miners and support crew were trapped 700 metres underground after a cave-in. At first no hope was held for the men, and the nation, still recovering from the terrible earthquake and tsunami of five months earlier, was plunged into a new round of mourning. Then, a miracle: after 66 days, one of the exploratory drills returned to the surface with a note attached: 'We are well in the shelter . . . The 33.' After 69 days in the depths of the earth, on October 13 all of the men were rescued. As I looked at the site of the now-abandoned mine, which was closed by the government, I thought what a resilient lot the Chileans are, and I draw strength from them as I run through their country.

There was a real treat when, near the town of Caldera, I came upon some major diggings and learned that this is where the complete skeletons of 75 pre-historic whales, which died between two and seven million years ago, were recently found. The skeletons lay side by side, and what is puzzling palae-ontologists is that they were 800 metres inland. Did they beach themselves on a high tide, or were their remains moved to the present spot by an enormous landslide or earthquake?

The dust is a hazard.

DECEMBER 5

Bernie and Katie are in Santiago, 550 kilometres down the road, organising the logistics of ending the run. Bernie is working out how to dispose of the trucks—hopefully we can sell them; if not we'll give them away—and how to get rid of any other gear we don't need to take home. He's also booking flights and working with Greg on my flight from Punta Arenas to the South Pole. Finally, he's checking out the latest information on the roads in the region. It's a lottery, because some roads that show up on maps no longer exist, while others have snaking twists and turns that take you way off your route.

It's looking like I'll have two weeks' running left when I fly back to Chile from the South Pole, but I understand that one of the routes we'd considered for this leg may be out of the question, because an active volcano has left a lot of ash in the area. It's the same type of ash that prevented all flights around northern Europe and Iceland not long ago.

Eric Philips, my Antarctic guide, has told us that there is a flight from the South Pole back to Chile on January 19, which I can be on if I can get to the South Pole the day before. This is going to mean, given the route Eric has now mapped out for me, running between 50 and 60 kilometres a day for 20 days. Such a feat has never been achieved before, but there have been many firsts on this run. I'll do it. I am so fired up. I have a need to show those who doubted me that I do what I say I will do. So many people laughed when I asked them to support this run.

I also have a point to prove to Eric. At the North Pole, we didn't get on well. I have come to believe that he was a little contemptuous of a bloke like me not only trekking through the Arctic—the whole way, not just the last few kilometres, as many adventurers do—then running more than 20,000 kilometres and, for good measure, ending up at the South Pole. He is a tough man who has no time for dilettantes and must have been doubtful of my ability to achieve this. I don't blame him, though, because he didn't know me well. I hope that when we reunite in the Antarctic we can share a fresh respect for each other, because I have done everything I promised.

As I run, I'm aware that my mind is a bit all over the shop. It's deep fatigue, I suspect. All I think about is finishing this quest and

Basic foodstalls along the road.

being with my kids again. In a way, this intense focus is good, because it means I don't dwell on the logistics. If I did that, I might go mad. I'll leave that for Bernie and Greg. What is weird is that, for no apparent reason, some days I am aching and sluggish, and running my 90 kilometres is a despairing grind, while on other days I fly the distance. No doubt there is a physiological or psychological reason. But I don't have the time or inclination to rationalise it. I just run.

Thinking of food takes my mind off the task at hand. I have heard that Chilean food is excellent, especially the steaks, but I haven't had anything special to eat here yet. The towns we've gone through have been small, and the food available very basic. I am looking forward to reaching Santiago in six or seven days' time and sampling the local delicacies with Brooke and Dillon. I bet Bernie has found time for some hearty meals, despite the fact that he recently, thanks to my Australian dentist friend Tony Collins, who joined us a few weeks back, had some emergency dental surgery on the run to fill three large and infected cavities.

I have to mention that yesterday we entered a road and were hit with an US$18 toll. *Eighteen dollars!* Never again will I moan about paying $3 to cross the Sydney Harbour Bridge.

DECEMBER 7

Bernie has called to say that he is making progress in Santiago and is also checking out some likely Antarctic gear for me. One item I won't have to worry about is my skis. At a Red Cross breakfast on the road a couple of weeks ago, I spoke to a ski company's photo expert, Clemens Stieboeck, who is sending me some special skis with skins attached. He says these are a necessity, because there is a constant incline from the Union Glacier to the South Pole, and the skins give the skis more grip for trekking uphill.

DECEMBER 10

As I ran this evening, a beautiful fat and yellow full moon rose over the mountain range, and its light was so strong I was casting shadows on the road.

I've struggled the last few days. I think what's happening is that

Some days I struggle; others are a breeze.

my body knows it's done nearly 17,500 kilometres and, with roughly 4000 to go, the run is nearing its end, and so it is shutting down and wanting to stop running. This means I have to work my mind overtime, having it impress on my legs and heart that, yes, we've come a long way, but there is still a lot of serious business to be done, keeping up my 90 kilometres a day until it's time to fly to Antarctica, and then running across the ice to the South Pole. The old body could use some physio. I have had only five sessions since the beginning of the run, and the last one was in Colombia, thousands of kilometres ago. Perhaps I can find a masseur to stretch me and loosen my back and legs before flying out to the ice. If I can, it will help to open up my running gait and speed me up.

I left the desert behind two and a half days ago and am passing along the west coast through populated areas now. The roads are increasingly clogged with people and vehicles as I get closer to Santiago. The weather has changed a bit. The last couple of days have been overcast and cool. Stupidly, I was lulled into a false sense of security and I ran all day yesterday without my protective hat and sunglasses.

Why I have been so badly burned here became obvious when I read a newspaper online and discovered that an 11 million square mile hole in the ozone layer over Antarctica is allowing ultraviolet radiation to bombard parts of Chile. In Punta Arenas, where I will be catching a plane to the Antarctic, 120,000 residents had been warned to remain indoors for their own protection. The risk of getting badly sunburned, and contracting skin cancers and cataract damage was so high, the government was warning anyone who had to venture outside to wear sun-block, a wide-brimmed hat, long sleeves and sunglasses.

Of course, I got badly burned and I am paying for it today. My face is an angry red, and my busted lips have become swollen again.

There are a lot of police cars on the road: the police are having a blitz on drunk drivers, just like they do at home. A truck that I've noticed passing me in both directions over the past few days pulled up alongside me this morning. The driver got out and told me, through Gustavo, that he was a haulage carrier and kept driving out of his way to watch me run. I told him why I was running, and this big bloke picked me up in a bear hug and told me that I was an inspiration. I hope Gustavo was telling me the truth, and that he wasn't actually saying that I'm a crazy fool for running from one end of the earth to the other.

The other day I emailed a Christmas video to Robert Tickner, chief executive of the Australian Red Cross, wishing him and the organisation a happy Christmas from the road and giving them an update on my progress. The message pinged on his computer just as he was addressing a conference of 500 Red Cross people. He projected the video onto a big screen and the crowd cheered.

There has been another personnel change. Katie, my niece, has unexpectedly left us to return to Australia. She was meant to be leaving with Bernie at the end of December, but she has departed early. She has been a rock for the entire run. I don't know how we will replace her, even though there is little more than a fortnight to go until I fly to the Antarctic. Katie is the only crew member not to have taken a major break during the run, and she needed to go home to get a few things sorted with her house, family and 'real job' at the gym. She has been loyal, super-efficient and a joy to have around.

Bernie went to collect Brooke and Dillon from the airport today and should be bringing them back up the highway to me. He called at one-thirty to say they had arrived safe and well, and I expected them to get to us by four o'clock, but now it's ten o'clock and there is no sign. My eyes are peeled for every set of headlights in the distance, hoping it's them.

DECEMBER 13

At last the kids are here again. It's funny how having them around makes the road seem shorter and me seem stronger. Remember Popeye and his spinach, well that's the effect Brooke and Dillon have on me.

I'm determined to set the record for the fastest man to cross the ice to the South Pole. I plan to run 65 kilometres a day. The current record was set by a Norwegian who trekked, I'm told, at an average of 18 kilometres a day, although he was alone and unassisted, and had to erect and dismantle his own tent. I'll be accompanied by Eric and Ming. I will happily settle for the assisted record.

DECEMBER 16

Today has been like running in Technicolor, as I've passed through fields of vivid yellow canola and wheat, red and yellow wildflowers, and green rice plantations and vineyards, all under a bright blue sky. Chilean wine is delicious, and I had a chance to sample some last night, the first wine I've sipped since Longyearbyen many, many months ago. We came by the wine when we filmed a live cross with Channel Nine's *Today* show in the parking lot of a general store, off the busy highway. I felt odd using the car park without repaying the owner so asked Bernie to load up on provisions there. The lady who ran the place was so delighted that she pressed two bottles of excellent white wine into Bernie's hands and insisted he accept them with her compliments. We enjoyed her largesse. Chile's wines have won many international awards, and Chile is the fourth highest supplier of wine to the United States. Naturally, with a four o'clock start this morning, I didn't overindulge, but not because I didn't want to. I've

Brooke, my running mate, is back.

gone a long time without wine. I've gone a long time without a lot of things.

Brooke and Dillon have fitted right in, as if they've been with us from the outset. They are willing workers and do anything that's asked of them. This frees up Bernie, Ming and Gustavo. My kids run alongside me for 5-kilometre stretches, and yesterday Brooke ran to catch up with me while carrying a bowl of fresh strawberries, bananas and honey. Maybe not recommended running fuel, but prepared with love. I wolfed it down. Brooke also sings and plays her guitar for us at night, in the short period between when I stop running and fall asleep.

I am now around 300 kilometres south of Santiago, near a town called Parral. Normally I would have stopped in Santiago, Chile's capital, to do media engagements and meet Red Cross officials, maybe have a run with the locals, but I powered right on through in a bid to maintain my 90 to 95 kilometres a day and to get as far as I can before being driven to the airport for a December 29 departure. In fact, I have just learned that we might be flying out a day or two earlier. ALE, the group that is flying us down to Antarctica, is worried by deteriorating conditions near the South Pole and is thinking that the earlier we can get in and out, the better.

I am about to sleep with the crew in a petrol station. I was just talking to a bunch of local men who followed us today. They cheered me on and wanted to be photographed with me. I happily obliged. We don't speak the same language, but with Gustavo as interpreter we all have an idea of what the other is saying . . . more or less! They told us that they come from the nearby cities of Concepción and Chillán, which were close to the epicentre of the massive 8.8-magnitude earthquake and consequent tsunami that devastated Chile, with enormous loss of life and property, in February 2010. It was the sixth-largest earthquake ever recorded and claimed around 550 lives. Some 10 per cent of the population of Chile was left homeless. Roads and bridges were buckled and torn to pieces, and large areas were inundated with water from the tsunami. The fishing industry in the tsunami zone was wiped out. The effects of the quake and tsunami were even felt in the United States and Japan. I've been noticing a lot of road works and bridge repairs in the last day or two, and the men informed me that this was still the mopping-up work after the quake. The road works have been a problem. The white dividing line

Rest stop by the side of the road.

on the highway is often obliterated, so vehicles feel free to use both sides of the road. The construction sites also impede my vision when I run, and I have lost count of the times I've had to jump into a ditch to avoid being hit by a truck that's loomed out of nowhere. The days have been slow, hot and frustrating, with the air filled with dust from the road works. Also, the running area has been too narrow to have anyone from the crew running with me, making for long, boring stretches.

Today I've been thinking again about how close we came to death in the desert. Thankfully, Bernie didn't panic. If he had called the emergency services to search for me, chances are they would have ended the run then and there. He and I have spoken about it since, and he said that if I hadn't turned up within 48 hours he would have considered it. He said, 'I have faith in you, brother.' The near disaster was a significant part of this run, because it changed my thinking. Fatigue and monotony had made us careless—we've tightened up since then.

Eric has arrived in Punta Arenas. He'll be busy organising the food and equipment we'll be taking with us to Antarctica. He said all is going to plan and he's looking forward to the adventure continuing. I've been in touch again with Robert Tickner of the Australian Red Cross, asking him to send me a Red Cross flag that I can raise when I reach the South Pole. It will look great in the photographs.

DECEMBER 18

Christmas has come early. Just when I was beginning to wonder if my run is really making a tangible difference, I received an email today from Bob Tickner telling me that the East Timor project that Pole to Pole has helped to fund is going great guns.

> All materials have been procured, and negotiations with the community have been reached for completion of the project works over the next weeks. Tap stands and storage tanks will go in for January in Com and again in February for the school and health clinics and the schools should have latrines in February as well. In Pato the latrines and well rehabilitation is scheduled for completion in March.

Messages like this make all the aches, all the pain, all the near disasters and the hardships worthwhile.

DECEMBER 19

Today was all about running with Brooke and Dillon and catching up on things in the real world. Their life is school and skateboard parks and basketball hoops, concerts and plays, fun and laughter: exactly what I need to hear about to take my mind off the daily grind of this endless run.

The time has been moving so quickly since my children arrived. They are great company on the road, and I am now up to speed with everything going on back home in Australia. Dillon has excitedly told me about a monster BMX park where he and his mates ride their bikes and skateboards down ramps and into huge pools of soft foam while trying to do tricks, and how he can now drop off the lip into the skateboard bowl at Bondi Beach. He wants to get an old car and do it up with me, just as I did with my dad. Brooke has filled me in on her first

The kids help out around the van.

job, at a cafe in Bronte, and it's good to hear of her dream to do well at school and enter a university course that teaches stage performance and communications. As we run, I tell them all about the places I've seen and the people I've met along the way. I am so blessed to have the support of my family and to have my children here with me in Chile sharing in my run and learning, along with me, that nothing is impossible.

The scenery here is a carbon copy of a part of Canada that I ran through, with rivers flowing from mountains and plantations of pine trees. There are no black bears here, but they do have huge flies whose bites are painful, like Canada's infamous march flies. This is an agricultural area, with citrus trees, corn and grapes being grown. Chile has a population of about 17 million—not many for such a huge country—so the people have plenty of space, and the population is spread out.

Chileans seem to me to be happy with their lives, in stark contrast to the Peruvians. Their homes are more permanent: made of bricks and timber rather than makeshift thatching. The cars are all reasonably new, and the trucks are in good condition. This is great for me, because there are no detached vehicle parts or busted tyres lying on the road ready to trip me up when I run in the dark.

DECEMBER 20

With Karl Stefanovic taking his Christmas break (crewing on a yacht in the Sydney to Hobart classic—some break!), Michael Usher interviewed me for Channel Nine today. There was a chance there would be a live cross on Christmas Day, but this has turned out to be impossible, so we sent our Christmas message today to all those who have followed and supported us since the North Pole.

I am having trouble getting my skis for the South Pole. Apparently they are held up in customs in Santiago. I can't be preoccupied with this stuff; I still have to do all the kilometres. It is frustrating leaving these things to my crew to sort out, though, and then hearing from them the tales of bureaucracy and red tape. I have asked Bernie to ask the Austrade representative in Santiago to get to the bottom of the problem.

The scenery got better and better today. It was a clear, sunny day, and we were surrounded by fields of canola and maze, with their contrasting colours of yellow and green. We had clear views of the Andes, with snow on the tops of the mountains.

Brooke and Dillon made me their trademark plate of pancakes with bananas and strawberries to pump me up at the 50-kilometre mark, and it worked a treat. Food is so important to me, not just because I need the energy but because it stimulates my brain and gives me something else to think about. Those pancakes took my mind back to breakfast in bed on Father's Day, at home in Australia—I'm looking forward to being at home for the next one.

DECEMBER 21

Today I started at five in the morning and finished at five in the evening, early for me. What a spectacular day: clear blue skies, 35 degrees, ever-present snow-capped Andes views, and the great news that my skis have been released from customs and a courier is speeding them to me on the road, in plenty of time for the Antarctic. This is a great result, and I appreciate the support of the Australian ambassadors and Austrade in each country we pass through.

Though the days are hot, the nights are cold. The temperature plummets alarmingly as soon as the sun sets. The chill reminds me of what I'm in for at the Antarctic. I am getting a little scared of the ice and blizzards to come and the prospect of my hands freezing again. My mind turns back to the below-freezing conditions of the North Pole, the strong winds and the torturous pain in my right hand every time I closed it to eat something. Hopefully my body is better prepared now than it was then; if it's not then I'll just have to deal with it anyway.

Each day when I start running I am crippled by pain in my knees and neck. I walk around like a 90-year-old until I warm up, and each day my warm-up period is taking longer. Pain has become my companion on this journey, and it's going to be with me all the way. Sometimes, I've found, it's best to go into things without thinking too much about possible problems. But the end of this event can't come soon enough. I need some recovery time, but that won't happen until I'm back in Australia, a world away.

DECEMBER 22

The weather has turned rainy and chilly. The last time raindrops fell on us was in Colombia, and I haven't needed to run in a jumper since Canada.

More comings and goings in the crew. Bernie returned home today, for good. He wants to have Christmas with his family in Canberra, and he has planned a surprise. Both he and his son Daniel, who lives in New York, will materialise on the family doorstep. I'd like to be a fly on the wall. He has missed Deb, his wife, and his other children so badly, ringing them every single day when the communications have allowed, and I know they have missed him too. Bernie and I had no emotional farewell. He simply walked a couple of kilometres with me this morning, then we said, 'Goodbye, mate. See you in Oz,' shook hands, and he was gone. I know he appreciates the job I'm doing, as I appreciate all his cool-headedness and hard work, which have made this event happen.

The reason Bernie was able to leave is that Katie has returned. She went home for a short while, caught up with her loved ones, and now is back on board. She will go to Buenos Aires with Brooke and Dillon on

December 26, put them on the flight to Sydney, then hang out in the Argentinean capital, relaxing and seeing the sights, before rejoining me for the last leg of the run after I return from the South Pole.

 THE PLAN

Here is the latest plan, ironed out during the past day by Bernie, Eric Philips, ALE and me.

I'll get as far south as I can past the Chilean port town of Puerto Montt before being driven back to it on December 26. The further south I go, the less distance I will have to run when I return.

Eric, Ming and I will fly from Puerto Montt to Punta Arenas, meet Eric, and at eight o'clock in the evening on December 27 we will fly to Union Glacier, on the Heritage Range of the Ellsworth Mountains, on the Antarctic's Ronne Ice Shelf. Departure day was to be December 29, but ALE is insisting we leave early, because the weather is worsening, with temperatures of –22 degrees Celsius (–32 with wind chill factored in), high winds and blizzards. We will camp by the ice shelf landing strip, and I will start running first thing the next morning.

There are two flights out of the South Pole available to us: one on January 19 and the other on January 26. I am aiming to be on the January 19 flight. This means covering the 1100 kilometres from the ice shelf to the pole in 22 days, trekking 50 kilometres every day. People tell me this is impossible. We shall see.

After reaching the pole, we will fly back to Punta Arenas and catch another plane to Puerto Montt. I will head to the exact spot south of Puerto Montt where I stopped running on December 26 and recommence my run from there.

It is around 2500 kilometres from Puerto Montt to Ushuaia in Tierra del Fuego, which is regarded as the bottom of the Americas. Bernie tried to talk me into finishing the pole-to-pole run at the South Pole, but I simply couldn't live with myself if I hadn't covered the entire distance. To have come so far and cut a corner at the end is not my way. So, if all goes to plan, if I can run 80 or 85 kilometres a day during that last leg, the run will end on February 17 or thereabouts.

DECEMBER 24

We rang home today so that Brooke, Dillon and I could Skype our loved ones on Christmas Day Australian time. After Brooke made me a breakfast of pancakes, I ran 70 kilometres during the morning and early afternoon, then we contacted the family. It was overwhelming to see them all. I longed to be there with them. Mum said, 'Get home as soon as you can. Your Christmas pudding will be waiting for you.'

DECEMBER 25

My children and I celebrated mass in a little church along the way. It's strange to think that on Christmas Day 2010 we worshipped in Sydney's great St Mary's Cathedral, where I approached Archbishop George Pell and asked him to pray for me. After mass, we found a cafe in the lovely town of Puerto Varas and had lemon meringue and caramel pie. Despite having to do without ham, pork, seafood and our usual pudding, it was a Christmas feast we will never forget. Brooke and Dillon told me it was one of the best Christmases they had ever had, even though we were all feeling a little sad and nostalgic, missing Lisa, and we knew that time together here is running short for us. But now I must focus. There is too much for me to accomplish before I'll dare to look forward to being back in Australia.

I had no time or money to get presents for the children, so I gave Dillon my watch and enough money to have it engraved when he's home. On the back it will read: 'Make every minute count . . . Love from Dad.' I gave Brooke a little Russian doll handmade by a woman in Longyearbyen. There is supposed to be a series of ever-smaller dolls inside, but this one was empty, so I wrote a note: 'Dear Brooke, I love you, and no matter where I am in the world I am always watching over you.' They presented me with a T-shirt they'd bought in Sydney. The message on the front? 'Life is a highway.'

DECEMBER 26

I said goodbye to Brooke, Dillon, Katie and Gustavo this morning, then flew to Punta Arenas after a day's run. Katie by now will have put my kids on a plane for Sydney. Gustavo has gone home to Mexico. Greg

Lenny and Rex Quail in Punta Arenas with all the gear for the South Pole. *Courtesy of Eric Philips*

Quail met us tonight, with his wife and children. They're here in Punta Arenas to farewell Ming and me as we leave, with Eric, on the ALE flight to Union Glacier tomorrow evening. Greg has arranged to sell a couple of the vans, after, of course, salvaging all the expensive film and broadcast gear out of Ming and Gustavo's vehicle.

I have received hundreds of messages from people wishing me well in the Antarctic: very special Christmas gifts. Of course, in my replies I put on a brave face, but to be honest I am scared about being back on the ice. For fear that my mind and body will relax too soon, I have been willing myself not to see the Antarctic as the final leg simply there for the taking. Recalling the ordeal of the Arctic quickly disabuses me of that notion. Thoughts of facing –40 temperatures, roaring winds and blizzards bring back memories of the terrible conditions on the Arctic leg of my run, and the pain I experienced when I was frostbitten. In some ways, the Antarctic leg is more daunting, because, unlike when I was preparing for the North Pole, this time I know exactly what I am in for. This is going to be hard, and I am by no means certain of finishing. A bitter feeling it would be to fall at the final hurdle after coming so far.

My feet and toes are, quite literally, a bloody mess, the skin shredded and blistered, covered in bleeding sores. My damned right knee is hurting. That said, I am physically and mentally strong, as strong as at any time on the run. It has been a trek, and I am looking forward to it ending. It will be bliss to use a toilet in a bathroom instead of having to huddle under a bush on the roadside. I have to banish negativity from my mind and keep pressing on, putting one foot in front of the other until I prevail. That philosophy has seen me through so far.

Back in Australia, I've learned, not as many people as I'd hoped know that I'm doing this event. That is a worry in terms of donations, but that aside I'm not concerned. More and more, this 21,000-kilometre run has been about me doing what I said I would do: run from the top of the earth to the bottom and make as much money for the Red Cross as I can. In a few weeks I will have done that. A wonderful by-product is that I am a changed man. I know now that I am once again the man I was before I embarked on my political career and a quest for material things, which changed me from the simple bloke with whom Lisa fell in love. Once again I can appreciate beauty and family and friendship and, like Louis Armstrong sang, what a wonderful world this is.

DECEMBER 28
• •

We're still in Punta Arenas. Today, the wind has been blowing at 100 kilometres per hour. It's as cold as charity, and I am a five-hour flight away from the polar ice shelf. Just like we did at the North Pole, we have encountered bad-weather delays here. The strong winds grounded us last night and all of today, and Eric, Ming and I will not take off until tomorrow. So most of the day has been taken up with going through the clothing and supplies. It's important nothing is left to chance. But Eric is very organised, and although he has travelled this route dozens of times, he checks, double-checks and triple-checks everything.

I did another live cross to Channel Nine, and viewers were able to see how bad the weather is. I explained how the conditions have forced me to run the South Pole leg before I finished completely with the mainland. When I think of all the unnecessary pressure I put on myself trying to make a deadline that was already predetermined by Mother Nature to be impossible, I could cry. Everyone else just cares about whether I complete the journey or not, and fair enough. I would have preferred to have finished the run sequentially instead of back-tracking, but what can you do?

The bad weather has been my wake-up call, a reminder of what I have taken on. I'm a little scared: there is a lot of concern over whether I can finish this leg, and, if I can, much expectation over what time I may be able to achieve—quite frankly I could do without the pressure. Everyone is talking about polar records, which of course would translate into dollars and cents for tour operators in the form of advertisement of the region. ALE are the main players in Antarctica and are into adventure promotion in a big way. At the planning meeting at ALE headquarters, things were changed at the last moment. The staffers here are hungry to see me set a new record for running to the South Pole so want to leave nothing to chance, and this means that, instead of disembarking the plane and then kicking off at Hercules Inlet some 58 kilometres further south of Union Glacier, I will start from the moment we land at Union Glacier. This will add an extra 58 kilometres, which is a pain, but it means that there will be no disputes when I finish over whether I have run from the very north of Antarctica. I certainly won't be going back to have another shot; I will do it once and do it properly.

The hotel foyer here has been filled with adventurers, people from all walks of life, with all sorts of abilities. No matter what language they speak or what country they come from—China, Russia, America, Norway or Australia—they all share the same spirit: the desire to squeeze more out of this life than the average, to push the limits, to leave the office behind and get back to the roots of existence, to a place where cunning, strength and basic survival instincts are the tools of trade rather than a computer and phone.

Punta Arenas looks and feels very European, with beautiful little shops cluttered with handmade toys, clothing and furniture. It sits on the Straits of Magellan and has a thriving restaurant and cafe culture. Greg Quail and his family joined us again for dinner this evening, and it reminded me of the period just before the start of the run, when we were all together in New York. I have had my criticisms of Greg, of everyone in fact, but they have done nothing but try to make my dream become reality. Happily, not least because of my near-death experience in the desert, I have lost my stubborn, pig-headed attitude. I have been humbled by this earth and all it has thrown at me.

Above: Flight to a white hell: The Ilyushan Il-76 cargo plane that delivered me to Union Glacier.

Below: While we waited for the six-wheel drive to arrive, I was happy to run alongside the skidoo.

Above: The Antarctic's changeable weather produced some amazing skies.

Below: The ALE's monster six-wheel drive proved more hindrance than help.

Above: My 'gorilla suit' gear and a cup of something hot every 10 kilometres kept me going.

Below: One of the hardest daily tasks was exiting my sleeping bag.

Above: Footsteps—I've made a few.

Right: A welcome rest break.

Below: In the Antarctic ice I felt like an alien—and looked like one.

Above: Antarctica's breathtakingly beautiful—and deadly—landscape.

Below: The beautiful sastrugi—ethereal ice sculptures created by the wind.

Above: Ming, the gallant photographer.

Left: I much prefer running in shorts and a T-shirt.

Below: Scotty made an ice sign to celebrate Brooke's birthday.

Above: Running through the aftermath of a blizzard.

Right: My goal is almost in sight.

Below: Nearly there! The South Pole station lies ahead.

Above: The South Pole at last. I reach the summit of my dreams at the bottom of the world.

Left: There's still a way to go before I can head for Sydney.

🌐 CHRISTMAS MESSAGES

Christmas Facebook messages to me have been as much appreciated as presents under the tree. Here's a sample:

Merry Christmas to you and your crew and family. We think and talk about you every day. My son just asked yesterday if we could be in the south pole when you got there. We love you all so much and wish you the best blessings.

Go Pat go, what a wonderful effort!!! Merry Christmas to you and your crew!!!!

Thinking of you, Bernie, Brooke, Dillon, Katie and all the crew. You are our inspiration and our rock . . . when things get tough we turn to Pat Farmer and [are] shown that nothing is impossible and nothing is out of reach for a willing mind. You do it all with service in your heart and for the greater good of others. We love you and can't wait to see you! Merry Christmas mate and our love.

Pat it is fantastic to see you looking and sounding so well [on TV] after the year you have put yourself through. Clearly your team has done an excellent job and kept your spirits high. Good luck with the rest of Chile and Antarctica.

Wonderful to see you with your beautiful children Pat. Sooo proud of you. Unfortunately there is no coverage on Dutch TV for your spectacular run yet. I'll keep sending them your link.

Amazing. You are an amazing human being Pat. Utterly amazing.

It was lovely to see you and the kids on *Today* this morning. I love that you can now see Light at the End of the Tunnel (The South Pole).

Hey Pat, still following your amazing trek and sending my thoughts and prayers your way. Any chance of giving us a rough idea how many miles you are behind now and how many stand between you and the South Pole? Would like to count down the miles with you. Also, will your communications be affected during the South Pole leg? Will be thinking of you and your crew and family and friends at Christmas. God couldn't be here to give clean water to the underprivileged . . . so he sent Pat Farmer!

STAGE 6
ANTARCTICA

··

December 29 to January 21

🌐 **DISTANCE TO COVER:** Officially around 1100 kilometres, but as much as 100 kilometres extra due to detours around mountains and crevasses

🌐 **TERRAIN:** Ice with sastrugi

🌐 **TYPICAL WEATHER CONDITIONS:** Temperatures of sometimes lower than −40 degrees, ferocious winds and blizzards

🌐 **HAZARDS:** The cold and wind, crevasses, mechanical issues with the vehicle

🌐 **KEY EQUIPMENT:** Polar clothing—long, thick woollen socks, merino wool underpants and thermal undergarments; fleece pants and top; light-down under jacket; outer jacket, balaclava, face mask, goggles and hood with fur ruff; skin-tight gloves, mitts and hand warmers; boots and boot covers

🌐 **PERSONNEL:** Polar guide Eric Philips, cameraman Ming d'Arcy, and driver and mechanic Scotty

DECEMBER 29

I am in the Antarctic: it's time to face the music.

We flew out of Punta Arenas in a Russian-built Ilyushan Il-76 cargo plane piloted by a Russian crew. It's the perfect machine for polar regions: it has plenty of cargo room—it can even fit vehicles on board—and the power for short take-offs. The pilot came down to my seat and introduced himself, then said, 'Welcome, Mr Patrick, to my plane. I would be honoured if you and I could have a photo.' I grabbed Ming, our cameraman, and the two of us went up to the cockpit to check out the view from there.

Arriving at Union Glacier.

By the time we landed on the blue ice runway at the ALE camp near Union Glacier tonight, I had realised that my worries that Eric did not respect me were baseless. He believes in me and has promised to do everything in his power to get me to the South Pole safe, sound and as quickly as possible. It is now entirely up to me to show the world what I'm made of and reach the South Pole in time to catch that plane out on January 19. (Eric thinks January 26 is more likely, which I must talk to him about.)

After we landed, true to my word, I started running as soon as I reached the bottom of the steps and put my bags down. It was an easy 8 kilometres to the main Union Glacier base. There, we met our driver, Scotty, who informed us that our support vehicle wouldn't be ready until the day after tomorrow. So, after all the concerns about using ski-doos, we'll have to manage with them for a while.

DECEMBER 30

I was able to clock up 70 kilometres by the end of my first full day. Just outside the Union Glacier camp there were lots of crevasses, which meant that for the first 30 kilometres I had to use snowshoes or skis to give me a greater surface area on the snow and less chance of falling into a crevasse. After that, it was strictly my new snow boots all the way. I would never normally run in new footwear, but there is nothing normal about this run!

The weather has been reasonably fine so far, with good visibility. I need to get my big kilometres in before the weather turns sour. One thing this run has taught me is that things can and will inevitably change, for better or for worse, so it's important to make the most of good situations.

The snow is very soft, and although I am light I'm still sinking into it with each step, which makes progress a struggle. The temperature is around –33, but this quickly drops to –40 or lower when the wind increases. Unlike at the North Pole, I have hand warmers in my mittens, which are staving off the aching cold in my fingers.

The major difference between the Arctic and the Antarctic is that down here there are no leads or pressure ridges impeding the way. There are, however, lots of crevasses. Fall down one of those and you're dead. The great Antarctic explorer Douglas Mawson lost his companion Belgrave Ninnis to a crevasse, along with a dog team and fully laden sled, in 1912. One moment they were travelling behind Mawson, the next they had disappeared. Mawson, who himself narrowly missed death when he fell into a crevasse and his sledge wedged into the ice and stopped his fall, never saw them again.

Eric is adamant that we won't be flying out until January 26. I've told him I plan to be there to raise the Red Cross flag on January 19. He's sceptical, but he has learned that I usually do what I say I will.

DECEMBER 31

I woke at 4.48 am still dressed from last night. (The use of the word 'night' is not strictly correct, as the sun shines here for 24 hours a day. We have remained on Chile time.) I had a quick stretch, put my bib and brace overalls on and took off down the designated track used by scientists and explorers that leads to the South Pole. Ming and Eric had their breakfast, packed up the camp, then jumped on their ski-doos to rendezvous with me later on the ice.

The snow seems to have a different structure here from at the Arctic where I found the ice shifting and giving way beneath me. It's more solid and like large raw sugar crystals and reflects the light like diamonds. There have been periods when it has been knee-deep. Mostly, though, the ice surface is like sand—gritty and crunchy underfoot—and it's as though I'm running on a beach. I've run through the deserts of Central and South America, and now this place is like a desert, too, with no flora or fauna, but instead of roasting heat there's freezing cold. I've had to modify my running style to accommodate the new conditions. My low-cut snow boots are keeping my battered feet warm and the ice out. My feet are torturing me, but my bad knee is holding up okay so far.

It is easy to get snow blindness here, but, as I'm without a powerful filter on my goggles, I'm finding it difficult to tell the difference between hills and holes. Also, my nose and mouth pieces are icing up more quickly than they did at the North Pole. I must be breathing more heavily here. After all, at the North Pole if I ran 20 kilometres it was an outstanding day; here, I'm running 70 kilometres per day at an ever-increasing altitude. The air will become thinner and thinner, and it will become increasingly difficult to breathe and more difficult to maintain this pace, which is why I have to push hard while I can.

There are no cars here to contend with, no fear of crossing a white line and being hit by a tired driver. My enemy here is the wind. It whistles and roars and makes me think I'm hearing voices. I have to lower my head and focus on putting one step in front of the other, only occasionally looking up, as I get nearer to a food break. Eric and Ming are giving me food and drink every 10 kilometres, but it's more difficult to eat and run here than on the mainland. I am reluctant to take my hands out of my mittens to eat, because they freeze within minutes. I'm eating chicken soup, chocolate (*lots* of chocolate), cheese and butter in hot water, oats in hot water . . . in fact, *everything* comes in hot water. Thank God for the thermos. Food breaks are my only luxury here. I am sustained by the prospect of getting some chalky butter or cheese to chew on. I am in a world of my own: all I have are my thoughts, and my mind drifts back to my childhood, playing backyard footy and cricket. It helps to block out the white noise that is currently my world.

The mittens are enormous but essential.

Ming, Eric and Scotty—who has joined us at last in the six-wheel drive truck—were not happy about the midnight finish today.

This is the quietest and most lonely New Year's Eve of my life.

JANUARY 1, 2012

My New Year's resolution is to exercise less.

I've completed my third full day of running in the Antarctic. My aim is to cover 60 or 70 kilometres a day, and today I have again run 70. This is the fastest that anyone has ever travelled on foot in the

Antarctic. I'm running for 16 hours a day, and I am buggered when I stop. I won't be able to maintain this pace until the end of the run to the South Pole. But if I can run 60 or 70 kilometres for the next few days, it will put me ahead of schedule and give me the leeway to slow up a bit or cope with the terrible weather we have been told to expect as we near the pole.

Tonight, the ground as far as I can see in any direction is white, and the sky is white, and the horizon line, separating the two, is a red-yellow rim. It's magic.

JANUARY 2

From the start of the day there was an icy headwind, and it has been relentless. It seems to cut all the way to my soul. I am covered in icicles, slowly becoming encased in ice. We regularly have to deviate to avoid the crevasse fields—vast areas where there are small and large crevasses covered with thin snow and ice. ALE recently lost a tractor down a deep crevasse, and it will cost them millions to try to recover it.

The six-wheel drive with all our gear finally arrives.

Fortunately, they were able to save the driver. Because I said no to skis and insisted on running this leg, Scotty, our support driver, refuses to deviate from the marked waypoints on the six-wheel drive's GPS. Skis would have given me a bigger surface area and less chance of punching through the ice. Consequently, to cover 70 kilometres a day of the distance to the pole, I actually have to run closer to 80 kilometres. A 1.30 am finish.

JANUARY 3

I purposely slept in this morning, as the wind was blowing in excess of 100 kilometres an hour. Somehow, though, I still did my 70 kilometres; I finished at two in the morning. It has been a tough day.

As I ran from Canada through the United States, and Central and South America, I passed literally thousands of little monuments by the roadside commemorating the lives of those who had been killed there. I said a prayer every time I encountered a cross or pile of stones and felt an affinity with my fellow travellers. Now I'm in the Antarctic, I can feel the spirit of the great explorers Douglas Mawson, Robert Falcon Scott and Roald Amundsen and their gallant teams, who risked, and in some cases lost, their lives exploring this dangerous and remote icy realm. As I experience the same cold, the pain, the sense of being overwhelmed by unimaginably huge expanses of ice, I feel at one with them, without ever daring to compare myself to those brave souls. I've said a prayer for those long-gone heroes, too.

I continue to make excellent time, despite today's blizzard-like conditions. For the fifth day in a row, I have completed 70 kilometres. In a few days I will be able to decrease that figure to 50 kilometres and, barring disaster, make it to the South Pole by January 17, the 100th anniversary of Scott's arrival there, which will see me on the January 19 flight back to Chile. Running fewer kilometres will allow me to sleep longer and recover more effectively.

But I have too much respect for the Antarctic to believe there will not be mishaps and challenges that could threaten my plan. Looming to the west are enormous black clouds that promise a blizzard tomorrow. It's a fact, too, that it will get colder and windier the closer to the pole I get. As I write this, it is −30 degrees, and the wind is pounding my face. At times in the past couple of days the wind-chill factor has seen

A 10-kilometre food break.

POLE TO POLE

the temperature fall to −40. It is so bloody cold. Despite the state-of-the-art polar clothing I'm wearing, every piece of me is freezing.

Eric has been wonderful. In the Arctic we were at loggerheads, because he had my safety at heart while I was preoccupied with travelling as far and as quickly as I could each day. He thought I was foolhardy and headstrong, and I admit that I was. Back then, I had so far to go I wanted to get off to the best possible start. Eric was sceptical when I told him I would run 70 kilometres a day here in the Antarctic and be at the South Pole by January 19. He told me I was foolish to think I could cover such a distance so quickly. Now I am doing it every day he believes in me. He respects me. Every 10 kilometres, when I pull off the icy track for a 'pit stop', Eric is waiting to feed me and give me water, take off my boots for a few blissful minutes, adjust my zippers and flaps to make sure the cold stays out, and then send me on my way. I could not have a better man in my corner than Eric Philips, polar guide extraordinaire. Ming is doing brilliantly, too. He is taking great footage and lots of photographs.

Around us is a vast white ocean of ice whipped with sastrugi— wind-formed confections of ice left after the softer snow has been blown away. I've seen a formation that resembles the Batmobile, one like a Sydney Harbour hydrofoil and another like a whale. The sky is blue with streaks of vivid orange sunlit clouds. Ahead of us, to the south, the bright white ground slopes upwards. The South Pole is around 2800 metres above sea level, and since I left the Union Glacier five days ago it has been a steady climb.

JANUARY 4

This might be my last 70-kilometre day as long as the weather doesn't get too bad and I find myself having to play catch-up. From now on I can do 50 kilometres a day and still make the South Pole by January 17 or 18. It's getting colder as we climb towards the pole. The altitude is starting to be noticeable.

JANUARY 5

Those terrifying black clouds that were coming in from the west arrived today and brought with them a monster blizzard. Yesterday I was running well, making reasonable progress into a southerly gale, and the sky was blue. Today, the clouds were upon me and I was engulfed in driving snow. I have never experienced snow like it. I could hardly see a couple of metres in front of me. I had Scotty take the six-wheel drive a little way ahead to flatten out the track so I could run on it, and Eric on a skidoo was behind it, dragging a red sled that I could just about see and follow. I prayed I would not fall into a crevasse. I was worried that Scotty would refuse to drive in the blizzard, because it was definitely dangerous, but, thank God, he toughed it out. Tonight I have an even greater appreciation of what Scott and Mawson endured.

The blizzard passed after a few hours, and suddenly the sky was blue again. They say it's never brighter than when you emerge from the darkness, and it's true.

I made 60 kilometres for the day, despite it being –20 degrees. If I can maintain 60 or even 50 kilometres a day for the next ten days, I will finish this sector in 18 or 19 days, which will blow away the old record of 24 days, 1 hour and 13 minutes for getting from Union Glacier to the South Pole, although, as I've said, the existing record was set by a lone

Eric on the skidoo drags the red sled that guides the way.

skier, Norwegian Christian Eide, in January 2011, and my attempt is assisted. More than setting a record, though, I just want to get the hell out of here and back to the mainland as quickly as possible, because the sooner I do that, the sooner I will be back home in Australia.

I ran through a section today where yesterday's massive snow dump made running on the track like negotiating wet cement, and in other places it was an ice rink. I slipped and fell many times. I've avoided frostbite so far, because I'm trying not to expose my skin to the cold. I'm cocooned in my gear and resemble a big blue mummy. Nevertheless, icicles form on my face, and when I blow my nose blood flows out, because the snow and ice that get in and harden there cut the membrane lining. My right knee is now giving me tremendous grief.

Sometimes the only thing that can alleviate my pain is to run out of sight and sound of my crew and stand on the ice and scream. Scream at the top of my lungs. Once I have released the anguish from my body I run on. I am not ashamed to admit this.

Running in the Arctic has definitely helped me down here. My experience there has conditioned me to the extremes I'm facing and has made me understand that the pain, the numbness and the fatigue will eventually go away.

I cannot praise Eric enough. He is tremendous. He is supporting me in every way. I appreciate his kind and gentle manner, which has helped me to keep my own emotions under control.

Eric, Ming and I sleep in a tent, and Scotty sleeps in the vehicle. All of us are doing our jobs well and combining as a team, and, importantly, our spirits are high, while we are not underestimating the enormous task that I still must undertake.

JANUARY 6

Today began cold and black. My alarm went off at five o'clock and I went outside to find that it seemed darker, colder and even more depressing than before. My boots were still cold and my feet ached, and I hadn't even started. Eric heard me poking around before I left and insisted on making me a cup of tea first. I think he could see I was upset, and as I left he gave me a pat on the back and said, 'Good on you, mate. I'm proud of you.' I ran for about 500 metres but then broke down and cried. My tears froze to my goggles and face mask, and my eyelids were stuck together. I pulled them apart, pulled myself together and struggled on for the next 10 kilometres, until Eric, Ming and Scotty caught me up after packing the tents and gear. Eric had some hot porridge for me, and it helped enormously. By the 30-kilometre mark the sun had started to shine through the clouds, and my spirits lifted. Another 60 kilometres down.

JANUARY 7

Today I passed the halfway point between Union Glacier and the South Pole—only 550 kilometres to go, and then this will all be a memory. I guess you could say I'm on the downhill run, even though I'm running uphill! The weather was beautiful, with clear visibility.

During the course of this run, particularly in the extreme cold of the Arctic and when I was lost in the Peruvian desert, there have been moments when I have pondered dying. Equally, there have been times when I have felt total joy and euphoria, especially when I have received

Doing it tough.

the support of the folk along the way, often people living a hard life and having few material possessions. Even before this run started, when I went to East Timor and saw the locals dying because they had no clean water . . . well, you can't do or see what I have without being changed. Today, I am a man whose life has changed dramatically, and it has changed forever. I've always had compassion, but I am a far more compassionate person today than I have ever been. I have promised myself that I will dedicate the rest of my life to doing whatever I can to help those who are less fortunate. To do anything else would be to waste this amazing experience.

Today Eric filed a report of our progress to an explorers' website. In part, he wrote:

> In all my years as a wilderness educator and polar guide, I have never met anybody with the physical and mental resilience that Pat draws on daily and I regard him as one of the world's greatest endurance athletes.
>
> Sitting next to Scotty in the van, both tapping on computers, with Ming 5 km in arrears on the skidoo, Pat pounding the ice behind, I stare through the windscreen towards the white austere southern horizon and contemplate the second, and most exacting, half of Pat's run to the South Pole.

JANUARY 8

There were some distractions today—people! Six kite skiers came towards us from the direction of the South Pole and asked if I was 'the runner'. Among them was Christian Eide, the current record holder for the fastest unassisted man on foot to the pole. He was leading a group of fellow Norwegians, skiing and kiting to commemorate the feat of their countryman Amundsen a century ago. We shook hands and wished each other well, though I'm sure I saw Christian tense up when I told him I planned to eclipse his record, despite being assisted. Felicity Aston from the United Kingdom also passed by, following her 59-day ski from Hercules Station to the South Pole, which made her the first woman ever to make a solo trek to the pole. What special people they are.

Eric cooked bacon for dinner and, wow, it tasted great. I have a ravenous appetite and would be pleased with anything, but it's wonderful to have a change from the freeze-dried dinners.

People have contacted me to ask how I deal with the isolation, the lack of people apart from my crew. I've never been one for big crowds, and I don't really enjoy running in cities clogged with people and traffic: I feel I have to live up to their expectations. But in the polar regions or the desert, I've found that I have to be true only to myself. I enjoy being alone with my thoughts, mulling over problems and making plans. I've been doing that a lot here in Antarctica, probably the most remote and isolated place on earth.

JANUARY 9

My feet hurt as I squeezed them into my boots this morning. My toes are a mess; they feel like they have been through a mincer. I took one step, and the pain nearly made me jump through the tent roof. How am I going to cope with another eight days of this? All I can do is focus on something else, something completely different from what I'm doing now, and concentrate so hard that there's no room in my mind for pain. For a while, I thought about Dillon playing basketball and Brooke singing at school, and it helped.

JANUARY 10

The two things that were supposed to help me the most—the vehicle and its driver, Scotty, whose devotion, I suppose understandably, to safety first at all costs—are becoming the biggest hindrances. I woke at quarter to five, dressed as usual, went out of the tent at five and started to run, only to be stopped by Scotty claiming that there was thick fog and there was a possibility that the vehicle could fall down a crevasse. He said it would be too hard for him to see the trail. So it seems that the six-wheel drive vehicle that is supposed to be able to go anywhere can now go only on a designated trail. It has GPS, and the South Pole is easy to find, but Scotty said it wasn't in his contract to go off the trail, and so I had to wait for hours for the fog to clear. I have since learned that there will be another late start tomorrow—at eight o'clock—because Scotty says he won't start before then.

The vehicle also broke down today: the air-pressurised suspension

The van is crammed to the brim.

stabilisers packed up. In fact, it keeps breaking down. I'm only as fast as the slowest member of the team, and lately the slowest member has been this incredibly expensive truck. At one point the alternator broke, and Scotty had to repair it because the spare we had was the wrong size. And, while I'm having a whinge about the vehicle, there's no room in it. It was supposed to be an emergency shelter, but the back half is taken up with a floor-to-roof fuel tank, and there is room in the back only for Ming's computer and gear, with Eric and Scotty in the front. Added to these problems, it was two days late arriving. It's not my favourite piece of equipment in the world. For the first couple of days before the truck caught up with us we travelled with skidoos, and they were great.

There is no wildlife down here, at least, not on the track I'm taking. Having said that, though, I did encounter some wildlife in the form of Cas and Jonesy. Soon after I finally set out today I saw coming towards me from the south two trekkers who turned out to be the Australians James Castrission and Justin Jones, young adventurers skiing unassisted from Union Glacier to the South Pole and back again to raise funds for You Can, which builds cancer centres across Australia. Our paths crossed at the start of my run, in the Arctic, when we were all training for the challenges ahead. When we recognised each other, our faces lit up. It's said that no matter where you go in this world you'll run into an Aussie, and I guess that's true. Before we went our separate ways, we reminisced about the delights of meat pies and beer, and promised to catch up back home and experience those delicacies rather than just talk about them.

Things went pear-shaped again soon afterwards. All day there had been no wind, and as a result a thick fog settled, reducing visibility to 20 metres. Scotty said it was too unsafe to drive the vehicle in these conditions in a known crevasse field. He was scared he would get bogged or fall into a crevasse. Look, I understood and sympathised with what he was saying, but that didn't stop it being bloody frustrating. Because of the delays, I have to make 55 kilometres a day from now on to be at the South Pole by January 17 or 18 at the latest. For three endless hours until the fog lifted I sat cooling my heels, not knowing how long I'd be held up for. I called a meeting and pointed out to Scotty that a nine-to-five mentality is out of place on this run. The sole reason for us being here is for me to get to the South Pole in the fastest possible time. I don't work eight-hour days; I run for 12, 14, maybe 16 hours, and my team stays with me—whatever it takes to get the distance done. I told him that unless we are in huge danger, which I conceded we could have been in this morning if we'd set out in the fog, we have to keep going. Eric backed me up. It was a hard conversation but one that had to happen. Scotty took what I said onboard, and we started up again. We finally stopped at 2 am.

JANUARY 11

Just when I thought it couldn't get any colder, today strong south-easterly winds and bleak grey skies saw the temperature hit −45 degrees with the wind-chill factor. Both Eric and Scotty are now refusing to work such long hours and have said I must be finished running by ten in the evening, or they will pull the plug. Eric is worried that overtiredness could cause errors. We're also still having late starts because of bad weather. But I must rely on the others. I can't wait to finish the South Pole leg. I hate it here.

With all the gear on, it's difficult to move, let alone run.

JANUARY 12

I'm losing a lot of weight. My body is literally consuming itself to cope with the energy I'm expending through running and trying to keep warm, because I simply cannot ingest the 8000 calories a day required to maintain myself in these conditions. My clothing feels heavier the weaker I get; it's like running in a gorilla suit and army boots. My lips have split open again and bleed constantly. Today was the coldest it's been down here without the wind-chill factor—about –40 degrees. My clothes are not thawing at night, and I'm starting each day with ice in the ruff of my jacket and my pants. I sleep with my gloves and socks on to keep them dry. My only sanctuary from the cold is in my sleeping bag.

Despite the conditions, this place is indescribably beautiful. Sometimes I think it's like running on a solid sea with frozen white caps, and at others like traversing a giant lemon meringue pie with wispy peaks of ice and snow. Then, in a flash, a blizzard or fog can descend and things turn sinister. When in years to come people ask me what the Antarctic is like, I'll tell them it's beautiful and it's deadly.

JANUARY 13

Today after a late start I took the wrong trail during a blizzard and hit a crevasse field. I had to detour around it to find a different track. Eric tells me it's more likely a runner will go through ice than a vehicle. We are now at 2450 metres above sea level and the ice formations are getting bigger. I'm scared that bad weather might end the run. I have never experienced conditions as vicious as these.

I used some visualisation techniques to see myself arriving at the South Pole just a few days from now. All that can stop me is the weather, a crevasse or my failing body. I find myself wondering if, for all my longing to be at home, I will be able to fit in there after what I have endured on this epic run. Today was a bad day—only 35 kilometres.

JANUARY 14

It is becoming hard to write, because I am losing the use of my thumbs. I am seriously concerned that I have done permanent damage to my

The ice is sculpted by the wind into amazing shapes.

fingers and toes, they hurt so badly. I tell myself that quitting would cause much greater pain that would last a lifetime, so I put that thought out of my mind.

Last night I had a dream, probably inspired by the weird shapes of the sastrugi. I dreamed that a great white whale, just like Moby-Dick, came lunging at me out of the ice. I was terrified that it was going to harm me, but instead it led me to safety.

The altitude now is over 2600 metres, and it is hard to breathe. With that and the driving wind and snow, I am averaging a desperately slow pace. The heavy, powdery snow is sapping my energy. With some steps I sink in it down to my knees then have to drag my leg out to take another step. I'm not the only one struggling: the bloody vehicle keeps getting bogged.

I've been thinking of home and of Brooke's approaching birthday, figuring out a way to send her something to remind her of how much I love her.

JANUARY 15

I am now within striking distance of the South Pole—after today's good run of 60 kilometres, there are just 145 kilometres to go. I'm fading, but so is the vehicle. Sometimes I think this is a race between me and the machine, to see who breaks down first. Put your money on me coming in ahead. I have to confess the truck *looks* better than I do—I have ice caking my hair and eyebrows and snot-icicles hanging from my nose. At least there was no wind today.

I can see the horizon from end to end and discern the curve of the earth. To reach the support vehicle 10 kilometres ahead I have to run to the horizon twice. I really am at the pointy end of the planet. I saw a rainbow in the distance today, near the pole, caused by the sun shining through the falling snow. It's beautiful, ravishingly beautiful, but the going is too hard now for me to take much solace in the beauty.

JANUARY 16

The will remains strong, but the amount of energy I need simply to survive is beyond what is left in my brutalised body. I don't know how, but I am still moving. I am like the walking dead, oblivious to anything or anyone around me. I am focused on the snowflakes on the ground and the line that is left in the snow by the skidoo up ahead. I am mesmerised by that track.

I ran 60 kilometres today. The truck broke down again. Just 85 kilometres to go.

JANUARY 17

I am aiming to reach the pole in the mid-afternoon tomorrow, because I have media commitments with the Nine Network, and they are adamant that I am to go to air live on the *Today* show at 7 am, which is about 3 pm here. The media is absolutely critical if I am to raise the needed funds for the Red Cross. If I can somehow impart to viewers how hard I'm doing it, perhaps they will be inclined to donate.

Scott arrived at the pole 100 years ago today. I won't get there till tomorrow—it's been slow going and I've only made 50 kilometres today.

JANUARY 18

I am at the South Pole. I have survived, and what's more, set a new record for running with assistance from Union Glacier to the Pole: 20 days, 9 hours and 2 minutes.

Today is the day I have been looking forward to since I started running back in early April, at the North Pole. I have dreamed of reaching the South Pole for so long, and at the start of the day it was within my grasp. I'll forgive you for thinking that adrenalin would have allowed me to float the last 35 kilometres to the pole or maybe enabled me to turn on a sprint to get it over and done with, so I could break out the champagne and celebrate, but those things did not happen. For reasons I cannot fathom, I had to fight mentally and physically for every step through to the finish. I have seen marathon runners stumbling to the end of a race with no comprehension of where or who they are, and then just before the finish line their legs fold beneath them and, with the crowd willing them on, they crawl to the end of the race.

At last! I run past the sign that welcomes travellers to the South Pole station.

Weirdly, it seems, the closer you get to the end, the more your mind and body rebel. That happened to me today.

I was in terrible pain as I trudged through the soft snow, having to use both hands in places to drag a leg out of the snow and place it down again in front of the other. Also, because the snow was so soft, I was sinking much deeper than usual, and the snow and ice slipped in through the top of my boots. My pants are designed to stop this happening, but they are also designed for skiing, not running—completely different motions—and are torn and shredded around the calves from the continuous rubbing.

Twenty kilometres from the pole, the support vehicle became completely bogged in the soft snow, and the over-revving on an already damaged and oil-leaking turbo charger caused the impeller to overheat and seize. That was it. I did outlast the bloody vehicle. That six-wheel drive truck, which was plagued with problems right from the start, was left behind like a wounded and dying mammoth, half-buried in the snow. Scotty remained with it and was eventually rescued by staff members at the South Pole station. Eric and Ming took skidoos ahead and used them to make my path through the snow.

As I trudged the last 5 kilometres, I saw two lone skiers closing in on the pole from another direction. Eric went ahead to meet them and returned with the news that it was Johan Ernst Nilson from Sweden and his crew, who were also travelling from pole to pole—sailing, dog-sledding, skiing and biking their way down—and with whom I shared a helicopter ride a world away, back at the North Pole. Amazingly, we were simultaneously closing in on the finish line. He had been given the same instructions as me: to leave the mainland at the point he had reached by late December, do the South Pole leg, then return to finish his trek to the bottom of Argentina.

As Johan and I rounded the ALE hangar, for both of us, me running and him skiing, the pain, discomfort and negativity were overwhelmed by our competitive streak to reach the pole first. Eric picked up on what was going through my mind when he saw that I had dramatically increased my pace. He drove the skidoo back alongside me and yelled, 'Come on, we can beat them! Push it!' And I did. After more than 19,000 kilometres, I sprinted to the pole with a dome on top that marks the official South Pole. The staff of the US science base and the

A reunion—I last saw Johan at the North Pole.

ALE cheered us on. I beat Johan by 10 metres. He grabbed me in a big bear hug and called me whatever is Swedish for 'bugger!' The emotion burst from each of us, and we cried in each other's arms.

I was greeted by the officials here, and I broke down. A few minutes later, when I ran, holding the Red Cross flag aloft, along an avenue of the flags of all the nations that have ventured to this remote place, I cried again. And I blubbed when I planted the flag in the ice right by the official South Pole.

I went straight to a tent to bathe my swollen hands and feet in a bowl of hot water. When the station doctor inspected and treated my feet, my blistered face and lips, my crook right knee and all my other pains and sprains, I cried once again, not from the pain but from gratitude. Then she brought me a mug of hot chocolate and a bowl of hot beef stew. Heaven! After a quick glass of champagne it was time to talk to the *Today* show's Ben Fordham, followed by interviews with Radio 2GB, the *Daily Telegraph*, *The Australian*, *The Age* and other newspapers.

Now, writing this entry in my diary, I am still weeping. The emotion that has built up over the last ten months, born through pain and exhaustion, frustration and loneliness, and the joy that I have all but finished my trek have burst free. I know I haven't finished, that tomorrow I must fly back to Chile and continue running for a further 2000 kilometres, but that will be a piece of cake compared with what I've endured here.

I am so proud of what I've achieved, and I am prouder still that I will be instrumental in providing clean water to some of the people in our world who need it. I understand from Greg Quail that we have inspired people to donate more than $100,000, and it's certain that my completing the run will lead many more to dig deep for the cause. I have received messages of congratulations from Prime Minister Julia Gillard and Opposition Leader Tony Abbott, and those messages mean so much to me. I'm hoping that the Australian government will make a donation to the Red Cross, to make those congratulations tangible.

The satellite phone is going crazy. As well as doing all the media interviews, I've spoken to Brooke and Dillon, who are happy and relieved, to Greg Quail, my brother Bernie—now back home in

At the geographic South Pole.

Canberra—my sisters and other brothers, and my mum. I've received scores of calls from Australian TV networks, radio stations and newspapers wanting to set up more interviews. I can't deal with them all, but I'll do my best—anything to get the message out there.

It was so good to take off all my polar gear. It is wonderful to know that I will never in my life put it on again.

I have lost track of time. I lie here in the tent feeling more content in my heart and soul than I have since I set off from the North Pole ten months ago. Of course there is still work to do but so far, so good. So very good. I have raised donations for the Red Cross, I have been tough and strong and done what I said I'd do. I know myself better than I ever have and I believe I have found my essence. Best of all, I am loved by those I love. There will be challenges ahead. I know that after surviving this run I will never be able to settle for a quiet life. Yet whatever life brings, success or failure or something in between, I'll always have Pole to Pole.

JANUARY 19

Bad weather prevented us flying out from the pole today—it was simply too dangerous—so I spent the day trying to organise the logistics of getting back on the road in Chile. I have 2000 kilometres still to run, perhaps more, depending on the roads, from just south of Puerto Montt, in Chile, to my final finish line in Ushuaia, Tierra del Fuego, at the bottom of Argentina. My route will take me over the mountains from Chile into Argentina, and then I'll zigzag between the two countries, taking the route of least resistance to Ushuaia. The logistics are tricky, because with each border crossing come the bureaucracy of customs and having to produce documents and explain to incredulous officials, for the millionth time, what I am doing. There is also the question of what vehicle will accompany me. Do Katie and Javier Trujillo (our Mexican cameraman, who will return to be with us at the end) drive the fuel-guzzling van we've been using since Canada, or do we rent another vehicle? I am looking forward to catching up with Katie and hearing about her travels in Buenos Aires and Brazil.

I had a chance to check out the United States base. Some 250 people live here in summer and 150 in winter, when it is dark for 24 hours a day. The airport can handle jumbo jets but almost permanently uses a C-130 Hercules, with which they ferry passengers between the pole and the mainland and bring in fresh food supplies fortnightly from New Zealand. (The South Pole operates on New Zealand time.) Most of the dozen major buildings are devoted to the United States government's climatology, glaciology and seismology work and its monitoring of space and climate conditions. At the Science Community building I read up on the research being done into global warming and its effect on the Antarctic. The researchers specialise in astrophysics and operate a huge radio telescope that stands 23 metres tall, weighs 254 tonnes and has a 10-metre-diameter dish. It studies the faint afterglow of the Big Bang; the South Pole's exceptionally clear atmosphere provides the ideal environment to observe the cosmic microwave background.

JANUARY 20

We flew from the South Pole back to the ALE base at Union Glacier to connect with my flight back to Chile. I had hoped to continue to Chile today, but once more the terrible weather has thwarted my plans. It is windy and overcast, the sky the same colour as the snow, and such conditions result in a lack of contrast that makes flying perilous. We are stranded here at Union Glacier, just like Douglas Mawson was on his return from the pole. It seems that once the Antarctic gets hold of you it is very difficult to escape.

Thankfully, I am in good company. As well as Eric and Ming, Union Glacier is currently sheltering people who between them have climbed every significant peak in the world, including Mount Everest and the Matterhorn, and I never tire of hearing the stories of these high achievers. One fellow here took his submarine and a Russian team below the North Pole ice shelf to place a Russian flag in the dead centre of the geographic North Pole. There are researchers, explorers, pilots and doctors who operate in the most remote and dangerous regions on earth, every one of them leading an extraordinary life. The workers from the Antarctic are a unique group of people, from as far away as Alaska and London. Some of them are heading home and some heading to their next adventure in the North Pole and the Arctic. The season for the North Pole starts in March, and they simply continue doing everything they have been doing, just in a different hemisphere.

JANUARY 21

I'm still stuck on the ice at Union Glacier with nothing to do but recover from some mild frostbite and attend to my badly swollen and infected toes. It's a good opportunity to drain them of the poison that has built up, and although lancing my toes is extremely painful, the relief is immediate. Normally, you would simply take antibiotics and allow the medication to get rid of the infection, but I do not have that luxury in this isolated location.

I am enjoying comparative comfort after the hardships of the Antarctic leg. The vegetable soups and meat stews make me feel stronger, and being able to sit on a toilet instead of squatting over a hole I've scratched in the snow is a highlight of my day.

The final leg of this event is the equivalent of running from Sydney to Melbourne and back again, only through a lot of windswept and God-forsaken terrain. I am trying to get my head back in the right space to conquer it. I have to treat it like a mountaineering expedition: I've reached the summit, but I have to climb back down to camp 4, camp 3, camp 2 and base camp before I'm finished. I must remember that it is deadly to relax and become complacent; as soon as you do so, disaster strikes. Many climbers die on the way down a mountain. Here at Union Glacier I have befriended a wonderful man, Dr Robert Miller of Austria, who specialises in rescuing people stranded on Mount Everest. He has reinforced my belief that I cannot take it easy now that the 'summit' of Pole to Pole has been reached. If I don't get home safely, it will all have been futile. Robert said I have made the right decision to return to South America to finish the run rather than pretend that the South Pole was the finish line and go straight home. Not to follow this run through to the very end would betray my promise, my ideals and the people I am trying to help.

FINISHING THE JOB

JANUARY 22

We got away today, after a rousing send-off from the expeditioners at Union Glacier. A few were themselves soon to depart for Longyearbyen, where it all started for me, to begin preparation for the North Pole season. I'm glad it's them and not me. I don't know how they do it. They are very, very tough.

After I meet up with Katie and Javier in Puerto Montt, we have to drive to the exact spot where I stopped running, about 200 kilometres south. In the meantime, they have been busy getting fuel, changing our Chilean pesos into Argentinean pesos, organising internet connection, broadcast equipment and phone communication. The phones have been a bugbear. There were satellite phone systems in the Arctic and Antarctic, and these are expensive and temperamental, and there is also a different phone system in every country we have passed through that we have had to link with.

JANUARY 23

It's Brooke's birthday tomorrow. I remember asking Lisa, when she was pregnant with Brooke, if she could hold on until Australia Day, because it would be great for her to be born on such a significant day. I won't repeat the reply I received. Chile is a day behind Australia, so my thoughts are with Brooke today. I wonder if she has received the basket of flowers, chocolates and fruit I ordered for her.

Today has been a crazy day of re-packing ice gear and rushing to catch planes in order to meet up with Katie and Javier. I finally arrived at Puerto Montt, and as I walked to the luggage carousel I could see them through the glass. I felt overjoyed to see them. I am sharing the dream again. I don't feel so alone anymore. With Katie, I have someone I can talk to about our family, someone who knows me and understands me. It's not going to be easy, but I know we will find a way to make it to the end.

I left Ming at Union Glacier. He's staying there for another week, covering the story of the Australian skiing adventurers Cas and Jonesy, then he will catch us up somewhere in Argentina. Tomorrow I'll be back running on solid ground again, and I will need a good 80-kilometre day to boost my confidence.

JANUARY 24

We crossed the border from Chile to Argentina today. The people at the border were efficient and friendly, and there were no problems. The army commander there simply wanted a photo with me, and he offered his support if there is anything we need while here in Argentina. I am happy to be here: this is the 14th and final country on my list. I still have some serious running to do and many mountains to cross, but my head is in a good place.

It's hot, and just like when I left the North Pole and hit Canada I have to be careful not to get sunburned. My body has been encased in five layers of clothing for the past month, and I am vitamin D deficient. Luckily, I have vitamin supplements.

I've noticed that the Argentinean people dress well, which indicates to this blow-in that the economy is prospering. The Argentinean peso is missing three of the zeros that the Chilean peso had. The very popular prime minister, Cristina Fernández, has had a cancer scare, and the people are concerned about the direction in which the country may be taken should she be unable to govern. As well as being a champion of human rights and of those Argentineans living in poverty, she has stabilised the country's economy, and now Argentina has the respect of Central and South America.

It's said that Argentineans see themselves in the same way as a small cat looking in the mirror and seeing a big lion. I think that's great. There is an old saying here, as well, that when people of other countries wish to speak to God they must make a long-distance phone call, because heaven is so far away, but Argentineans need only make a local call, because God resides in Argentina.

Cas and Jonesy didn't look in great shape when I met them.

JANUARY 25

My thoughts drift towards Cas and Jonesy, and I wonder if they will make it out of that God-forsaken place on time. They looked in bad shape when I met them: their supplies were low, and their faces were covered in wind burn and cold sores. All I can do for them is say a silent prayer and keep them in my thoughts as I run down the highway.

After the ice, my legs feel thick and heavy, like tree trunks. Swelling and bruising appeared as soon as I started running on roads again. I have cut the toe boxes out of my running shoes to give my toes some space.

JANUARY 28

This is a beautiful country. I am near to Río Mayo, and I've been running through wide plains and farmland. The wild life is also astounding. So far I've seen a type of native cat, llamas, silver foxes, skunks, a creature that looked like a mink or a mongoose, rabbits, hares and glorious pink flamingos. Many people fish in the streams. The drivers are friendly, and many know who I am and why I'm here. The word has spread quickly.

Towards the end of the day's run, the scenery became akin to sheep country back home: dry-looking with big open plains. The wind blew up and was so strong that it knocked me over four times. Adding to my injury list are another two lost toenails (I'm now just about out of nails) and gravel rash on my shoulder and hands from where I tried to break my falls.

JANUARY 29

This is the second day in a row that the wind has beaten me. Yesterday I ran only 61 kilometres and I was exhausted, and today I pulled the plug at 70 kilometres, after being pushed around the road like a puny kid by a schoolyard bully. The wind has been my enemy for a lot of the run, and it seems it won't give up until it breaks me. I don't know how long I can go on; instead of feeling closer, the finish seems to be moving further and further away.

Rugged up against the wind.

I was listening to a song by Adele, 'Make You Feel My Love', in which she says that she would go to the ends of the earth to make her lover feel her love. I thought, 'Yeah, so what else?' I suppose that, although I am a romantic, going to the ends of the earth to prove my love won't be enough anymore. I have raised the bar. It kept me busy, thinking what more I would, or could, do for love.

The wind won this round. I simply couldn't endure it any longer, so I decided to turn eastwards, onto National Route 26. This will take me off National Route 40, which heads down the western side of Argentina close to Chile, to the east coast, where I'm hoping that the Atlantic Ocean and the south-running National Route 3 may be a little kinder. It's a 270-kilometre trek to the coast. I hope I'm making the right decision. At least communications should be better on that side of the country; the west is beautiful, but it's predominantly national parks.

JANUARY 30

Today included the good, the bad and the ugly.

The good were flocks of flamingos and getting our communications sorted. Katie and Javier found the nicest lady in town, who, even though she had a five-month-old baby to look after, helped us to fix our internet and then gave us a spare sim card that she had. Yet another Samaritan. There have been so many, God bless them.

The bad was the relentless gale on the vast petroleum fields. The wind really does seem determined to stop me; it bounced me all over the place like a ping-pong ball. I could never be a sailor.

The ugly was me falling off the pavement time after time as I was buffeted by the wind. I now have gravel rash on my knees, elbows, arms and hands, plus a chipped tooth. Did I mention that I hate the wind?

FEBRUARY 2

Finally, I have been rewarded with a view to die for: the Atlantic Ocean. The sky is red, with the sun setting behind the mountains, and the ocean is blue-green. The sand is white. I have a smile on my face. After eating dust stirred up by mining operators and strong winds for the past week, I can now breathe without a bandana over my face.

Today I passed Comodoro Rivadavia, in the province of Chubut, from where the region's petrol is distributed, and then I was heading south again. I have been running a lot of dead kilometres from west to east, but I didn't really have a choice. I needed to cross the country to get away from the wind, and I took the shortest route to do so.

It's hard to believe that by the end of this month I'll be home.

FEBRUARY 4

Ming has arrived and he is a welcome sight. He caught a taxi from Comodoro Rivadavia and met up with us around noon today. It was great to hear about the wrap up of the South Pole—where all the people went, how they got all of the things back to the mainland, from tents to vehicles to tractors to ablution blocks, and what they left behind. A lot of the machinery and gear that ALE are going to use next season is simply buried and preserved by the freezing conditions, then dug up and de-iced.

It is also good to have a runner around—Ming runs 10–20 kilometres with me from time to time, which gives me some company and conversation on the long boring stretches. With Ming back on deck, things should be easier for Javier and Katie, now they have another driver, cook and companion. And he is an athlete, so he understands the strain of backing up with such high mileage day after day after day.

We're all sleeping in the van together each night. It's a bit cosy, but that's the least of our worries!

FEBRUARY 5

I could only manage 70 kilometres today in the strong winds. I was continually being pushed over and held back by strong headwinds. It is so difficult to run through this wind, especially as I've lost weight, having dropped from around 68 to 59 kilograms. My energy and strength are very low. The fat padding on the soles of my feet is depleted and it is just skin and bones hitting the tarmac. Any strength that I do have comes from my heart, not my legs. This whole journey is about will-power, perseverance, stubbornness and determination, none of which you can measure in a laboratory.

FEBRUARY 6

Today marks 10 months since I began my journey in the North Pole. It is hard to believe that I am so close to the finish after only 10 months. When I first started this journey the world seemed such a big place, so many countries to cover, so many mountains to climb, so many kilometres to run. But, in a relatively short space of time, I've managed to traverse almost the full length of this planet. Every morning before I start I study the map and measure and re-measure the distance to the finish. All I can think about now is the end.

FEBRUARY 7

The terrain in this part of Argentina consists of windswept plains, and hills covered in brown grass. There's still plenty of wildlife, including guanacos, armadillos, rheas and skunks, the last of which I'm giving a wide berth. At times, the sky has seemed full of birds.

We met back up with the coast when we arrived in Puerto San

Rolling plains and guanacos.

Julian today, the only town we've seen for several days. I have been running through some of the most desolate places on earth but now it's a chance for Katie, Ming and Javier to catch up on the outside world and get some internet coverage.

FEBRUARY 8

The winds are blowing the van around. Both Javier and Ming are having trouble keeping it on the road so Katie is taking over the driving—she can drive and reverse a truck better than anyone I've seen, which has got to be hurting the boys' egos. The wind and the sleet have brought the temperature down to 2 degrees. Even the locals are saying that this is unusual weather for this time of year.

I have completely worn out my last pair of shoes, but I am trying to hold on till we can buy just one more pair in Río Gallegos in three days' time. This is not helping the alignment of my knees and ankles but I simply don't have a choice.

The guanacos are everywhere in large numbers now and are quite curious. They often come up close to me to try and figure out just what I am doing in their territory.

FEBRUARY 10

The day started the same as every other day since I returned to South America from the South Pole—cold and windy with plains as far as the eye can see. I am finding this part of the run uninspiring; there are not many people around and the days blur into each other.

I put my head down and switched to autopilot; at the 70-kilometre mark Katie interrupted me to tell me I had a visitor. One of the Red Cross workers from Río Gallegos had driven up to meet us, along with a couple of guys from the local radio station. He introduced himself as Pablo.

Pablo told me about the work the Red Cross were doing in the region. I never cease to be amazed at the dedication and selflessness of the people in the Red Cross. When I asked him about fundraising he mentioned that they were doing it tough. It's a very poor region and they don't receive any support from the government.

I took Pablo on a tour of the van, and asked him if this type of

Some of the wonderful people from the Argentinean Red Cross.

vehicle would be useful when they were working a long way away from the towns or when they were working through the night. The answer was yes. I told him the van was theirs but that I just needed to borrow it for a week longer.

He was reduced to tears. Today was a good day.

FEBRUARY 11

About 25 kilometres north of Río Gallegos, after I'd completed 60 kilometres of my day's run, we were joined by some runners who wanted to run the last section with me.

One of the runners was called Elvis. I noticed Elvis as I ran up to the 60-kilometre mark because he was jumping around a lot and doing some incredible contortions as warm-ups. As I suspected, Elvis took off in the lead, and it was clear that he only knew one speed: flat-out. I can't figure out why people do this, but it happens regularly. Running alongside and having a chat is far more civilised.

Elvis definitely had me on the flats and the downhill. It wasn't easy to match him but I didn't run from the other end of the earth to get my ass kicked either. There were a number of big hills coming up that dragged on for kilometres and these are my passion—the steeper the better. I decided to hammer the hills from the base and see what Elvis was made of. As we hit the top of the third hill, some 15 kilometres on, he gasped and turned to ask me if I ran at this pace all the time. Only if I am tired, I said. He stopped, covered in sweat, and called up the support vehicle.

Thank God, I thought. I was about to collapse myself but I wasn't going to be the first to break. This business really is all about the mind.

FEBRUARY 12

Tierra del Fuego is divided between Argentina and Chile so we have to cross another border, but the customs officers are all aware that I am coming and have streamlined the process for us.

The Río Gallegos Red Cross members were with me every step of the way and they saw firsthand just what it takes to run two marathons each day. By the time I reached the border they had tears in their eyes. They saw me fall and get up many times today.

The border officials stopped work so that we could get a group photo. No one seemed to mind, not even the truck drivers who were waiting patiently to cross the border. My motivation takes a hammering as I leave Argentina. I have to keep telling myself that the next border crossing will be the final one on this whole run. We will only be in Chile for 100 kilometres or so.

FEBRUARY 14

It's raining today; no, it's snowing; no, it's sleeting: it seems the weather can't make up its mind what it wants to do. It's so cold today that I decide to run in my polar jacket and pants topped off with a balaclava.

The edge of the road is very muddy and it's playing havoc with my shoes. I'm slipping all over the place, and the cuts I put in the toe box area are allowing the grit and mud in and squeezing my toes out.

I put my head down, run hard and focus on tomorrow when I will cross my last border.

FEBRUARY 15

Back to Argentina. Word of our arrival had preceded us and the customs people were waiting outside to grab a photo; they even offered me a shower if I wished, but I wanted to get a few more kilometres done before I stopped. As I ran off they yelled 'God bless you, Pat'. It made me cry.

The crew can feel the finish is only days away—there is mounting excitement. These have been tough miles for them as well, especially Katic who has been with me from Canada.

FEBRUARY 16

It is now under 200 kilometres to Ushuaia—in striking distance. I joked on the phone to my friend Larry back in Australia that even if I had to crawl I could still make it from here. I have finally let my guard down and am planning the finish.

The last stage—running past Lake Fagnano, just north of Ushuaia.

FEBRUARY 17

I haven't seen a tall tree since I headed across from the east of Argentina until today. The severe winds prevent trees on the plains growing beyond shrubs but in this last section the mountains provide some protection. I am relieved that the surface has changed from flat open road to hilly and mountainous territory, this gives my muscles a variation in the length of my stride and stops a lot of the leg soreness. I don't feel so fatigued at the end of the day.

While I was running I remembered how, when I was about to start this event, I likened it to being sentenced to ten months' hard labour and how, like a prisoner, I had no choice but to keep my head down and do my time. Now it's as if I am in the last few days of my sentence and about to be released, but instead of euphoria I worry about how I will adapt when my every waking hour is not regimented. I've heard of ex-prisoners who cannot cope with freedom when they get out of jail and long to return to their cell. How will I cope when I have choices? It's almost time to set new goals and face new challenges.

I don't know how I will fare but, as I always say, your next step is the most important step of your life.

FEBRUARY 19

My job is done. At ten o'clock this morning I completed the pole-to-pole run: 20,919 kilometres in ten months and 13 days. I stopped last night 30 kilometres from Ushuaia so that I could be in the town centre this morning, by the statue of Eva Perón, to be greeted by Red Cross officials, the mayor, sports administrators, police, the fire brigade and a throng of locals. I didn't sleep a wink.

I covered the final few kilometres easily and quickly, in spite of the wind and sleet. Nothing could dampen my spirits today; I breezed down that road. Funnily, though, at the moment I crossed the finish point, my right knee collapsed, and I stumbled. It was as if it had been holding on until the very last, but now that the run was over it gave up. I was feeling no pain, however.

After the hugs and handshakes I downed some thick, tasty seafood chowder and a couple of colas, had a bath and donned clean clothes—luxury. Then Radio 2GB was on the line, and Karl Stefanovic's producer

Ushuaia at last!

at the *Today* show was organising our live cross. I was interviewed by reporters from Australia and from North and South America. Dillon and Brooke called me. One fellow from New York took the trouble to email and congratulate me, saying he could remember me dragging tyres in New York's Central Park in December 2010. A group of Australians showed up to say well done. From Sydney, Brisbane and Melbourne, they had been on a tour to the edge of the Antarctic, and when they heard I was finishing in Ushuaia they came across. No matter where I have been on this monumental run, I have bumped into Australians.

Tomorrow, I have a day off, my first in 10 and a half months. I think I'll sleep in.

ACKNOWLEDGEMENTS

I would like to give special thanks to the following people for their enormous support throughout my run from Pole to Pole: Greg Quail, Sharon Davson, John Gerathy, Scott Kaylen, Carolyn Grant, Robert Tickner, Bernie Farmer, Katie Walsh, Brooke and Dillon Farmer.

This is my raw core, as I was and as I am. This book reflects my thoughts and feelings each day as I ran from pole to pole. I have not returned to revise my words, even though I am a different man today than I was when in the Arctic, the United States, Nicaragua or Chile. This run has changed me forever. My aim has been to chronicle the days and nights of my run exactly as they happened and as I experienced them in the moment.

And thanks to Larry Writer for assisting me to turn my thoughts and experiences into words for this chronicle.

🌐 OUR SPONSORS

Pat Farmer's Pole to Pole Run would like to acknowledge the assistance of the Nine Network, especially the *Today* show, radio station 2GB, Tardis Group, Blackmores, the SOC Exchange, Champion System, Inglis Bloodstock, Davson the Artist, Alphapharm, Mont, Fugen, Sell & Parker Pty Ltd, Metropolitan Demolitions Group, the legal firm Shaw, Reynolds, Bowen & Gerathy, Baffin, Snowgum, Smith Optics, Wests Packaging Services and Sea to Summit.

Com school students enjoying the clean tap water from a project already funded by Pat's run. *Courtesy of Danielle Parry/Cruz Vermelha de Timor-Leste (CVTL)*

Australian Red Cross
THE POWER OF HUMANITY

Australian Red Cross congratulates Pat Farmer on his amazing achievement.

But Pat's superhuman effort was about much more than breaking records or personal glory. His purpose was to raise awareness and money for Red Cross water and sanitation programs around the world, a cause about which he is extremely passionate.

Pat might have finished his run, but he's even more keen now to raise funds for this vitally important purpose. And it's not too late to support him by making a donation to the Red Cross Pole to Pole Run For Water Appeal.

'Unsafe water and poor sanitation have claimed more lives worldwide over the past century than any other causes; some four million people continue to die each year from diseases associated with the lack of access to safe drinking water, inadequate sanitation and poor hygiene,' says Australian Red Cross CEO Robert Tickner.

Money raised through the Pole to Pole Run for Water Appeal has already been used to fund a project in Timor-Leste, laying pipes to connect a school and a clinic on the outskirts of the town of Com to the settlement's clean water supply. The money will also be used to build extra school toilets and fund hygiene education for students and teachers.

But there is still a huge amount of work to do...

'Pat's willingness to push his body to the limits of human endurance to draw attention to the desperate plight of millions of people makes him a humanitarian legend. He has cemented his place in the history books, and has already gone a huge way towards changing the lives of people in Timor-Leste.'

Stand up and show the world you care. Support Pat's amazing effort by making a donation to the Australian Red Cross Pole to Pole Run for Water Appeal at redcross.org.au or by calling 1800 811 700